*More Praise for*

# YOU'RE WEARING *That?*

"Tannen shines brightest in her blow-by-blow dissections of actual conversations—the seemingly trivial exchanges that take place in a kitchen, or on the phone, or via e-mail or text-messaging."
—*Houston Chronicle*

"Deborah Tannen has hit upon another hotbed of miscommunication: the mother-daughter relationship."
—*Seattle Post-Intelligencer*

"Deborah Tannen's groundbreaking book *You Just Don't Understand* improved male-female relationships about, oh, 100 percent. Now she's poised to do the same for moms and daughters. . . . Listen, and get ready to make peace!"
—*Glamour*

"Deborah Tannen decodes the veiled insults, *hmms,* and *oh, really's?* between mothers and daughters. . . . The . . . implications behind the spoken words . . . are so familiar, it hurts when you laugh."
—*O* Magazine

"[Tannen] describes the intense connections between mothers and daughters—and how we press each other's buttons."
—*Good Housekeeping*

"So many women say, 'I thought when my daughter grew up we'd be friends,'" says . . . Deborah Tannen. In her new book, she explores why that can be tough—and what can help."
—*People*

"Tannen's astute observations get at the heart of conversations between mothers and daughters." —Fredericksburg *Free Lance-Star*

"This book, at the least, will strike a chord; at the most, it will help you, whether you be a mother or a daughter, to strike a balance and heal old wounds."
—*Taconic Press*

"[A] provocative study of conversation between mothers and daughters."
—*Deseret Morning News*

# YOU'RE WEARING *That?*

# YOU'RE WEARING That?

Understanding
Mothers and Daughters
in Conversation

## DEBORAH TANNEN

BALLANTINE BOOKS   NEW YORK

LIBRARY OF CONGRESS CATALOGING-IN-PUBLICATION DATA

Tannen, Deborah.
You're wearing that?: understanding mothers and daughters
in conversation/Deborah Tannen.
p.   cm.
Includes bibliographical references and index.
ISBN 978-0-8129-7266-5
1. Mothers and daughters.  2. Parent and adult child.
3. Interpersonal communication.  4. Communication in the family.
5. Conversation analysis.  I. Title.
HQ755.86.T366 2006        306.874'3—dc22        2005048591

In memory of my mother

Born DINA ROSIN
Minsk, Russia
*May 3, 1911*

Died DOROTHY TANNEN
USA
*July 23, 2004*

# CONTENTS

# INTRODUCTION
## TO THE PAPERBACK
## EDITION

One of the great privileges that come with writing books about relationships is that people who read those books, or hear me talk about them, invite me into their lives by telling me their own experiences. When *You're Wearing THAT?* was published, in English and in translations, I particularly looked forward to hearing from women who grew up in countries other than the United States. I was eager to learn whether the patterns I describe are universal, since my research was based on observations and examples drawn mostly (though not exclusively) from middle-class Americans, albeit Americans of varied ethnic, regional, and racial backgrounds. As responses to this book began to flow in by e-mail or in comments by callers to talk shows or members of audiences at public talks, I was pleased to hear from women in other cultures and countries that the insights rang true for them, too. For example, I received an e-mail from a Guyanese professor, Belle Tyndall, who recognized the title of my book as what her mother said, word-for-word, one afternoon when her daughter showed her a dress she was planning to wear to a wedding the next day. Professor Tyndall wrote: "The fact that I was already 46 years old and dean of the Faculty of Education at the University of Guyana made no difference." It made no difference in her mother's freedom to comment, and also no difference in the daughter's response: she stayed up nearly all night and sewed a new dress.

Though few middle-class American women sew their own clothes (they'd be more likely to buy a new dress), the basic pattern is the same: a mother renders her opinion about her daughter's clothes, and the daughter picks up her meaning, even if it is implied in a question rather than stated outright. The Guyanese mother didn't say, "That dress isn't appropriate; you'd better sew yourself a new one, quick," because she didn't have to. Refraining from praising the dress was enough to get her meaning across.

I was also fascinated by an e-mail I received from a Muslim woman in the small Arab country Oman. Here, too, the particulars of mother-daughter comments she related are different from those I heard from Americans, but the underlying dynamic is the same. The Omani woman told me that aspects of daughters' appearance that I call the Big Three—hair, clothes, and weight—are not common points of maternal inspection in her own or her friends' experience. Instead, their mothers focus on covering up. Whereas American mothers might say, "Put on a little lipstick," the Muslim woman's mother, like her friends' mothers, would say, "Put on a head scarf." Or, "Tighten up your head scarf," "Put on an abaya (the robe that Muslim women in her country customarily wear)," or "Why is your abaya so tight?" Just as American women often feel that they can never do things correctly enough to avoid comment, the Muslim woman told me of a friend who always wears a head scarf as well as wide, loose-fitting clothes that cover her up completely. Yet her mother finds something that could be improved (or something to disapprove of, depending on your point of view). This modest woman doesn't wear socks because of the heat. "Wouldn't it be better if you had socks on?" her mother urges. "I can still see some hair."

Wanting their daughters to present themselves to the world in the best possible light, many Western mothers focus on helping them appear attractive, while Arab Muslim mothers in the Arabian Gulf typically focus on their appearing decent—that is, covered up.

Comments about appearance topped the list of personal anecdotes I heard from daughters. Some of these anecdotes helped me see new aspects of dynamics I had described. For example, among the memorable comments I heard from women about their mothers, I especially love this one, which was told to me by Ellen Levine, editorial director of Hearst Magazines: "My mother is losing her eyesight, but she can still spot a pimple across the room."

I heard so many mothers' comments about pimples that I began to add complexion to the Big Three. One woman said she dreaded the first moments of homecoming because she was so often greeted by her mother's disappointed look and the comment, "I can see your face is breaking out again." A family who were filmed for a *20/20* segment on the book were able to joke about just this. The daughter said that everyone in the family knew she tended to break out when she drank "dark pop." So when her mother asks, "Have you been drinking dark pop?" the daughter quipped to her mother on camera, "You might as well just say, 'Hi, pimple face!'"

A remark one woman made helps explain why daughters find the appearance-check so unnerving. In a letter she sent to Bea Lewis, a columnist at the *Palm Beach Post,* the woman said that her mother's frequent comments about her hair or her weight make her feel that she can't just be herself around her mother; herself is never enough. Reading this, I thought of the parallel complaint expressed by mothers, and I noticed an irony. Mothers have told me that once they understand why suggestions, advice, and helpful comments can come across as criticism, they are able to hold back. They are pleased that, as a result, they get along better with their grown daughters. At the same time, though, the need to continually watch what they say leaves them with the less pleasing feeling that they can't just be themselves around their daughters. In other words, each one's wish to be accepted as-is can be at odds with the same wish in the other.

I got an insight into some of the complex motivations of mothers when a woman told me something her mother had said that seemed unconscionable. The woman recalled that when she was in high school, her mother had urged her to lighten her brown hair with blond highlights. When the daughter resisted, her mother said, "All the popular girls have blond hair."

Why would a mother say something like that? Surely she was aware, having been a teenage girl herself, that concern with the popular girls can be overwhelming, a source of anxiety if not misery. Many years later, when mother and daughter talked about this, it emerged that the mother herself had suffered as a teenager because of what she perceived as mousy brown hair, and she herself had eyed the popular girls with envy. She had begged her own mother to let her lighten her hair, but her mother wouldn't hear of it. She was trying to spare her daughter the unhappiness she herself had suffered. This desire would be even more urgent because she felt responsible: her daughter had inherited this hair from her.

A woman who was born and raised in the Philippines recounts a similar cross-generational experience in a "My Turn" column that appeared in *Newsweek* June 19, 2006. Tricia Capistrano writes that while growing up, she was keenly aware that her wide nose, like other features of her classic Filipino looks, was considered less attractive than those of her more Caucasian-looking peers. Her mother had taught her "to pinch the bridge daily so that the arch would be higher, like my cousins." Her mother, too, had a personal stake in this project: "My Mom, whose nose I acquired, has one of the widest among her brothers and sisters." So not only was her mother responsible for what she viewed as an unattractive feature on her daughter's face, but the comparison with her siblings was also being passed down.

The solution, these anecdotes imply, is for mothers to bite their tongues. Though this is surely a good thing, it isn't the whole answer, as I was reminded by women who find themselves in both roles. A conversation with one woman helped me understand how the issue spans generations—and how challenging it is. This woman has thick, curly hair, which her mother was always after her to comb and keep down. She even recalls that this was the subject of one of the few comments she ever heard from her grandmother, whom she met only once. (Her family had been living abroad, and the old woman died not long after.) One of her few memories of that meeting is hearing her grandmother say to her mother, "Can't you do something about that child's hair?" Note that this criticism of the little girl's hair was phrased as criticism of her mother, who, the grandmother implied, had fallen short of her maternal responsibility. Well, the girl grew up into a woman who had a daughter of her own—a little girl who inherited her hair! "I try not to say anything," the woman told me, "but the not saying anything is in itself an obsession. Other people mention it all the time." And when she does try to comb her daughter's hair, the little girl cries.

What exactly is a mother to do? Cut it all off? Few little girls in our culture will allow that. The dilemma is built into the relationship, given that girls and women are judged by appearance, that society has standards of beauty that no individual can escape, and that mothers are held responsible for their daughters' appearance.

Other comments I heard from women indicated that a mother who routinely bites her tongue is not assured her daughter's lifelong gratitude. More than one woman approached me to say that her mother never criticized her—and she wished she had. In some cases, I was told, "It was as if she didn't care." In others, the daughter said she really wanted her mother's guidance: "Whatever clothes I buy my mother says they're great; they can't all be great! I want her opinion." With all these nuances and potential grounds for complaint, the ultimate lesson—and it is one that readers tell me they do indeed glean—may simply be to cut each other a little more slack.

Throughout the book I made efforts to represent both mothers' and daughters' points of view. But the examples I've given so far of comments about appearance were all made by mothers to daughters. That's not because I didn't hear about similar comments made by daughters to mothers. I did, though not as many. More importantly, mothers who told me, "My daughter says to me, 'You're not going to wear that, are you?'" usually laughed as they said this. I got the impression they found it more funny than deeply hurtful that their daughters critiqued their hair and clothes (though not necessarily their weight). I didn't perceive the depth of feeling, the sense of injustice and hurt, that I sensed when daughters told me that their mothers critiqued their appearance. It seemed that mothers' opinions of their daughters have greater force than the reverse. This difference—the power of a mother's judgment—might also explain why quite a few women told me that they had read the book expecting to gain understanding of their relationship with their daughter, but found themselves equally, if not more, captivated by the insights it gave them into their relationships with their own mothers. I did hear anecdotes from mothers that revealed a deep sense of injustice and hurt, but they tended to reflect feeling rejected, neglected, or left out—as well as feeling unjustly accused of criticizing or being judgmental. As one caller to a talk show put it, "My daughter takes everything the wrong way."

Among the issues that frequently surfaced in reaction to the book was the question, Can mothers and daughters be friends? I heard many new examples that captured how a daughter reacted negatively to comments from her mother that would no doubt roll off her back if they were made by a friend. For example, one woman recalled a conversation she had recently had with her grown daughter—a daughter, I should add, with whom she has an excellent relationship. The mother had begun a conversation with her daughter by saying, "I miss you." It's a comment a woman might well make to a friend, who would likely respond, "I miss you too. How've you been?" But the daughter's reaction was different. She asked, "Why do you miss me? I talked to you a week ago." Her daughter perceived the comment as implying she should have called her mother.

The same goes for casual suggestions or questions about even the smallest things: "Did you remember to turn on the headlights?" "Are you going to put more water in the broccoli?" You might think of asking a question like this of a friend, but you probably wouldn't say anything. And if you did, the friend might be annoyed because you're a pest—but not take it as evidence you think her incompetent. It's a mother who seems always to stand as a judge of competence, so her judgment carries much more weight than a friend's would. Daughters and mothers who, like friends, confide in each other and spend recreational time together tell me they are reassured to understand the source of these frictions.

As I talked about the book to audiences across the United States and in other countries, I encountered, above all, great sighs of relief. The remark I heard more often than any other was, "It's a relief to know I'm not the only one." And it was a relief to realize that there is a fundamental tension built into the relationship—a tension I would now summarize this way: From the daughter's point of view, the person you most want to think you're perfect is the one most likely to see your faults—and tell you about them. From the mother's point of view, your job has always been to help and protect your daughter, give her guidance based on your greater experience, and ensure that all goes as well as it can for her. But any advice or suggestion you offer implies criticism, because someone who is doing nothing wrong does not need suggestions or advice.

It has been deeply satisfying to hear from readers that the book helped them. Sometimes that means they changed their way of talking, which changed the reactions they got and consequently improved the relationship. But sometimes they tell me that simply understanding what motivates their mother, their daughter, or themselves, gives them more compassion and a more generous attitude. Because this is the first book I've written that is aimed primarily at women readers, I've been pleased to hear such comments from men as well. One man wrote, "Obviously, I'm neither a mother nor a daughter, but I've had close association with some of each." He went on to say that the book helped him understand what's gone on between the mothers and daughters in his life, "as well as some other family dynamics I've been involved with."

Nothing makes me happier than hearing that my work has helped people improve their relationships. For that, I thank my readers.

YOU'RE WEARING *That?*

# PREFACE

They are the best of conversations; they are the worst of conversations. Talk between mothers and grown daughters can be both: a remark coming from your daughter or your mother is more healing or more hurtful than the same remark coming from someone else. The relationship between mothers and daughters is the literal "mother of all relationships." It is among the most passionate of women's lives, the source of the deepest love and also the deepest anger—even hate—that most women experience. It brings us face-to-face with reflections of ourselves and forces us to confront fundamental questions about who we are, who we want to be, and how we relate to others both within and outside our families.

The mother-daughter relationship continues to hold tremendous power throughout our lives—for daughters, long after we are grown and even after our mothers are gone; for mothers, long after daughters have become adults and, in some cases, mothers themselves. Words exchanged between daughters and mothers—in the moment or in memory—can carry enormous weight. In *You Just Don't Understand* I showed how women and men can walk away from the same conversation with completely different ideas of what was said and what was meant. The same is true for conversations between mothers and grown daughters, even though both are women and in many ways speak the same language—indeed, partly *because* both are women and in many ways speak the same language: a language in which intimacy and closeness as well as power and distance are constantly negotiated. Improving communication between mothers and daughters, much like breaking down barriers to communication between women and men, requires, above all, understanding: seeing the situation from the other's point of view. In this book I provide that understanding as well as concrete suggestions for improving mother-daughter conversations and therefore relationships.

The challenge in every relationship, every conversation, is to find ways to be as close as you want to be (and no closer) without that closeness becoming intrusive or threatening your freedom and your sense that you are in control of your life. In this, relationships between daughters and mothers are like all relationships, only more so. They combine, on one hand, the deepest connection, the most comforting closeness, with, on the other, the most daunting struggles for control. Each tends to overestimate the other's power while underestimating her own. And each yearns to be seen and accepted for who she is while seeing the other as who she wants her to be—or as someone falling short of who she should be.

Women are healed by, or ache for, satisfying conversations with their mothers and grown daughters, in some cases to build on already excellent relationships, in others to break out of cycles of misunderstanding that can turn amiable conversations into painful or angry ones in the blink of an eye. Both want to maximize the gifts of rapport and closeness while minimizing the inevitable hurts that come along with any close relationship but can be especially intense in this one.

*You're Wearing THAT?* grows out of my last book in much the same way that *You Just Don't Understand* grew out of the book that preceded it. My first general-audience book, *That's Not What I Meant!,* introduced my concept of conversational style and illustrated its power in every aspect of our daily lives. Of the book's ten chapters, the one that got the most attention and the most enthusiastic response was the chapter devoted to conversations between women and men. That led me to turn my research to the topic of male-female communication and to write *You Just Don't Understand: Women and Men in Conversation.* In a parallel way, of the nine chapters in *I Only Say This Because I Love You,* a book about adult family relationships, the one that got the most attention was "I'm Still Your Mother," and the parts that most captivated readers were those devoted to the complex and superloaded relationship between mothers and adult daughters. Prompted by this response, as well as by my desire to get to the bottom of my evolving relationship with my own mother, I turned my research to conversations between mothers and daughters in order to delve more deeply into this uniquely intense relationship—one that continues to evoke powerful emotions long after it has ceased, ostensibly, to be the center of our personal lives.

Much of what I say about mother-daughter conversations is also true of talk between mothers and sons, fathers and daughters, and fathers and sons. By focusing on daughters and mothers, I do not mean to deny this. I have not conducted a comparative study. As a professor of linguistics specializing in sociolinguistics, I use a case-study method in my research. Reflecting the "linguistic" part of sociolinguistics, I base many of my findings on close analysis of transcribed, tape-recorded conversations. Reflecting the "socio" side, I also analyze conversations I am party to or overhear, much as some sociologists or anthropologists—like fiction writers— become observers and analysts of the interactions around them. Many of the examples I present are reconstructed from interactions I took part in, overheard, or was told about. Any conversation I encounter, with people I know well or have just met, is a potential source of examples, as women who hear the topic of my book often volunteer their own experiences. The foundation of my research, however, is close analysis of transcribed audiotaped conversations. In this book too I analyze word-for-word transcriptions of conversations that were tape-recorded by students in my classes in connection with written assignments they handed in as part of their coursework and gave me permission to use.

I also arranged to have more focused conversations—interviews, you might call them—with women I knew, and women they knew, in order to hear in more depth about their experiences with their mothers and daughters. When I talked to someone in person, I audiotaped the conversation and had it transcribed; when I talked to someone over the phone, I wore headphones and typed notes as we spoke; and when interchanges took place on e-mail, I printed them. In several cases I spoke to a mother and then, separately, to her daughter or vice versa. In two instances, I talked to groups of women together at meals hosted by women I knew to which they had generously invited friends I did not know. My interviews (conversations, really, because I did not ask a preset series of questions) included women of a range of ages, races, and ethnic groups. But I did not attempt to make generalizations about members of groups, so I don't specify the race or ethnicity of women whose experiences I include, although many of the examples I present come from Asian-American and African-American as well as European-American women and, for that matter, from deaf as well as hearing women, and lesbian as well as straight women.

I never use an example without getting permission from the person who was its source. So that people will speak freely to me, and simply as a matter of integrity (using my students, friends, and family as sources of data might otherwise seem somewhat vulturish), I always let people see how I intend to use their life experiences, in order to make sure that I got them right and to confirm whether they want to be identified by name or pseudonym.

Pseudonyms are always first name only; when I identify the source of an example, I use both first and last names.

My analyses of the examples I present are based on insights and concepts I've developed over the quarter century that I have been doing academic research since receiving my doctorate in linguistics at the University of California, Berkeley. All the concepts I introduce here, as well as explanations of my research methods, are developed in more technical detail in academic publications. (Anyone interested can find references on my website: www.deborahtannen.com.)

When asked why I decided to write for general readers instead of sticking to academic articles and books, I typically respond, "I wanted to write books that my mother could read." When I say this, "my mother" stands for the general reader who would never pick up a scholarly book, regardless of how much the topic interested her. But "my mother" also stands for my mother: the person who is, on some level, the first audience for all my accomplishments, the ultimate judge of all my deeds. That my mother died while I was writing this book made the task of writing it, in many ways, harder, but it also made it more urgent. The book became a way to honor her memory as it forced me to examine the enormous impact she has had—and continues to have—on every aspect of my life. Acknowledging this impact in turn reinforced the importance of understanding, and improving, conversations between daughters and mothers.

*1*

## CAN WE TALK?
## MOTHERS AND DAUGHTERS
## IN CONVERSATION

M y daughters can turn my day black in a millisecond," says a woman whose two daughters are in their thirties.

Another woman tells me, "Sometimes I'll be talking on the phone to my mom, and everything's going fine, then all of a sudden she'll say something that makes me so mad, I just hang up. Later I can't believe I did that. I would never hang up on anyone else."

But I also hear comments like these: "No one supports me and makes me feel good like my mother. She's always on my side." And from the mother of a grown daughter: "I feel very lucky and close with my daughter, and particularly since I didn't have a close relationship with my mother, it's very validating for me and healing."

Mothers and daughters find in each other the source of great comfort but also of great pain. We talk to each other in better and worse ways than we talk to anyone else. And these extremes can coexist within the same daughter-mother pairs. Two sisters were in an elevator in the hospital where their mother was nearing the end of her life. "How will you feel when she's gone?" one asked. Her sister replied, "One part of me feels, How will I survive? The other part feels, Ding-dong, the witch is dead."

The part of a daughter that feels "How will I survive?" reflects passionate connection: Wanting to talk to your mother can be a visceral, almost physical longing, whether she lives next door, in a distant state, in another country—or if she is no longer living on this earth. But the part that sees your mother as a wicked witch— a malevolent woman with magical power—reflects the way your anger can flare when a rejection, a disapproving word, or the sense that she's still treating you like a child causes visceral pain. American popular culture, like individuals in daily life, tends to either romanticize or demonize mothers. We ricochet between "Everything I ever accomplished I owe to my mother" and "Every problem I have in my life is my mother's fault." Both convictions come laden with powerful emotions. I was amazed by how many women, in the midst of e-mails telling me about their mothers, wrote, "I am crying as I write this."

Women as mothers grapple with corresponding contradictions. The adoration they feel for their grown daughters, mixed with the sense of responsibility for their well-being, can be overwhelming, matched only by the hurt they feel when their attempts to help or just stay connected are rebuffed or even excoriated as criticism or devilish interference. And the fact that these pushes and pulls continue after their daughters are grown is itself a surprise, and not a pleasant one. A woman in her sixties expressed this: "I always assumed that once my daughter became an adult, the problems would be over," she said. "We'd be friends; we'd just enjoy each other. But you find yourself getting older, things start to hurt, and on top of that, there are all these complications with your daughter. It's a big disappointment."

## SMALL SPARK, BIG FLARE-UP

Especially disappointing—and puzzling—is that hurt feelings and even arguments can be sparked by the smallest, seemingly insignificant remarks. Here's an example that comes from a student in one of my classes named Kathryn Ann Harrison.

"Are you going to quarter those tomatoes?" Kathryn heard her mother's voice as she was preparing a salad. Kathryn stiffened, and her pulse quickened. "Well, I was," she answered. Her mother responded, "Oh, okay," but the tone of her voice and the look on her face prompted Kathryn to ask, "Is that wrong?"

"No, no," her mother replied. "It's just that personally, I would slice them."

Kathryn's response was terse: "Fine." But as she cut the tomatoes—in slices—she thought, Can't I do anything without my mother letting me know she thinks I should do it some other way?

I am willing to wager that Kathryn's mother thought she had asked a question about cutting a tomato. What could be more trivial than that? But her daughter bristled because she heard the implication "You don't know what you're doing. I know better."

When daughters react with annoyance or even anger at the smallest, seemingly innocent remarks, mothers get the feeling that talking to their daughters can be like walking on eggshells: they have to watch every word.

A mother's questions and comments which seem to imply that a daughter should do things another way can spark disproportionate responses because they bring into focus one of the central conundrums of mother-daughter relationships: the double meaning of connection and control. Many mothers and daughters are as close as any two people can be, but closeness always carries with it the need, indeed the desire, to consider how your actions will affect the other person, and this can make you feel that you are no longer in control of your own life. Any word or action intended in the spirit of connection can be interpreted as a sign that the other person is trying to control you. This double meaning was crystallized in a comment that one woman made: "My daughter used to call me every day," she said. "I loved it. But then she stopped. I understand. She got married, she's busy, she felt she had to loosen the bonds. I understand, but I still miss those calls." In the phrase "loosen the bonds" lies the double meaning of connection and control. The word "bonds" evokes the connection of "a close bond" but also the control of "bondage": being tied up, not free.

There is yet another reason that a small comment or suggestion can grate: It can come across as a vote of no confidence. This is annoying coming from anyone, but it's especially hurtful when it comes from the person whose opinion counts most—your mother. Unaccountable as this may seem to mothers, the smallest remark can bring into focus the biggest question that hovers over nearly all conversations between mothers and daughters: Do you see me for who I am? And is who I am okay? When mothers' comments to daughters (or, for that matter, daughters' comments to mothers) seem to answer that question in the affirmative, it's deeply reassuring: all's right with the world. But when their words seem to imply that the answer is No, there's something wrong with what you're doing, then daughters (and, later in life, mothers) can feel the ground on which they stand begin to tremble: They start to doubt whether how they do things, and therefore who they are, really is okay.

## YOU'RE NOT GOING TO WEAR *THAT,* ARE YOU?

Loraine was spending a week visiting her mother, who lived in a senior living complex. One evening they were about to go down to dinner in the dining room. As Loraine headed for the door, her mother hesitated. Scanning her daughter from head to toe, she asked, "You're not going to wear *that,* are you?"

"Why not?" Loraine asked, her blood pressure rising. "What's wrong with it?"

"Well, people tend to dress nicely for dinner here, that's all," her mother explained, further offending her daughter by implying that she was not dressed nicely.

Her mother's negative questions always rubbed Loraine the wrong way, because they so obviously weren't questions at all. "Why do you always disapprove of my clothes?" she asked.

Now her mother got that hurt look which implied it was Loraine who was being a cad. "I don't disapprove," she protested. "I just thought you might want to wear something else."

A way to understand the difference between what Loraine heard and what her mother said she meant is the distinction between message and metamessage. When she said "I don't disapprove," Loraine's mother was referring to the message: the literal meaning of the words she spoke. The disapproval Loraine heard was the metamessage—that is, the implications of her mother's words. Everything we say has meaning on these two levels. The message is the meaning that resides in the dictionary definitions of words. Everyone usually agrees on this. But people frequently differ on how to *interpret* the words, because interpretations depend on metamessages—the meaning gleaned from how something is said, or from the fact that it is said at all. Emotional responses are often triggered by metamessages.

When Loraine's mother said "I don't disapprove," she was doing what I call "crying literal meaning": She could take cover in the message and claim responsibility only for the literal meaning of her words. When someone cries literal meaning, it is hard to resolve disputes, because you end up talking about the meaning of the message when it was the meaning of the metamessage that got your goat. It's not that some utterances have metamessages, or hidden meanings, while others don't. Everything we say has metamessages indicating how our words are to be interpreted: Is this a serious statement or a joke? Does it show annoyance or goodwill? Most of the time, metamessages are communicated and interpreted without notice because, as far as anyone can tell, the speaker and the hearer agree on their meaning. It's only when the metamessage the speaker intends—or acknowledges—doesn't match the one the hearer perceives that we notice and pay attention to them.

In interpreting her mother's question as a sign of disapproval, Loraine was also drawing on past conversations. She couldn't count the times her mother had commented, on this visit and on all the previous ones, "You're wearing *that*?" And therein lies another reason that anything said between mothers and daughters can either warm our hearts or raise our hackles: Their conversations have a long history, going back literally to the start of the daughter's life. So anything either one says at a given moment takes meaning not only from the words spoken at that moment but from all the conversations they have had in the past. This works in both positive and negative ways. We come to expect certain kinds of comments from each other, and are primed to interpret what we hear in that familiar spirit.

Even a gift, a gesture whose message is clearly for connection, can carry a metamessage of criticism in the context of conversations that took place in the past. If a daughter gives her artist mother a gift certificate to an upscale clothing store, it may be resented if her daughter has told her again and again, "You're too old to keep dressing like a hippie, Mom." And criticism may be the impression if a mother who has made clear she can't stand her daughter's messy kitchen gives her as a gift an expensive organizer for kitchen utensils. The gift giver may be incensed that her generosity has been underappreciated, but the lack of gratitude has less to do with the message of the gift than with the metamessage it implies, which came from past conversations.

The long history of conversations that family members share contributes not only to how listeners interpret words but also to how speakers choose them. One woman I talked to put it this way: "Words are like touch. They can caress or they can scratch. When I talk to my children, my words often end up scratching. I don't want to use words that way, but I can't help it. I know their sensitivities, so I know what will have an effect on them. And if I'm feeling hurt by something they said or did, I say things that I know will scratch. It happens somewhere in a zone between instinct and intention." This observation articulates the power of language to convey meanings that are not found in the literal definitions of words. It highlights how we use past conversations as a resource for meaning in present ones. At the same time, it describes the distinction between message and metamessage, a distinction that will be important in all the conversations examined in this book.

## WHO CARES?

While talking casually to her husband, Joanna absentmindedly tugs at a hangnail until the skin tears and a tiny droplet of blood appears. Unthinking, she holds it out before her husband's eyes. "Put on a Band-Aid," he says flatly. Her husband's non-reaction makes Joanna wonder why she showed him so insignificant an injury. And then she realizes: She developed the habit of displaying her wounds, no matter how small, to her mother. Had she shown the ever so slightly broken skin to her, her mother would have reached out, taken Joanna's finger in her hand, and examined it with a soothing grimace. Joanna was looking for that glance of sympathy, that fleeting reminder that someone else shares her universe. Who but her mother would regard so small an injury as worthy of attention? No one—because her mother would be responding not to the wound but to Joanna's gesture in showing it to her. It isn't only, isn't really, concern for the torn hangnail that her mother shares but a subtle language of connection: The tiny drop of blood is an excuse for Joanna to remind her mother "I'm here" and for her mother to reassure her daughter "I care."

Many women develop the habit of telling their mothers about minor misfortunes because they treasure the metamessage of caring they know they will hear in response, though, like Joanna, they may not notice until they get a different response from someone else. This also happened to a student in one of my classes, Carrie, when she was sick with the flu and called home. Carrie usually talked to her mother when she called, but this time her mother was out of the country, so she spoke to her father instead. This is how Carrie recounted the conversation in a class assignment:

Carrie: Hey, Daddy. I'm sick with the flu. It's absolutely awful.

Dad: Well, take some medicine.

Carrie: I already did, but I still feel terrible.

Dad: Well then, go to the doctor.

Carrie: But everyone else at school is sick too. I couldn't get an appointment for today.

Dad: Well then, I'm sorry. I can't help you there.

In commenting on this conversation, Carrie explained that she knows perfectly well to take medicine and go to the doctor when she's sick. What she had been looking for when she called home was a metamessage of caring. In her words: "I am used to talking to my mother and having her fuss and worry over the smallest of my problems." In contrast to her mother's characteristic response, her father's pragmatic approach came across as indifference and left her feeling dissatisfied, even slightly hurt.

## THE ANGEL IS IN THE DETAILS

Mothers and daughters don't need to be feeling sick to talk to each other at length, in person or on the phone. In telling me what they most appreciated in their relationships with their mothers, many women mentioned their frequent conversations about the smallest details of their daily lives: "Who else could I tell that the sweater I've been eyeing finally went on sale? Who else would care?" That is one of the precious aspects of talking to your mother: no one else cares what you wore, what you ate, or exactly what someone said and what you replied. For most women, being interested in the insignificant details of another's life is a sign of intimacy and caring.

The exchange can go from mother to daughter as well. In an assignment for my class, Kate Stoddard examined e-mails she received from her mother. In one, her mother updated Kate on decisions she'd made about clothes she had purchased with Kate's help:

> (Love the items I ordered but will return the 2 purple tops
> . . . The green sweater (snapped front) and shell are perfect
> and I love them, (thanks for finding them!) and the navy
> cardigan is great too.)

By enclosing this information in parentheses, Kate's mother showed that she regarded it as more by-the-way than newsworthy, yet recounting these details helped maintain her close relationship with her daughter, who was away at college.

If exchanging details of daily life reflects and creates intimacy, then not being interested in the details—or getting them wrong—can be a sign that intimacy has fled. In her book *The Love They Lost: Living with the Legacy of Divorce,* Stephanie Staal, who lived with her father after her parents divorced, recalls times when she was a teen that she was truly enjoying her mother's company during her weekly visits. "But then," Staal writes, "she might ask about a friend I hadn't spoken with for years, or get my current boyfriend's name all wrong, and I would give her a tremulous smile and feel the distance between us." That her mother did not know the day-to-day specifics of her life was a painful reminder of what Staal had lost when her mother moved out.

## THE GRAND INQUISITOR

Alison Kelleher is another student who explained, in an analysis she wrote for my class, that talk about small details forms a large part of her conversations—and her relationship—with her mother. She zeroed in on the role played by her mother's questions.

According to Alison, she is very close to her mother, and that closeness is created and reinforced when they talk about "the littlest occurrence or tiniest detail" of her life. Alison describes one of those conversations this way:

In a recent telephone conversation with my mother I was telling her about my day and what I did. I told her I had gone to lunch with Larry, my brother, chapel choir and the movies with my friend Rob. She proceeded to ask, "What did you wear?" "What did you eat?" "What kind of dressing?" (to my response "steak salad"), "Did you have anything to tell Larry or just a regular lunch?" "Did you ask him or he called you?" "Did you wear the same thing to choir and the movies, or did you change?" "What time did you go to bed then?" "Didn't you have to work?" "Did it take long to finish?" and so on.

Reading these questions, you can see why Alison and her brother call their mother "the Grand Inquisitor," but Alison says this with affection, not irritation. She does not mind her mother asking all these questions, because she likes to tell stories about her day (though she does sometimes get annoyed when her mother has to repeat questions because while Alison was answering them, her mother was talking over her, asking three more!).

Anything that can signal intimacy can seem like an intrusion if the intimacy is unwanted. Just so, attention to details about your life can be resented rather than welcomed if you don't want to be that involved with the person asking questions. A mother who wants to know all the details of her daughter's life may seem like a best friend or an interrogator, and many daughters may not share Alison's appreciation of that role.

A daughter might wish her mother would ask fewer questions when they are reminders of a topic the daughter would rather not dwell on. This was the case with another student, Colleen, who wrote:

I recently went through a difficult time when I broke up with my boyfriend of 4 years. Although I generally confide in my friends when it comes to such issues, I thought that my mom might be able to provide a different perspective than my friends. And she did. She was more than willing to listen, to comfort me and to offer her opinion. However, she was also quick to remind me why I hesitated to talk to her about things like this in the past. Ever since that talk, she has repeatedly managed to steer our conversations back to the breakup, asking questions like, "How are you dealing with things?" "How about Chris, is he okay?" "What are you going to do about this summer?" "Have you met anyone else interesting?" and so on. . . . I finally had to tell her that I really didn't want to talk about it anymore because she was just making things harder. She was upset.

Knowing of someone's troubles always presents a dilemma: Should you avoid mentioning the topic and risk seeming callous, or mention it to show your concern and risk causing further hurt—and seeming intrusive? Colleen's mother chose the latter, but her daughter would have preferred the former. Clearly, her mother asked these questions as an expression of caring and a way of preserving and nurturing the closeness that Colleen had initiated by confiding in her. But whereas Colleen had appreciated her mother's input when she asked for it, she did not appreciate her questions when it was her mother who raised the topic, and she did not appreciate how often her mother raised it. No doubt her mother was upset because making things harder for her daughter was the last thing she wanted to do, and because telling her not to ask questions curtailed the closeness between them.

If a mother craves information as a way of being close to her daughter, then the ability to offer or withhold that information gives a daughter power in their relationship, power she may use to enhance their closeness or to limit it. This is one of many ways that a power shift occurs when daughters become adults.

## INVOLVEMENT OR INVASION

Lillian has very different conversations with each of her two daughters, both women in their thirties. From the time she was small, the younger daughter, Andrea, was a private child; Lillian could not pry information from her. When children are young, a mother needs to know what's going on in their lives in order to protect them. But probing questions inevitably caused Andrea to clam up, snapping shut as surely as does a literal clam when it senses a threat. Lillian learned early on that she would glean more from Andrea if she acted uninterested and let her volunteer information in her own time. Andrea was like a well-protected castle, and Lillian had to wait outside until the drawbridge mysteriously lowered, opened invisibly from inside.

Lillian's older daughter, Nadine, could not be more different. From the time she was small, she talked freely with her mother about whatever was going on in her life. She confided her worries, asked for advice, and seemed to have few secrets she did not want to divulge. Yet, ironically, it is with Nadine that Lillian now has conflict. They'll be talking congenially on the phone, Nadine telling her mother about some personal matter, Lillian asking questions and offering comments much as any woman friend might do. But then Lillian asks a question—one that seems to her similar in spirit to the many she has asked before—and Nadine flares up in anger, even hangs up the phone. Lillian is left staring at a silent receiver, smarting as from a blow. She knows she overstepped some boundary but wonders how she could have known where that line was drawn. To Lillian, Nadine is like an unpredictable hostess who invites you into her home, then kicks you out and slams the door in your face. At those times, she thinks it would have been better had she not been invited in at all.

It seems ironic, even unaccountable, to Lillian that these problems arise with Nadine, the daughter who has always talked so freely to her, rather than with Andrea, the one who had always held her at arm's length. But this development is not surprising, because talking about personal topics provides opportunities for comments that can hurt feelings and therefore spark anger. And this explains why mother-daughter conversations can be especially troubling as well as especially comforting. Discord at times results from the kinds of conversations many women have with other women they are close to. Flare-ups triggered by a turn in the conversation that one or the other resents are therefore more likely when a mother and daughter talk at length about personal topics—just the sort of conversation that many women treasure as a sign of closeness.

One risk in such conversations is crossing an invisible boundary: Giving a certain amount of personal information does not mean a woman wants to reveal every aspect of her personal life. Knowing this, Lillian assumes that when Nadine becomes angry after Lillian asks her a question, the question she asked must have stepped into territory where her daughter did not want her to tread. But often what angers a daughter is not the kind of information a mother's question seeks but the judgment it seems to imply. And this can happen with an apparently insignificant exchange of details as much as with more emotionally laden talk.

### RAISING YOU UP OR PUTTING YOU DOWN?

Maureen is talking on the phone to her daughter Claire, a piano teacher with a full roster of private students, who was recently elected vice president of the music teachers' association to which she belongs. They are engaged in an amiable conversation, in the course of which Claire says, "I'm so tired. I was up half the night last night writing up my evaluations of the students who applied for our association's music scholarship, and tonight I'll be up late again typing up the minutes from our last meeting." Maureen responds, "You take on too much, Claire! Why can't some of the other officers do some of that? You shouldn't be typing minutes anyway; you're not the secretary, you're the vice president! I hate to see you allowing yourself to be taken advantage of." After this comment comes the explosion.

"Mom!" Claire bursts out. "You know how much I love working with the music teachers' association! I was thrilled to be elected, and it was my choice to continue as chair of the scholarship committee. I like being a judge because it helps me prepare my students for competition. And I volunteered to take minutes this one time because the secretary couldn't make the meeting. Why are you always putting me down? Why can't you just be supportive?" Maureen defends herself: "I'm *not* putting you down. I *am* being supportive!" She feels unfairly attacked. Where on earth did Claire get the idea that her mother was putting her down? Isn't it supportive to encourage her daughter to stand up for herself? And if Claire doesn't agree with her mother's suggestions, why does she get so angry? Why did such a small comment spark such a strong response?

The reason is metamessages. What Claire heard is that her mother doesn't think she has made the right choices, and that she can't perform well the tasks she has taken on. Saying that Claire lets herself be taken advantage of doesn't only impugn her judgment; it transforms her image of herself. The many tasks she has been trusted to fulfill were testament to her colleagues' respect for her abilities. Doing them all, while tiring, also made her feel important and competent. Her mother's admonitions made her feel instead like a doormat, a powerless dupe. Her colleagues' trust and respect were reframed as exploitation.

Maureen wonders, "What does she want from me?" What Claire wants from her mother is a sign of caring: "I can feel in my bones how tired you must be, but the work you're doing is important and I know you'll do a great job. You'll catch up on sleep over the weekend." She was angling for her mother's sympathy and comfort, an adult analog to the gesture of a child showing her mother her scraped knee so her mother can kiss it and make it well. How disappointed the child would be if the mother instead bawled her out for falling, which mothers sometimes do—to their children's consternation. That's the double frustration that fueled Claire's outburst: Not only did her mother fail to offer the sympathy she was seeking but, worse, the advice she offered implied that she had no confidence in Claire's judgment and competence. But consider Maureen's point of view. She was watching out for her daughter, demonstrating the quality that so many women say they value in their mothers: always being on her side. That's why Claire's reaction is so unexpected, and its unexpectedness makes it all the more painful. Maureen thought she was riding happily and comfortably along the road with her daughter when suddenly she was cast out of the car with a thud.

Both Maureen and Claire were caught off guard by the other's response to her words. It is just such differing interpretations of the same way of speaking that make frustration so common among grown daughters and mothers. The sequence goes something like this: A daughter reveals something personal in the spirit of closeness. Her mother, wishing to protect her daughter and to see things go well for her, offers advice; the metamessage she intends is caring. But the daughter hears a different metamessage: that her mother disapproves of what she is doing and therefore of her. This implication hurts the daughter's feelings, so she lashes out, hurting her mother's feelings in turn. Both are tied up in the knots created by the double meaning of advice: while it offers to help, it also implies that you're doing something wrong; otherwise you wouldn't need advice. The knots are hard to untangle because, more often than not, the threads that form them are found not in the messages, which are easy to pinpoint, but in metamessages, what the words imply.

The way the argument between Maureen and Claire arose shows why conversations between mothers and daughters can be the best and also the worst: the risks and the gifts grow from the same roots. Having self-revealing conversations about personal matters brings many women great rewards: knowing that someone cares about the details of your life and understands what you're going through, someone to whom you can open your heart and reveal what's in it. Through these conversations, women also gain insight into their situations, see more options for what to do, and are reassured that they are not alone, that others have had similar experiences. But these kinds of conversations are also risky: You are giving another person information so close to your sense of yourself that if she doesn't react as you'd wish, you are deeply hurt—as you could not be if you had been talking, say, about politics or current events. There is nothing more hurtful than thinking you are in the embrace of a safe conversation, sharing personal details that reinforce closeness, and suddenly feeling that the person you trusted with information about your life and yourself is using it as a weapon with which to strike. You may then lash out, thinking you are striking back, but if the other person thought she was offering a constructive response, she will perceive your reaction as a first blow.

Here are two examples of conversations that left both daughter and mother feeling wounded, each blaming the other.

## "I CAN'T BELIEVE YOU SAID THAT!"

Martha was delighted that her daughter Vicki was telling her about her life. "I'm so worked up about the election," Vicki said, "I can't stop talking about it. I've been volunteering to call voters in the swing states. I'm actually thinking of going down for a week to help get out the vote." Martha responded in a way that she thought was full of praise. "Vicki," she said, "I love hearing you so passionate about something. You've been in such a funk lately, I can't remember the last time I've seen you excited about anything. I'm so happy." Suddenly, out of nowhere, came an outburst: "I can't believe you said that! Who cares if you're happy or not. This isn't about you! I should have known I can't tell you anything."

Martha felt baffled and hurt. She thought she had said something positive and reinforcing. She had no idea this would set her daughter off. It was outbursts like this that made her feel like she was walking on eggshells when she spoke to her daughter. But on hearing this conversation, I could see why Vicki reacted as she did, why what Martha thought was praise and reinforcement had the effect of hurting her daughter—because, after all, when people get angry it's usually because they feel hurt. Under the guise of saying she was glad her daughter was passionate about something now, Martha said that Vicki had previously lacked this positive quality, passion. Built into the effusive "The way you are now is great," is an implication, "The way you were before was crummy." It was the contrast of the current positive with a past negative that turned Martha's comment from a compliment to criticism. Whereas Martha regarded the positive part as what she had really said, the negative part overshadowed that from her daughter's point of view.

This disappointment was not what Vicki expressed when she said "This isn't about you!"—the accusation that most hurt Martha. I can think of several reasons why Vicki accused her mother of being self-centered rather than complaining about her insulting evaluation of Vicki's past state. First, at the time you are hurt, you often don't know exactly what you're reacting to. You just know that you had been feeling good and now you're feeling bad. Second is the distinction between message and metamessage. The hurtful implication was not explicit in her mother's words, so Vicki focused on what was: the "I" in "I'm so happy" to hear this. Furthermore, Vicki may well have sensed that accusing her mother of being self-centered was something that had a good chance of returning hurt for hurt. (There is no way to know whether, as I am inclined to think, "I'm so happy" was just an idiomatic expression, much as saying "I'm so sorry" can be a way of expressing sympathy, or whether Vicki was right that on some level her mother was focusing on her own emotional experience rather than her daughter's.)

This conversation has much in common with another one that I heard about from the mother who took part in it and was upset by it. The conversation also began as a comfortable interchange about everyday happenings and feelings. "I've been really down lately," Judy confided to her mother, Eva, on the phone. "That bad evaluation has really gotten to me. I don't know why I can't just shake it off, but I can't." Eva tried to offer helpful advice. "Maybe you should consider taking Prozac," she said. "I've noticed you have a tendency to get depressed, and so many of my friends tell me that Prozac really helps them." Suddenly the cozy atmosphere of casual talk was shattered. Judy exclaimed, "I can't believe you said that! I've never been depressed! Just because I'm having a bad day you want to make me out like some kind of a

mental case!" Eva was caught completely off guard by this explosion. She had no idea why her daughter had reacted so strongly to
her well-meaning suggestion.

## LARGER THAN LIFE

As in the previous example, Judy was asking for sympathy for
what she was feeling now, and Eva responded with a general observation about her daughter. I have no way of knowing whether
or not Eva was right that Judy has a tendency to be depressed. But
I can see that Eva, because she cares so deeply about her daughter,
would wish to find a way to help her feel better, and would believe
that taking an antidepressant might do the trick. In other words,
Eva might be making more of Judy's unhappiness than someone
else would precisely because, as a mother, she cares more. I can
also see that, whereas a suggestion which Judy thinks is an over-
reaction might be annoying coming from someone else, coming
from her mother it might seem like a damning judgment, because
her mother's estimation of her carries great weight. If so, behind
Judy's fury is the fear that her mother might be right: what if her
feeling down really isn't just a normal case of the blues but evidence of mental instability?

Because of explosions like these, talking to a grown daughter
or a mother can feel like picking your way through a minefield.
Even if she could understand Judy's being annoyed by her advice,
Eva found her daughter's reaction grossly out of proportion to the
slight. Okay, so you don't agree that you tend to get depressed, she
thinks. What's the big deal? Surely what I said couldn't be *that*
bad! A daughter's response to her mother's words often seems out
of proportion to the current slight because it really isn't a reaction
to the words just spoken; it's a response to the weight of her
mother's opinion. This knowledge should comfort mothers who
don't understand the proportions of their daughters' anger: To a
daughter, a mother is larger than life, so any judgment coming
from her can seem like a life sentence. "When I was a kid," one

woman told me, "and my mother got mad at me, she'd scream that I was the worst child in the world. I'd scream back that she was the worst mother, but underneath I feared she was right. And even now, if I have a fight with my husband or I think someone is mad at me, I hear my mother's voice and I think maybe I really was the worst child, and now I'm the worst adult."

Hurtful generalizations can go from daughter to mother as well. Marilyn was a craftsperson who took great pride in her work. She had developed a following for the jackets she made out of patchwork fabric she created herself. But lately she had been experimenting with a whole new use for her fabrics: wall hangings that mixed colors and textiles in an original and unique way. She was proud of her new line but also apprehensive about how her clientele would respond. Indeed, the first time she displayed her hangings at a crafts show, Marilyn was disappointed that very few of them sold. She told her daughter about this experience, fully expecting to hear encouragement: "Your wall hangings are beautiful, Mom. I'm sure the customers will come." Instead her daughter said, "You really should stick to making the jackets because you know you're good at that and that's what your customers want." Marilyn felt knocked down. It was devastating to be told she had been wasting all those hours trying to develop in new directions, and it was all the more hurtful coming from her own daughter. It felt as if her daughter wanted to hurt her, and knew her well enough to choose the best target, the aspect of her life where she was most vulnerable.

## GREAT EXPECTATIONS

The negative aspects of the mother-daughter relationship may result in part from the magnitude of the positive ones. Daughters and mothers expect, and often get, so much from each other that their frustration is proportionately vast when they don't get it. The actress Liv Ullmann expressed the ideal that every daughter craves and some find, at least at times. Ullmann said in describing her relationship with her daughter, "Whatever happens to her she knows she can come to me and she won't be judged and she will be supported and helped." And there is a parallel expectation, by at least some mothers, that their daughters will do whatever they ask. As one woman put it, "My mother is always telling me how much she did for her mother. I know she's thinking that I should be doing the same for her."

These expectations themselves can spark resentment. Margot gets a call from her daughter, Bonnie. "Hi, Mom," Bonnie begins. "I just found out I have a meeting to go to in San Francisco next Friday. Stan can take Friday off work, so we decided to make a weekend of it. We figured Jonah could spend the weekend with you, okay?"

Margot feels a tightening in her chest. "Gee, honey," she says hesitantly. "Saturday's my birthday, and your dad and I were planning to do something special to celebrate." Margot holds her breath. She hates to disappoint her daughter, and she rarely turns down her frequent requests to watch Jonah.

Bonnie is surprised. "You never cared about birthdays," she says.

"That's true," Margot allows. "But this one is my sixty-fifth, so it feels kind of special." Bonnie accepts this, but Margot feels terrible whenever she says no to her daughter. She herself believes, as Liv Ullmann put it, that she should be there to support and help her daughter whenever she is needed. And then she resents Bonnie for making her feel bad just because she wants to celebrate her birthday.

A daughter's resentment too can flow from her inability to fulfill expectations—her mother's and her own. Sharon is talking to her mother on the phone, and her mother asks if they can meet for lunch. Sharon knows how lonely her mother has been since her father died, and her heart goes out to her, but she doesn't have time in her busy life to keep her mother company day after day. Sharon has to say no, she can't meet for lunch. But because she thinks she should, she feels awful—and ends up blaming her mother for making her feel that way.

## A WIRE RUNS BETWEEN US

In situations like these, part of mothers' and daughters' resentment results from what each perceives her own or the other's obligations to be. But another part is the connection between them that makes each deeply feel the other's emotions. That certainly was the case for me and my mother.

One day, when my mother was in her nineties and living with my father in a retirement community, I came home to find her voice on my answering machine. She had been reading an article and she said, in a voice full of spontaneous excitement: "They *quote you*!" It made my heart expand to hear the excitement in her voice. I dialed her number, eager to hear her happiness firsthand. But when she answered the phone, I heard a different voice—a clipped, laconic greeting spoken in a flat, lifeless tone. I knew immediately that she was not happy.

"What's wrong?" I asked. "Don't you feel well?"

"No, I'm fine," she said in a voice that said she wasn't fine. "So what did you do today?" she asked in a sodden tone. I gave my typical answer: "I worked on my book." To this she gave her typical response: "You work too much. You should take some time out to have fun." This comment made my heart sink, as it always did, sounding like a dismissal of the life I'd chosen. My usual response was to say defensively, "I enjoy working. To me work is fun." This time, though, I thought, Oh good, I can tell her I did something to "have fun." I said, "But we went out in the afternoon. We met another couple and went to the FDR Memorial and then we went to dinner." She did not say, "Good, I'm glad you're finally doing something to have fun." She did not ask, "How was the FDR Memorial? What's it like?" She said, "We don't do anything. We just have dinner and go upstairs." Zap. I felt a pang, a familiar blow to my chest that I always felt when my mother was unhappy. Her disappointment with her life felt like an accusation, as if I were the one who had disappointed her, the one who failed her by not preventing her unhappiness.

I always felt as if there was a wire running from my mother's chest to mine, because her emotions were directly transferred to me. When I called her, I knew from the way she answered the phone which emotion I was about to absorb. If her intonation went up as she said, "Oh, hello, sweetheart, how *are* you?" my spirits lifted. But my spirits sagged if her intonation was flat as she said, "Hello. How are *you*." I now know that I'm not the only woman attached by this wire, and that the wire can conduct current in both directions. One mother of a grown daughter put it this way: "I can always tell by the sound of her voice how she's feeling. If she's down even just a little bit, it makes me sad. I pick it up in the first second. When she was going through her divorce, she was pretty much down all the time, so I was pretty much down all the time."

This mother also has two sons, but it is only with her daughter that this transfer of emotion occurs. I heard the same from many of the women I talked to: If they have both daughters and sons, they sense their daughters' moods more readily, and their daughters' emotions are more likely to affect their own. And daughters say the same for their mothers as compared to their fathers. The intensity of this effect varies, though. Some mothers tell me that they feel bad if their daughters feel bad, but the feeling does not last long after the conversation ends. And my two sisters, who had the same mother I did and also knew immediately what mood she was in, were not as deeply affected by it as I was. The range of intensity varies widely by individual personality and the nature of each mother-daughter relationship, but within that range, the tendency to absorb the other's emotions is typically strongest between mothers and daughters.

Women who have both daughters and sons also tell me that they talk more often to their daughters than to their sons, much as many women talk to their friends often and long. Talking more frequently is another reason that relationships between daughters and mothers can be more fraught than those between mothers and sons, fathers and daughters, or fathers and sons. "What do you girls find to talk about?" my father used to ask in genuine puzzlement when my mother talked for hours on the phone with me or one of my sisters. For daughters and mothers, as for any pair of women who are close, long rambling conversations can be among the most satisfying aspects of their relationship, a big part of what makes them close, whether they are engaging in serious discussion of personal problems or simply telling each other about the details of their daily lives. But frequent conversations also provide frequent opportunities to absorb negative emotions—and to learn to discern those emotions from subtle signals sent by the words spoken, by tone of voice, or by silence.

The invisible wire that transfers emotions from one to the other also accounts in part for why many women do not want to tell their mothers about what's going on in their lives—especially about anything major that might be worrisome, like significant illness or problems at work. I was quick to tell my mother of small misfortunes, in order to receive the balm of her concern. But I did not tell her of serious problems, because if I did, I'd be sure to hear from her the next day, "I was up all night worrying about you." My problems became her problems, and I did not want to cause my mother to lose sleep—or to have to shift from seeking comfort to providing it.

## OUT OF THE WOODS

It's impossible to know whether the verbal blows that mothers and daughters sometimes exchange are truly, utterly unintended or whether, sometimes at least, each may be aware on some level that she is hurling zingers but thinks she can get away with it by crying literal meaning. Two people who have been that close for that long are sure to have a history of hurts for which they may be seeking subtle revenge. But they also have a history of shared humor, shared stories, and shared language, along with deep caring about the other's welfare, that can make their conversations more intimate and more comfortable than talking with almost anyone else. Understanding the workings of message and meta-message, and the ways they negotiate connection and control, intimacy and intrusion, can maximize the times that words caress and minimize the times that they scratch.

Because talk plays such an enormous role in women's lives, understanding how conversation can lead to frustration and finding ways to improve conversations is key to more satisfying, less frustrating relationships between adult daughters and mothers. Our deepest wish is to be understood and approved of by our mothers and our daughters. We can get closer to that goal by listening to the ways we talk to each other, and by learning to talk to each other in new ways.

# 2

## MY MOTHER, MY HAIR
## CARING AND CRITICIZING

While visiting my parents in Florida, I was sitting across the dining room table from my mother when she asked, "Do you like your hair that long?" I laughed. (When I was younger and my mother stronger, I might have been hurt or angry.) Surprised, she asked what was funny. I explained that I'd laughed because in researching the book I was writing I had come across so many examples of mothers who criticize their daughters' hair. "I wasn't criticizing," my mother said. It was apparent that she felt slightly hurt, so I let the matter drop. But a little later I asked, "Mom, what do you think of my hair?" Without hesitation she replied, "I think it's a little too long."

Sheila's mother has come for a visit. One morning she says, brightly, "I love your hair when it's combed back. It looks so beautiful that way." Now this sounds like a compliment. And it would be, if she had said it when Sheila was wearing her hair combed back. But on this day, Sheila has let her hair fall forward onto her face. Complimenting her daughter on how her hair looks when it's fixed in a different way implies "I don't think your hair looks good the way you have it now." When Sheila responds, "Well, I'm wearing it this way today!" it's clear from her tone that she is annoyed. "What's wrong with you?" her mother asks, feeling singed. "Why are you so sensitive?"

The complaint I heard most often when I talked to women about their mothers was "She's always criticizing me." The complaint I heard most often when I talked to women about their grown daughters was "I can't open my mouth. She takes everything as criticism." Each of these complaints is the flip side of the other. Daughters and mothers agree on what the troublesome conversations are; they disagree on who introduced the note of contention, because they have different views of the metamessages their words imply. Where the daughter sees criticism, the mother sees caring: she was only making a suggestion, trying to help, offering insight or advice. Most of the time, both are right.

Whether or not Sheila's hair looks better combed back than it does falling forward, her mother thinks it does. And what if she's right? Isn't it a mother's prerogative, if not her obligation, to make sure that her daughter looks her best? Wouldn't a mother be derelict if she did not use her greater life experience to help her daughter better her life, including her appearance? That's the spirit in which making suggestions or offering help sends a metamessage of caring. But any suggestion or advice also sends a metamessage of criticism. After all, a mother who thinks her daughter is doing nothing wrong will see no need to offer advice or help. And when those offers of advice and suggestions are frequent, a daughter may feel as if her mother sees her as a reclamation project, and that makes the daughter feel like a wreck.

The metamessages of caring and criticizing are both there, bought with the same verbal currency. But each party to the conversation sees only one, so daughters feel unjustly criticized while mothers feel unjustly accused. When tempers flare, both feel blindsided. Neither sees the fastball coming, because they are focusing on different balls. To the daughter, the criticism causes her outburst. But to her mother, the outburst comes out of the blue, because she believes in her heart that her intention was not to criticize, much less to wound. So she feels wounded by what she perceives to be her daughter's surprise attack.

## WHAT ARE YOU LOOKING AT?

Implied criticism is not the only reason many women are dismayed by their mothers' comments about their hair. Any attention to their appearance—even praise—can wound because it seems to imply lack of attention to what daughters consider more important aspects of their lives.

A woman recounted that she eagerly anticipated her mother's pride at seeing her daughter appear on C-Span with the president of the United States during a bill-signing ceremony. It is easy to understand why her mother's first comment has stuck in her mind; it was "You looked like you needed a haircut." It occurred to me that this woman might have felt like borrowing the line yet another woman told me she used with her mother: "I'm sorry, my lifetime interest in the topic of my hair has been exhausted."

Hair is one of what I think of as the Big Three topics about which mothers tend to criticize (or advise) their daughters. The others are clothing and weight. (For some there is a fourth, but it is of a very different sort: how they raise their children.) Here's an example of the second—clothes.

When my book *You Just Don't Understand* was published, I went on a book tour that included local television appearances in many different cities. I asked friends who lived in these cities to videotape my appearances, and when the tour was over, I showed them to my parents. My mother was very excited to see her daughter on television, but she was also upset because I wore the same suit on all the shows. She was not mollified by my explanation that no one else watched all the shows. After that, whenever

I appeared on a national television show, I knew that if I wore that same suit I would hear about it from my mother, and I would earn her praise if I wore something else. If my mother was upset by my inattention to my clothes, I was upset that instead of paying attention to what I said, she was looking at what I wore.

My mother's obsession with what I wore on television was limited to a particular context, but concern with the third of the Big Three—weight—can surface in almost any situation. Here is one of the most extreme anecdotes I heard.

Jenny was one of many women who told me that dieting was a constant preoccupation in her family. When she was in the hospital, having given birth to her first child, she received a visit from her mother, who, unfortunately, happened to arrive just as Jenny was beginning to eat her first solid food in three days. As Jenny lifted a buttered roll to her lips, her mother appeared in the doorway and said, "I could rip that roll right out of your hands." No doubt her mother's remark had just popped out, an automatic response rather than a premeditated one, but at that moment, having given birth seemed to Jenny more worthy of attention than the caloric content of what she was eating.

Though many women mentioned comments about their clothing and their weight when they told me that their mothers were critical of them, the topic that surfaced most consistently—and in many ways, most interestingly—was hair.

## A HAIR STORY

When mothers critique their daughters' hair—or other aspects of their appearance—they may well be saying what others notice but don't express. You don't walk up to a stranger and say, "I can see you didn't wash your hair this morning. You'd look so much better if you did." But mothers—and later grown daughters—feel entitled if not obligated to put these observations into words.

Why, though, is criticism (and, for that matter, compliments) so often focused on hair? Two clues emerged in the comments made by a woman who, like so many others, was telling me about her mother's tendency to criticize her hair. "My mom tells me it's not professional to wear my hair long," Meghan said. "What's especially annoying is that I get so many compliments on my hair. Everyone else seems to think it's really pretty, including my husband. As a matter of fact," Meghan added, as she warmed to the topic, "my mom hates her own hair! She's always staring at herself in the mirror, trying to push it down or fluff it up or move it off her face or pull it onto her face." Pushing hair down, fluffing it up, moving it on or off our faces—Meghan's observations bring into focus a dilemma facing all women: the many options we have put all girls and women in a quandary about how to wear our hair. We have such a wide range of choices that any choice we make is guaranteed not to be the best one possible. This also explains why many women have such a hard time getting a haircut they like—and why just contemplating getting a haircut can inspire as much anxiety as optimism.

I was pondering this while riding a shuttle bus taking passengers from an airport arrival terminal to the main terminal. I scanned the women in the bus: There was not a single one whose hair I thought was the most flattering it could be; every one of them, in my view, would have looked better if she wore her hair differently. Of course, I would never tell them so—but perhaps their mothers would. I then scanned the men in the bus. Every one of them had a nondescript hairstyle, not a single one of which stood out as less than optimal. (Try this experiment yourself in any public place where strangers gather: a bus, an airplane, a supermarket.)

Boys and men can choose an unusual style if they want to: They can grow their hair so it reaches their shoulders, pull it back into a ponytail, leave it long and uncombed, or shave it off entirely. And if they do, there's a pretty good chance that some people, including their mothers, will think they'd look better if they wore it a different way. But most men adopt a style that attracts no special attention or interpretation, as all the men I was looking at that day had done. This is a luxury girls and women do not have. And that is why it is so likely that no matter how we wear our hair, some others—including our mothers and, when they're grown, our daughters—will think that a different choice would have been better.

The spirit in which Meghan told me that her mother hates her own hair was something like "It's not as if she's some kind of hair maven who has the answer to how hair should look." But the image of Meghan's mother trying to get her own hair just right as she stares in the mirror highlights another reason that many mothers tend to be critical of their daughters' hair: they are subjecting their daughters to the same scrutiny to which they subject themselves. That Meghan's mother looks at her daughter's face the same way she looks in a mirror suggests that she sees her daughter as a reflection of herself. This explains both why many mothers critique their daughters' appearance and why many daughters wish they wouldn't: The sense that our mothers see us as reflections of themselves clashes with our wish to be seen for who we are. At the same time, our mothers' scrutiny seems to confirm our worst fears: we are fatally flawed.

### A MOTHER'S EYE: THE GREAT MAGNIFIER

For a time, my mother was obsessed with a flaw she detected in my appearance. It began with a photograph I showed her, a close-up of my face. She peered at the picture with particular intensity. "Look," she said. "This eye is smaller." Then she turned to examine my actual eyes. "Yes, it is," she concluded, looking concerned. "The left one is smaller. You'd better have a doctor look at that. It could be a sign of thyroid disease." I looked again at the picture, and I could see it too. It was the same face I'd always had, but now my left eye had become the most prominent feature in it.

For a while thereafter, every time I looked in the mirror, my left eye seemed to be at the center of my face. And during that period, every time I visited my mother, she would grasp my chin and examine my face: "That eye really is smaller. Have you talked to a doctor about it yet?" How had I missed this flaw all these years? Or was it really something new, a symptom of a disease? I did ask my doctor, who scoffed at my query and assured me there was nothing wrong with my thyroid—or my eye. The season of my smaller eye eventually passed. My left eye is still smaller, but it has ceased to seem a big liability. Only when my mother focused on it had it become a major flaw—had it appeared, taken shape, become prominent because it was the focus of her attention.

A mother's gaze is like a magnifying glass held between the sun's rays and kindling. It concentrates the rays of imperfection on the kindling of her daughter's yearning for approval. The result is a conflagration—*whoosh*.

In the case of my left eye, my mother's concern might have been excessive if not obsessive. I certainly thought it was. But where I saw critique of my appearance, I have no doubt my mother saw concern for my health. I might, after all—if not in this instance then in another—have a disease whose symptom was so subtle that only my mother's close inspection would reveal it. When I try to see this from my mother's point of view, I recall a time when I was the one who held a magnifying glass, and my mother was the one I trained it on.

Many daughters, especially when they enter their teen years, subject their mothers to harsh scrutiny. "My daughter doesn't like me very much," the mother of a teen said glumly. "She thinks I'm ugly, fat, and stupid." I felt for this mother, but her comment also made me feel guilty, because it reminded me of my stance toward my own mother when I was her daughter's age. Luckily for us both, my mother lived long enough to turn the tables on me.

In my teen years, I regarded my mother's protruding stomach with revulsion. I compared it to my own flat stomach with a smug combination of relief and self-satisfaction, even though I did nothing in particular to keep it that way. I was just a naturally skinny kid. And I knew that my mother had also been skinny when she was young; I often heard that she had weighed ninety-nine pounds when she got married. But this fact didn't affect the way I saw her. Later in my life, my metabolism changed, just as hers had, and I watched in horror as my stomach started to bulge. During a visit to my parents late in their lives, I stood beside my mother as she sat in a chair, which meant my middle was at her eye level. She poked my stomach with her index finger and said, "Hold your stomach in!" I was caught off guard, and hurt, but I also felt I had it coming to me: payback for the critical eye I had turned on her when I was a teen.

## WHY WERE YOU COMBING HER HAIR?

I had another opportunity to catch myself turning the same critical eye on my mother that she had turned on me—and to get a glimpse of what my mother's motives might have been. In the course of writing this book, I asked my sister whether our mother had ever criticized her hair. "Oh, yes," my sister said. "She always told me it was too short." I said, "She always told me mine was too long." At that, we laughed together. Then my sister added, "The funny thing is, *her* hair never looked good. Remember how it used to stick out on one side?" "You're right!" I said, and we laughed some more. But then I realized that sometimes I *told* my mother her hair didn't look good. And one of the first things I often did when I visited her during the last few years of her life was to fix her hair—and my sister said she used to do the same thing. And *then* I realized that I treasured those times. I could feel my affection for my mother swell as I combed her hair and smoothed it down. There was something so intimate about handling her hair, so moving about the way she trusted me to do it.

This memory helps me understand one reason why many daughters and mothers examine each other's appearance with such intensity. It is, in part, an expression of how close we are. We can touch each other's bodies, talk about them, and scrutinize them for flaws in ways we wouldn't do with anyone who was not so close. Touch plays a large role in creating intimacy between mother and child, and touching hair is a part of that intimacy. My grandmother lived with us until I was seven, when she passed away. Among my fondest memories of her are the times she let my sister and me unfasten the bun at the back of her head and comb her long, thin hair.

Playing with each other's hair is a frequent part of girls' intimacy as friends. In a study of conflicts among middle school girls, sociologist Donna Eder recounts a brief argument that flared up between sixth graders who were best friends. The subject of the conflict is the significance of combing another girl's hair:

Tami:    Why were you combing Peggy's hair yesterday?
Heidi:   I didn't.
Tami:    Yes you were!
Heidi:   I was not.
Tami:    You were feathering it back.
Heidi:   I was not.
Tami:    You were *too*.
Heidi:   I was *not*. You can go ask Peggy.
         *(Peggy walks by.)*
         Peggy, was I combing your hair yesterday?
         *(Peggy shakes her head no.)*
         See! What did I tell you?
Tami:    Whose hair were you combing?
Heidi:   I wasn't combing anybody's hair.
Tami:    Who was combing Peggy's hair?
Heidi:   I don't know. *(Pause)*

All this talk about who's combing whose hair sounds almost comically absurd, until you realize that what is at stake is the most precious commodity in these girls' social lives: the lines of friendship that girls at this age (and perhaps at any age) continually negotiate. When Tami accuses Heidi of having combed another girl's hair, she is accusing her of having betrayed their best friendship. Combing Peggy's hair means Tami was being more intimate with her than she should have been: If we are best friends, I'm the only one whose hair you should comb. For these girls, combing another's hair functions more or less as grooming does among primates: It reflects and reinforces lines of alliance.

I thought of Eder's study of middle school girls when a woman, Ivy, told me about a visit to her mother. Ivy had been annoyed when her mother commented that Ivy's hairdo needed improvement—and ran and got a brush and some conditioning mousse to improve it on the spot. Yet later in the visit, Ivy caught herself criticizing her mother's hair, and she offered to fix it for her. She too applied mousse; then she wound her mother's thin, gray hair around cans. When she left, Ivy felt a little guilty because her mother's new hairdo looked thick and stiff with dried mousse. But the next time they talked, her mother said how pleased she was that they had done each other's hair. She'd even told her best friend about it.

Why, I wondered, did Ivy resist letting her mother fiddle with her hair but later offer to fix her mother's? And why was her mother so pleased, even though the results had been less than flattering? I think it's about intimacy. When a daughter is grown, she may no longer want the intense physical intimacy she had with her mother when she was a child, but her mother may long to recapture it. I believe (and hope) my mother also felt that my attention to her hair reflected and reinforced our intimacy. But I'm willing to bet that that's how she felt about her attention to mine.

## THE FEARSOME JUDGMENT: BAD MOTHER

Even though fixing my mother's hair was an expression of our closeness, it is still true that I was critical of her hair, and she of mine. There is yet another reason that mothers and daughters cast a critical eye on each other's appearance: Each sees the other as representing her to the world, and women are overwhelmingly judged by appearance. This is especially urgent for mothers, because once a woman becomes a mother, her value—in the eyes of the world and often in her own eyes as well—resides largely in how she fulfills that role. And her children's appearance is only one of many criteria by which she is judged. This is true regardless of how successful she is in any other realm. In fact, if a woman is successful in another domain, the need to demonstrate success in the maternal realm is even more urgent, because many people immediately suspect her of shirking her motherly duties.

When a large corporation appoints a new CEO, how often do you hear questions raised about how the new executive's parenting will be affected? Almost never—unless she's a woman. Andrea Jung took over at the helm of the Avon cosmetics corporation in 1999. A 2004 *Newsweek* profile quotes Jung's surprise: "When I came into this role, I didn't expect that the microscope would be on how I raise my children." The article then assures readers what the microscope reveals: that Jung never misses the most important events in her children's lives.

Other examples of this double standard abound. After publication of her memoir *With a Daughter's Eye,* about her parents, Margaret Mead and Gregory Bateson, the anthropologist Mary Catherine Bateson remarked on how often she heard suggestions that Margaret Mead had neglected her daughter while pursuing her career as the best-known anthropologist of her time. But no one questioned whether her father had neglected his parenting responsibilities by leaving his family when his daughter was still a child.

Given this level of scrutiny, it is not surprising that once a woman has children, her sense of herself as a worthy person depends on avoiding that fearsome label "BAD MOTHER." And to do that, she needs to see her children as successful, happy, and presentable, because if there is anything wrong with them, she will be blamed. It was not so long ago that mothers were blamed—by the experts—when their children had conditions that we now know have biological causes. In the 1950s and 1960s, for example, it was generally believed that autism was caused by mothers who were insufficiently loving and warm—what came to be known as the "refrigerator mother" theory of autism.

We now know that autism is biological in origin, and we are horrified to think that mothers, in addition to the despair they doubtless felt on witnessing their children's disabilities, were further burdened with groundless accusations of having caused that suffering. Yet there is still a widespread tendency to hold mothers (and not fathers) responsible for almost any way that a child—or the adult that child becomes—is deemed wanting. And children themselves tend to hold this view. One woman commented, for example, that she still blames her mother for sending her away to camp when she was only five. In retrospect, she realized that her father must have weighed in on that decision as well. If Susan Maushart is right in *The Mask of Motherhood,* nearly all mothers have moments—in most cases, many moments—when they are so overwhelmed by the demands of caring for small children that they lose patience in ways they later regret. Their sense of guilt and shame is deepened by the belief that they are alone in these transgressions.

For all these reasons, few women feel completely satisfied with the job they did as mothers. This came through in a comment I heard from a woman who writes a column in her local newspaper. She said that criticism of her writing tends, most of the time, to roll off her back. She knows that readers might disagree with the positions she takes; if she's done her best, her conscience is clear. But any criticism, direct or implied, of the job she has done as a mother cuts to the quick. In that arena, she can never feel completely confident.

### "PUT ON A LITTLE LIPSTICK"

Ironically, if a mother's critical eye is sharpened by fear that she was not a good enough mother, that same critical eye can cause her to pass that fear on when her daughter has children of her own. Again, the topic is often hair.

"She would look so much prettier if she just brushed her hair," Jill's mother says, as Jill's eight-year-old daughter scampers across the room, full of energy and play. Jill bristles, because she is reminded of how her mother disapproved of her own appearance when she was a child. A tomboy from the get-go, Jill never shared her mother's concern for appearance. Her mother was always at her to brush her hair—and, when she was older, to dress more conventionally and wear makeup. ("Put on a little lipstick" was one of my own mother's refrains.) Hearing the same admonition now applied to her daughter brings back the helpless resentment Jill had experienced as a child.

Her mother's comments on her daughter's appearance remind Jill that she felt her mother never accepted Jill's own tomboyish ways, that she would have preferred a more conventionally feminine daughter. Jill always wanted her mother to focus on what she most values in herself: not how she looks but what she does—her volunteer work, her professional success, and now, her parenting. Though there's no reason to think that her mother means it this way, Jill hears the preoccupation with appearance as implying that her mother doesn't value her other accomplishments. So when her mother says Jill's daughter would look prettier if she brushed her hair, Jill cringes from double-barreled disappointment: First, her mother seems more concerned with the little girl's appearance than with aspects of her character that Jill deems more important, and second, she seems to be implying that Jill has fallen short as a parent.

Appearance is not the only way many women feel that their mothers disapprove of their children and, by implication, of their daughters' parenting. Hannah, for example, decided to raise her children in the Christian church to which her husband belonged rather than her own Jewish faith. Though Hannah is approaching her twenty-fifth wedding anniversary, her mother still seems to question that decision, repeatedly reminding her daughter that according to Jewish law, Hannah's children are Jewish because their mother is. Though Hannah knows this Jewish law perfectly well, each time her mother brings it up, Hannah repeats that her children are what they were raised to be: Christian.

I would wager that Hannah's mother is motivated by a desire to feel connected to her grandchildren: her Jewish heritage is such a fundamental part of her identity, she can't imagine having grandchildren who belong to a different, and alien, group. (This sense of loss helps explain why many foreign-born Americans want their American-born children to marry within the parents' ethnic group; if they marry outside the group, the grandchildren typically learn little of the traditions that form the foundation of their grandparents' lives.) Ironically, though, Hannah's mother's repetition of this concern has the opposite effect. Hannah doesn't invite her to attend—or even tell her about—the children's church-related activities like singing in the choir or starring in a Christmas pageant.

It is easy to see why such a fundamental difference could form an enduring point of contention between Hannah and her mother. But many mothers and daughters who experience no major conflict nonetheless find that a mother's repetition of legitimate concerns puts distance between them. Grace limits not how much time she spends with her mother but what they talk about. Grace's daughter is working as a waitress while she figures out what she's going to do with her life. It doesn't help Grace (or her daughter) when Grace's mother asks, each time she sees Grace, "When will that girl settle down? Is she going to fritter her life away?" It is likely that Grace's mother believes she is allying with her daughter, sharing a stance that she assumes they both take. And of course Grace too would like to see her daughter find her place in the world. But Grace also identifies with her daughter, so any disapproval of the young woman is implicit disapproval of her. Hearing the dismissive way her mother speaks of her daughter is hurtful to Grace; to avoid that hurt, she makes sure never to mention her daughter when she talks to her mother. And having to avoid so important a topic raises a barrier between them.

### AWAITING APPROVAL

"I don't think they liked it," said Ry Russo-Young to a journalist about her mothers' (she has two) reactions to a film she had made. Russo-Young, a twenty-two-year-old filmmaker, then sighed and added, "Do you ever stop caring what they think?" Reading this, I smiled to myself. If she is surprised at twenty-two that her mothers' approval is still precious to her, what will she say when she finds that it still is when she's forty-two and sixty-two, if she is lucky enough to have her mothers when she reaches those ages? Come to think of it, even after they are gone, she will probably automatically ask herself, when she makes a film, "What would my mothers think of this?"

A daughter wants to feel that her mother is proud of her, thinks she's okay. So any evidence that her mother's approval is less than total can be hurtful, and hurt can swiftly convert to anger. But how could a mother (or anyone) think her daughter (or anyone else she knows well) is perfect, doing everything right, every moment? All human beings could improve in some ways at some times, and people close to us are the most likely to see those ways. This means that the closer a mother is to her daughter, the more opportunities she sees for improvement—all the more because she wants to see things go well for her. But anything she says to help her daughter calls attention to perceived weaknesses, and that is the opposite of approval.

If any hint of disapproval can upset a daughter, how maddening it must be for a mother to see clearly what her daughter should do and not be able to get her to do it. One mother told me that she has learned to refrain from giving her adult daughter advice, but she nonetheless finds it difficult because, as she put it, "I have better judgment than many of the people she listens to." Whether or not a mother's judgment is always right, she believes it is, and that is a source of frustration.

In this ongoing struggle between daughters and mothers, each sees the other's power and overlooks her own. The daughter reacts strongly to any hint of disapproval—or, for that matter, of approval—because her mother looms like a giant. The fact that her mother's opinion matters so much gives her enormous power. But a mother often persists in her efforts to influence her daughter precisely because she no longer has the authority she had when her children were small and she could quickly address any threats to their well-being. Once her children are grown, she can't eliminate risks on her own; she has to get them to do it. Her constant repetition results from her feeling helpless to address these risks any other way. Where the daughter sees power, the mother feels powerless.

"How *can* I tell my thirty-five-year-old daughter that she has to lose fifteen pounds?" a caller to a talk show asked me. I replied, "You can't." But having to bite her tongue should be less devastating than the caller might fear. I added, "You don't have to. If you think your daughter should lose fifteen pounds, she probably thinks she should lose twenty. Nothing you say can make her try harder to lose weight; it can only make her feel worse about the pounds she wants to lose." I don't doubt it would be hard for the caller to refrain from commenting on her daughter's extra pounds, especially with all the talk these days about the health risks of being even slightly overweight. There is extra urgency when a mother (or later, a daughter) perceives a risk to health or safety.

## WATCH YOUR STEP

Sally felt her husband was being criticized when her mother reminded them, on every visit, that he should cut down the dying elm tree in the yard lest it fall and hurt somebody (it did eventually fall, though no one was hurt), and replace the rotting step lest someone trip (it never was and no one ever did). Anyone would find these constant reminders annoying. But imagine the worry that Sally's mother endured each time she saw these threats to her loved ones' safety—and her frustration that they didn't undertake the simple repairs to eliminate the danger.

Daughters who don't understand the depth of their mothers' concern for their health and safety may understand it better when their mothers age and refuse to take their daughters' advice—and their conversational roles reverse. Lauren was beside herself when her eighty-four-year-old mother insisted on flying alone to spend Christmas with another daughter in North Carolina only months after undergoing open-heart surgery. And when it was clear she could not dissuade her mother, Lauren told her (as she recounted to me in an e-mail), "All I'm asking now is, please, *get a cellphone.* But—no." Lauren's e-mail went on, "I actually heard myself saying to her, 'I don't want to argue about this!' and she actually said, 'You can't make me do it.'" There may be lessons for both in the happy ending: Lauren's mother made the trip without mishap—and learned to love the cellphone that Lauren gave her for Christmas.

A less happy ending concluded the experience of Trudy, who encouraged her mother to take calcium and other bone-strengthening medication, and to be careful lest she break a hip, as many women her age do. But her mother ignored her daughter's advice, convinced that her bones were strong. Imagine Trudy's dismay when her mother did fall and break her hip—while carrying a side table down a flight of stairs. Many old people, like young people, simply don't feel as vulnerable as they are, and nothing their daughters say can change that, any more than their mothers' admonitions changed their own perceptions when they were young.

Not all concerns are so obviously urgent as safety and health. Often the improvements a mother (or a daughter or, disastrously, a mother-in-law) believes are needed reside in a daughter's house, both inside and out. Roberta cringed when her mother peered at the stove in her kitchen, lifting the protective pan under the grill to check to see whether the crumbs had been cleaned from beneath the pan—which, of course, they hadn't.

In Paula's case, the disputed arena was home decorating. She described her mother's visit to me: "She walked into my living room—nobody's in there, but the eagle eye is roaming around. And she says, 'Do you want some help with your accessories?'" Paula saw this as progress. "In the past," she said, "my mother would come into my house and start rearranging stuff, or she'd tell me how I should change things. A few years ago we had a huge blowup. I rattled off a long list of times she had done that or said that, and she got all upset and said, 'Okay, now I won't say anything!' But she still had that look." Paula felt she and her mother had come a long way since that blowup. When her mother asked if she wanted help "with accessories," it was hurtful, but less so than moving things around on her own. And Paula was proud that she had put a quick and low-key end to the exchange by replying, simply, "No thanks."

Because decorating styles, like styles of hair and dress, are constantly changing, it is pretty much guaranteed that mothers and daughters will favor different styles in these domains. If a woman adheres to the norms of her peer group, she will be following trends in style that differ from those of her mother—and later, of her daughter. As a result, many women in middle age find that they are the filling in a disapproval sandwich, criticized by both their teenage or adult daughters and their older mothers. For example, Mara is an artist with a counterculture approach to life; when she was an art student, she and her friends decided not to shave their legs or underarms to demonstrate their independence from society's demands. Long after she stopped thinking about it in those terms, Mara simply kept the habit. But her mother never approved. To her, women who did not shave in expected places were simply unattractive, verging on unsightly. So Mara's mother refused to take her to the swimming pool at her condominium because she'd be embarrassed by her adult daughter's unshaven underarms and legs. And that wasn't all. Mara also had to contend with her teenage daughter, who did not want to be seen in public with her mother—not only in a bathing suit but also in shorts or sleeveless blouses.

## A QUICK SWITCH

Given mothers' overactive improvement glands and daughters' overactive disapproval sensors, mother-daughter is a high-risk relationship. Daughters really do overreact to subtle—or imagined—indications of their mothers' disapproval, and mothers really do sometimes go overboard in their attempts to influence their daughters, including helping them improve. That's why conflict can arise seemingly out of nowhere. Here's an example of how it can happen.

Ever since she left for college, Brenda has had a good relationship with her mother. They have become like friends. But Brenda still reacts swiftly and strongly whenever she picks up a hint of her mother's disapproval. And this can turn a casual, friendly conversation into a barbed one, like a rose that suddenly reveals a thorn. One day, mother and daughter are having one of those fleeting conversations that express and cement friendship between women: they're talking about their lives and their friends. At one point, Brenda complains about her friend Mary, and her mother agrees, being supportive. Then Brenda remarks, "Mary likes you a lot. I've never met her parents." Her mother's response seems innocent enough: "Yeah, it's very interesting. She doesn't seem to want us to either. I could invite Mary and her parents over for a barbecue." Suddenly the tone shifts, and Brenda is annoyed. "Well, Mom," she says with an edge to her voice, "I think that would be weird. Mary would be insulted by an invitation like that. She's twenty-two."

What happened here? Where did the tone of annoyance come from? What on earth did Mom say to warrant the accusation that she had insulted her daughter's friend? Brenda had been complaining about Mary, yes, but when she commented that she hadn't met Mary's parents, she had finished the topic "complaining about Mary" and moved on. Her mother, though, was still on that topic, so she interpreted Brenda's remark as a further complaint. The mother's next comment was intended to support that spirit of complaint, implying: "Yeah, what's wrong with Mary that she has kept you from meeting her parents? What is she hiding?" Brenda's antennae began buzzing here. She heard the new criticism of her friend Mary (one she had not meant to elicit) as an indirect criticism of herself: if she has a friend who is hiding something from her, there must be something wrong with Brenda. So she snapped back that there was something wrong with her *mother* for wanting to arrange a meeting among Brenda, Mary, and their parents. It smacks of a children's playdate. That's why Mary would be insulted, since "she's twenty-two." Poor Mom. She had simply tried to support her daughter and found herself being criticized— precisely because her daughter had mistaken for criticism her mother's intended support.

## NOT IN SO MANY WORDS

Brenda's antennae may be overly sensitive to criticism from her mother because she is newly independent, and their friendship, as opposed to their mother-daughtership, is still new, too. But Brenda is not necessarily paranoid to be listening for disapproval in implications, or metamessages, rather than in words. Many women, in telling me what they find frustrating about their mothers, referred to their mothers' habitual indirectness: "She never says what she means." But when I ask for specific examples, they almost always relate instances they perceived as indirect ways of communicating criticism. I suspect it is less the indirectness that rankles than the criticism it conveys: the studied casualness of a remark seems to belie the critical intent it attempts (but fails) to conceal. The wolf of criticism often comes disguised in the sheep's clothing of indirectness.

Given the depth of a daughter's yearning for her mother's approval, combined with their lifetime of experience talking to each other, it might seem to outsiders that they are speaking in code. Imagine a mother who comes to visit her daughter and comments, on entering her daughter's apartment, "It looks like no one lives here." Is this criticism? From the perspective of an outsider, it certainly could be. But to the woman who told me about this scene, it was a compliment on her housekeeping; at the time she felt pleased to have earned her mother's approval.

By the same token, even the most seemingly innocent remark can come across as criticism. "I don't know how you do it all," Evelyn says to her daughter Louise, who works as a freelance writer and has two children. This sounds like praise, no? Not to her daughter. Louise hears this remark as implying "You shouldn't take on so much; you should concentrate on being a mother to your kids." Evelyn might or might not have been thinking those critical thoughts when she said what she did to Louise. Our radar is so attuned to indications of approval or disapproval, it can pick up even the most subtle hints of either—or of a remark as innocent as a flock of birds making their way across the sky.

Indirectness is often the vehicle for criticism—perceived or real—of the Big Three of appearance: hair, clothes, weight. A mother remarks, "I guess you don't have to dress up at your job." Her daughter winces, knowing that her mother doesn't approve of her taste in clothes. "Do you really need that dessert?" a mother asks, and her daughter knows her mother thinks she needs to lose weight. And then there's hair—there's always hair.

Kim's mother is convinced that Kim's hair, curly and thick when it's freshly washed and fluffed, sits too flatly at the sides of her face when she hasn't had time to wash it. ("Flat" is a relative concept. Compared to naturally straight hair, Kim's curly hair is never truly flat.) Kim is hurt by the criticism, but what drives her mad is that her mother won't just say "Your hair looks flat. Fluff it up." Instead she'll say "What are we going to do about your hair?" Kim thinks (but doesn't say), "*We* aren't going to do anything about it. It's my hair, and anything I decide to do I'll do myself." Though her anger fastens on the words her mother spoke—the message, the literal meaning of "we"—Kim's reaction is to feeling hurt that her mother thinks she doesn't look good.

Rhonda's mother is an early riser and disapproves (Rhonda well knows) if she catches anyone in bed past 8:00 A.M. One Saturday morning, her mother calls at 9:15, and Rhonda answers with a morning voice. "Oh, Ronnie, did I wake you up?" her mother chirps. In fact, her mother has not woken her up; Rhonda has been awake, though still in bed. But in order to exaggerate her mother's offense, to return guilt for guilt, Rhonda replies "Yes" in the groggiest voice she can muster. "Oh, I'm so sorry . . . ," her mother says—but rather than an apology, her response quickly morphs into an accusation, as she goes on, ". . . you slugabed. I thought *everyone* was up by *nine o'clock*." And she closes the conversation with a reference to staying in bed all day—a remark whose laughing tone does little to mask its judgmental implication.

Sometimes a mother knows she's entering a danger zone, so she broaches a topic indirectly, thinking she's treading lightly, maybe even soundlessly. But the ground is well-trodden, so the daughter hears the steps coming, and the indirectness only makes her angrier. A student in one of my classes described in a written assignment her reaction to the indirect way her mother shows her disapproval. As with Rhonda, the point of contention is sleeping late, and the magic hour is 9:00 A.M. Kathy describes a typical morning. It is midsummer; she is home from college; and she has, of course, gone to bed very late the night before.

> As morning comes I have no idea because I am asleep. Then I hear it, "KAAAATHEEEE." It is my mother, waking me up before 9 am. Yelling from downstairs does not bother me, it is her motivation that makes me start the day off angry.

Kathy notes it is not the message—that her mother wants her to get up—that bothers her. What rankles is the metamessage. "I do not have to see her in order to know that 'KAAAATHEEEE' means 'The day is half over, the dogs need to go out, and you are still asleep!'" And this is why the alarm clock is preferable: "I get no metamessage from an alarm clock, but that metamessage I get from one word out of my mother's mouth." (It isn't even a word, really—just the drawn-out pronunciation of her daughter's name.)

Kathy's mother then uses a creative device to get her daughter up. She sends the family's pet dogs into Kathy's room. "I can hear the trot of my five-pound poodles walking into my room," Kathy writes, "prancing around and waiting for me to get up, which of course I do." Kathy notes that she gets up less angry when the poodles serve as her mother's emissaries, but "the dogs themselves carry almost the same metamessage as my mother's voice," because she knows her mother sent them.

### SPARE THE PRAISE

When a mother really does seem critical, her apparent disapproval may result from her sense of appropriate child rearing. In many cultures, it is widely believed that too much approval or praise will give a child a swelled head. Indeed, there are cultures in which traditional beliefs hold that if you draw attention to good fortune, you risk destroying it by calling down the evil eye, so praising children is assiduously avoided, as it would incur that risk. Traditional Greek culture follows this norm, as does traditional East European Jewish culture.

The Yiddish language provides a phrase you must say to ward off the bad luck that can come with praise, especially of a child. I heard this phrase often while growing up in Brooklyn; it sounded to me like "kunnahurra," but the linguist James Matisoff explains that it actually is *Keyn ayn-hore,* "no evil eye." (I had no idea it had anything to do with the evil eye, nor did my parents until I shared my new knowledge with them.) According to Matisoff, if a woman in a traditional Yiddish-speaking community saw a beautiful baby, she would say the opposite of what she was thinking: "Yech, what an ugly thing!" Could it be that some of those who laugh at belief in the evil eye have nonetheless absorbed the habit of refraining from praising their children? Could this habit explain why so many daughters who were never praised by their mothers are later surprised to hear from their mothers' friends, "Your mother is so proud of you. She never stops talking about you." (I heard the same surprise from a mother regarding her daughters.)

The logic behind saying "Yech, what an ugly thing!" of a particularly pretty baby also made me think of truly insulting remarks women told me their mothers had made, like "April has such beautiful curls. It's too bad you don't have hair like hers." (Never mind that April was always trying to straighten her hair.) Or, to a daughter whose med-student boyfriend had just broken up with her: "What would a doctor want with you?" (What he'd want, it turned out, was a wife: They soon got back together and, before long, married.) Harsh, even cruel, as these kinds of comments are—and I heard of many others like them—it seems at least possible that some mothers who spoke to their daughters this way were echoing their own mothers, passing on a practice that had developed over time from the sense that praising a child might bring bad luck, and that withholding praise builds character.

Related to the belief that children should not be praised is the tendency to discourage boasting or anything that could be interpreted as self-congratulatory. The Puerto Rican writer Esmeralda Santiago recalls a saying her grandmother would repeat whenever her grandchildren seemed to boast: *"Alábate pollo, que mañana te guisan,"* which Santiago translates "Boast now, chicken, tomorrow you'll be stew."

Swedish culture discourages praising children as well as any sign of self-promotion. It is common for Swedish parents to discourage a child's apparent self-aggrandizement with the rhetorical question "Do you think you're somebody?" This cultural convention might help explain otherwise puzzling and hurtful remarks. Karin, a Swedish woman now living in the United States, returned to graduate school to get a master's degree in counseling when her last child left home for college. One day she called her mother to say hello and mentioned, in the course of the conversation, how hard she was studying for final exams. "You seem to be making a lot out of it," her mother remarked. Karin felt stung but tried to be cheerful and self-deprecating. "Well, you know," she said, "when a middle-aged woman returns to school, she has to try harder." To this her mother replied, "How much longer do you think you can keep calling yourself middle-aged?" This rhetorical question didn't just sting; it hurt. Now her mother was telling her she was old.

Why would Karin's mother put her down like that? It's possible she intended to tease but hit a false note. It's also possible that she heard Karin's remarks—first about how much she had to study, then about how hard she tries—as self-aggrandizing, given the Swedish expectation that people should downplay their efforts and accomplishments and that parents must instill this stance in their children. Karin was not intending to boast—quite the contrary, she thought her remark was self-deprecatory—yet it may help to understand that her mother might have been enforcing a code of behavior she had imbibed from her own parents, fulfilling what she sees as her responsibility to teach her daughter the proper demeanor. In this view, a mother who deflates her child's spirit is simply taking care that her child develop good character. Continuing the job after the child is an adult is simply providing a periodic tune-up.

## SHE WANTS YOUR BLESSING

All these examples show that on hearing—or speaking—the same words, one woman sees caring, the other sees criticizing. Is there a path out of this thicket? Understanding the motives behind apparent criticism can help. But are there other things a mother or daughter can do to break the cycle of hurt which drives them farther apart? An obvious solution to the approval/improvement conundrum is for mothers to resist the impulse to give advice, offer help, and make suggestions once their daughters are grown. I heard this from many women who told me they have good relationships with their grown daughters. One remarked that she had been taught this lesson by her daughter: "Don't give me advice unless I ask," she said. "And don't hint advice, either." (This the mother could not promise, but she could try.) Another commented, "I'm biting my tongue so often, I'm surprised it's not bleeding." Yet another put it this way: "She doesn't want your advice. She wants your blessing."

But what if a mother really can't give her blessing? There are times when it would be irresponsible to do that. For every mother who regrets having opened her mouth, there is one who regrets having kept silent, failing to warn her daughter—or, having warned her, to insist on action—of a danger she foresaw. (The same is true for daughters when their mothers age.) How do mothers know when it is best to keep silent, to avoid implying criticism, and when it is truly necessary to speak up, to protect a daughter from harm? When children are small, the answer is usually easy: Do whatever is needed to protect them. When they become teenagers, it is usually hard: any effort to protect them will anger them, because their fondest wish is to prove that they no longer need protection. But what about when your daughter is an adult, and your responsibility for her is officially ended—but in reality never abates? Then the decision about whether or not to offer advice is not at all obvious.

Doris, for example, got a call from her daughter Zoe telling her that she had seen an orthopedic surgeon about her back pain. The surgeon had recommended surgery and Zoe had scheduled it for the next month. Doris was alarmed. She believed her daughter should be more cautious about undertaking such a drastic course of action. Surely Zoe should get a second opinion, and look into this surgeon's credentials and track record. But Doris held back from directly expressing these concerns. Instead, she asked, "Are you comfortable with that? Isn't that a bit soon?" Of course Zoe heard the implication—not the concern but the disapproval. "Mom," she protested. "I'm forty years old. I think I can judge these things for myself."

Doris backed off and let Zoe do it her way, though she still worried. But sometimes a concern about health is so urgent that a mother may decide no amount of anger on her daughter's part will dissuade her from pushing the matter. Another mother, Shirley, was glad she did. She was sure her daughter Becky should check out some symptoms she noticed, and she was so insistent that Becky actually stopped talking to her for two weeks. Still, Shirley did not give up. She called Becky's husband at work and prevailed upon him to make sure her daughter saw a doctor. In fact, Becky did have a grave illness, and Shirley's persistence had saved her life.

## THE GREAT POWER SHIFT

When Becky was a child, her mother did not have to convince her to see a doctor if she deemed it wise. She simply made an appointment and took her child there. No longer being able to do this is one of many ways that mothers really are less powerful when their daughters grow up. Indeed, when a daughter has moved into her own home, she can decide how often—even whether or not—to see and speak to her mother. Also, as a daughter's focus shifts, it may be the mother who deeply wants her daughter's approval—especially in our society, which places more value on the freshness of youth than on the wisdom of age. A mother may be hurt by her daughter's disapproval of her taste in clothes or jewelry, where she decides to live, or, if she is a widow, the man she chooses to marry—or the fact that she chooses to remarry at all. And only her daughter can give her the ultimate stamp of approval: reassurance that she did a good job as a mother. In these ways, a mother is at her grown daughter's mercy, just as her children were at hers when they were small.

If a daughter has children of her own, there is another way that her mother is at her mercy. One of the greatest joys of many women's lives is the gift of grandchildren. Few blessings compare to the pleasure of lavishing love and attention on these small, trusting creatures and receiving their love in return, unburdened by the responsibility that came with parenthood. But access to this precious resource is controlled by the children's parents, usually their mothers. And this gives adult daughters (or daughters-in-law) enormous power over their mothers. Part of many women's desire to avoid offending their daughters (or daughters-in-law) is a fear that access to the adored grandchildren will be limited or even withheld.

It is a challenge for mothers to deal with these many ways that their once-great influence has diminished. It should help to remember that a daughter's extreme reaction to her mother's words is testament that what her mother says still matters. It should also help to find other ways to exercise influence. One mother who has an excellent relationship with her daughter commented, "I try to make a point of telling her how nice she looks and how terrific the kids are." These are exactly the points on which many mothers are offering suggestions for improvement. Imagine if Paula's mother said, when she visited, "Your house looks so nice. You've done a fabulous job decorating." (And who knows, if she made a habit of saying this, she might also find Paula open to her offer of "help with accessories.") Like criticism, a compliment coming from a mother carries great weight. Seeing how important your praise is to your daughter provides reassurance that you still have a significant role in her life.

A mother who is hurt by her daughter's accusations of criticism might also be consoled to think that what's really going on is her daughter's exaggerated admiration. One woman explained how this worked when she was a teen: "This presumption of criticism is not necessarily because your mother criticized you. I don't honestly think my mother spent a lot of time criticizing me, but it often felt as if she did because I felt I didn't measure up to my mother. I wasn't as cool as she was, you know, I didn't perceive myself as having as many skills. Well, of course I didn't. I was fourteen!" But because she wanted so badly to measure up, "it was really kind of a self-criticism, but that's too hard, so you kind of project it onto her."

There might even be a sense in which knowing that her daughter does not take her advice all that seriously could be liberating to a mother. That sense is explained by a remark my father once made. After giving me advice which I received with a noncommittal "That's an idea," my father observed, "You're not going to take my advice." "You're right," I admitted. "I'm not." "It's just as well," he quipped. "If you took it, I'd have to be more careful about what I advise." In this spirit, knowing her advice will not be taken—and is no longer sought—can be a burden lifted off mothers as well as daughters.

Mothers may also bear in mind that if their daughters do take their advice and are guided by their wisdom, there may come a time when the daughters regret this pattern and go overboard in the other direction. "I allowed my mother to be a kind of arbitrator of what was okay and what wasn't," one woman said. "In a sense it programmed what I thought was okay and what I did." This daughter felt, later in her life, that surrendering her judgment to her mother's reflected a lack of confidence in herself. And she began to make a point of not seeking her mother's advice at all, so she would not be overly influenced by it. She even had a dream in which she encountered a statue of her mother—and knocked its head off. She awoke from the dream with a sense of release. A daughter who never paid so much attention to her mother's opinion would not later feel the need to decapitate her symbolically in order to free herself.

Maybe there's a lesson for mothers in Nathaniel Hawthorne's story "The Birthmark," about a man who marries a stunningly beautiful woman who is perfect except for a single birthmark. Obsessed with wanting to eliminate this imperfection, the man convinces his reluctant wife to have the birthmark removed. The story's sad ending is that the surgery doesn't make her perfect; it kills her.

If a mother can't resist the urge to correct, advise, or make suggestions, is there something her daughter can do on her own? One thing she can do is remind herself that her mother's attempts to improve her are evidence of how much she cares, and how weakened her power now is.

If all else fails, a daughter can think of her mother's scrutiny as the price she has to pay to have her mother in her life. Once a mother is gone, a daughter may find that she actually misses her tendency to criticize along with other aspects of who she was. Nicole got a glimpse of this when her mother underwent emergency surgery. She flew from California to Florida as soon as she heard the grave news. Filled with anxiety, she found her way to her mother's hospital room. The first thing her mother said when her daughter entered the room was "When is the last time you did your roots?" At another time, this remark would have made Nicole angry; she would have thought, Only the tiniest bit of gray is showing; why does she have to fasten on that? In this instance, Nicole found the remark profoundly comforting. It meant her mother had come through the surgery with her body—and her personality—intact. Her mother was still herself.

# 3

# DON'T SHUT ME OUT
## THE IMPORTANCE OF BEING FEMALE

I was being interviewed by a journalist about conversations between daughters and mothers, how they get bollixed up, how
they cause grief. She blurted out, "What *is* it about mothers and
daughters? Why are our conversations so complicated, our relationships so fraught? Why is it different from fathers and sons,
fathers and daughters, mothers and sons?" I had to think for a
moment before the obvious reply took form: It's because both are
women. And because these two women are so important to each
other, all the rewards and pitfalls that characterize girls' and
women's conversations are amplified. Talk typically plays a larger
and more complex role in girls' and women's relationships than it
does in boys' and men's. Daughters and mothers, more than sons
and fathers, tend to play out and negotiate their relationships

through talk—in many cases, lots of it. More talk means more opportunities both for comforting connections and for miscommunication and hurt feelings. Among girls and women, talk is the glue that holds a relationship together—and also the explosive that can blow it apart.

It is intriguing when animal behavior corresponds to our own, even though we wouldn't want to draw direct parallels. According to Joyce Poole, the scientific director of the Amboseli Elephant Research Project in Kenya, female elephants in the wild "talk" more than their male counterparts, and they, too, do so to negotiate relationships. In an e-mail to me, Dr. Poole wrote:

> Female elephants (though not males) are rather "talkative" and in certain situations they use overlapping or chorused calls (using a variety of call types) that appear to function to cement important relationships. These situations include reconciliation between friends, expression of solidarity with another's proposal/plan of action, provision of care for another's offspring (kidnappings, greeting of new baby, birth, infant/calf rescue, response to calf distress), collective decision-making/action in response to external threat (coalitions against other groups and attacking/fleeing from predators) and reinforcement of bonds with allies during an excited social occasion (greetings, mating, etc.).

I am not suggesting that animal behavior is equivalent to the human kind, yet I was fascinated to see Poole's observation not only that female elephants vocalize more but also that they use vocalization to "cement" relationships, just as I often say (as I did above) that for girls and women talk is the "glue" that holds relationships together.

Understanding that women tend to use talk to create and reinforce social connections explains why for every daughter who complained, "My mother criticizes me," there was a mother who complained, "My daughter shuts me out." To see how the role of talk in women's relationships leads to this widespread complaint, let's start by looking at little girls at play, and how their use of language tends to differ from that of little boys.

### TALK TO ME

A woman who has a ten-year-old son and a six-year-old daughter noticed a difference between her children when she readies them for summer day camp. "With Jason," she tells me, "there's no baggage. I tell him what shoes to put on and he's out the door. With Lucy, every day it's a long story. She'll say, 'I don't know if I should be buddies at the pool with Jodie or Lisa.' Then she'll go on and on—did she make any promises the day before? What will Jodie think if she chooses Lisa? What will Lisa feel if she chooses Jodie?" Intrigued by the contrast between her children, the mother asked her son, "Jason, who are the boys on your basketball team?" He replied, "I don't know them. But I really like playing with them because we won!" I asked this mother, "What if Jason is going to swim and needs to pick a buddy?" "He picks one," she said. "It's no big deal. I don't hear about it. And I hear this kind of thing from Lucy no matter what she's going to do that day."

Lucy and Jason are not unique. Researchers who study children at play have documented that girls' and boys' friendships tend to diverge in these ways. Girls' social lives are typically centered on a best friend, and girls create and gauge best friendship through talk. So they learn to use language to negotiate how close or distant they want to be with other girls. That's why Lucy's decision about picking a buddy is important—and complicated. In contrast, boys tend to play in larger groups, and for them the activity is central. Boys' groups are also more obviously hierarchical: Boys get and keep high status by taking center stage and telling other boys what to do, so boys learn to use language to negotiate their status in the group. Michael Gurian, an author who lectures frequently on gender differences, notes that if you give a little girl a doll, she'll usually talk to it. But if you give the doll to a boy, more than likely he'll pretend it's a truck or plane—or try to take its head off so he can look inside. According to Gurian, for him it's an object to do something with, but for her the doll represents a person to relate to.

Researchers have also observed that boys often combine talk with physical action—or use only physical action—in situations where girls use talk alone, such as to initiate play with another child. One boy shoves another, who shoves back, and pretty soon they're engaged in play. But this doesn't work with girls. When a boy tries to invite a girl to play by shoving her, she's more likely to try to get away from him. A *New Yorker* cartoon captured this contrast: It showed a little girl and a little boy eyeing each other. She's thinking, "I wonder if I should ask him to play." He's thinking, "I wonder if I should kick her."

When I give my students the assignment to watch children interacting, they always notice girls using talk to accomplish goals, in contrast to boys who use action. For example, Igor Orlovsky worked at Discovery Zone, a place where small children are brought to play. He described what happened when more than one child wanted the same toy. For example, an older boy wanted a maraca that a younger boy had, so he tried to take it away by force. But when a girl wanted a maraca that another girl had, she tried to convince the maraca holder to trade it away, by explaining that another toy was really better. This strategy was similar to the one used by Rebecca, a four-year-old girl for whom another student, Maria Kalogredis, was babysitting. Knowing that Rebecca loved to play house when she got to be Mommy and her babysitter took the role of baby, Maria tried something different: she said she wanted to be Mommy. Upset by this development, the four-year-old tried to convince Maria to change her mind: "Are you sure you want to be Mommy?" she asked. "Because it's more fun to be baby."

These patterns set in childhood become the basis for habits that tend to distinguish adult women's and men's social lives. Since talk is the stuff of which their friendships are made, most women talk to their friends often: weekly or even daily. A man might well regard as his closest friend a fellow he hasn't spoken to in months, if not years. Yet he knows, If I need him he'll be there. A man may bowl, play tennis, or go golfing every week with another man yet know little of what is going on in his personal life. If the friend announces he is getting divorced, it may come as a total surprise. A woman who discovers that her friend is getting divorced and never mentioned that she was having difficulties in her marriage might well question whether they were really good friends at all, since being friends means telling each other what is going on in their lives.

Given the role of talk in women's relationships, it's not surprising that, as numerous studies have found, mothers tend to talk to their children more than fathers do, and they talk more to their daughters than to their sons. The pattern continues when children become adults, and in addition, most daughters talk more to their mothers than to their fathers. If you don't talk to someone at length, you have less opportunity to feel close—but also less opportunity to ruffle each other's feathers.

In addition to the liabilities that come with all this talk, there is a particular aspect of women's relationships that explains some of the complexity between mothers and daughters: The type of talk they engage in leads to a preoccupation with being included and a fear of being left. The pattern begins when they are children playing with other girls.

Much of the talk that little girls exchange with their friends is telling secrets. Knowing each other's secrets is what makes them best friends. The content of the secret is less significant than the fact that it is shared: Exchanging secrets is a way to negotiate alliances. A girl can't tell secrets in front of girls who aren't friends, because only friends should hear her secrets. So when girls don't like another girl, they stop talking to her, freeze her out of the group. That's why when a little girl gets angry at a playmate, she often lashes out, "You can't come to my birthday party." This is a dreadful threat, because the rejected girl is left isolated. In contrast, boys typically allow boys they don't like, or boys with low status, to play with them, though they treat them badly. So boys and men don't tend to share (or understand) girls' and women's sensitivity to any sign of being excluded. (They tend to develop a different sensitivity: to any sign of being put down or pushed around.)

In other words, the coin of the realm in girls' friendships is inclusion and exclusion, the first a precious (if tenuous) gift, the second a fierce punishment. This explains why much of the satisfaction in mother-daughter conversation comes from feeling included, and much of the dismay results from feeling left out.

## WHY WASN'T I INVITED?

Muriel visited her daughter Denise shortly after Denise's first child was born. She had come to help out, and she was happy to do that. Soon after arriving, Muriel noticed a stack of boxes in the corner, then realized that they were brand-new baby items. At first she wondered what they were doing in the living room. Then it struck her: These must be gifts that were given at a baby shower. "Did you have a baby shower?" she asked her daughter, trying to sound offhand.

"Yes," Denise replied, sounding genuinely casual. "My friend Ida threw me a shower. Wasn't that nice?"

"Oh, yes," Muriel replied, "that was very nice." But what she was really feeling was a stab of hurt. She wondered why Denise hadn't told her about the shower and, more poignantly, why she had not been invited. At that moment, Muriel felt a bit like the little girl who learns that all her friends spent the previous day at a birthday party to which she had not been invited. And just as girls often have no idea what they did to be suddenly shunned by their friends, Muriel couldn't understand *why* she had not been invited to the shower. If she was close enough to come and help out when the baby was born, why wasn't she close enough to be included in a celebration before?

Denise did not intend to offend her mother by not putting her name on the list of potential invitees she had given Ida. It never occurred to her to do that; when drawing up the list, she thought of her friends. Had someone told her that her mother would be hurt to be excluded, Denise might have felt fine about inviting her, or she might have feared that an older woman, and a mother at that, would not fit in, or might even put a crimp in everyone's mood. Such rejections are inevitable, as daughters grow older and their social networks expand beyond their mothers'. The inevitability of exclusion, combined with the importance of inclusion to women, necessarily complicates relationships between daughters and mothers.

### LET ME IN

Feeling left out can be the culprit underlying discord without that issue ever being mentioned. In telling me how her mother frustrates her, one woman, Julia, said, "My mother always seems to want more attention than I can give her. But then she tells me I should pay less attention to her. It drives me crazy." When I press for specifics, it becomes clear that the type of attention Julia's mother wants is different from the type she objects to, even though they are both described by the same word. For example, Julia's mother came for a week's visit. Julia sensed that her mother was not happy; she especially seemed to sulk when Julia's attention was focused on her ten-year-old daughter. But when Julia asked what was wrong, her mother demurred, "Nothing, nothing." Julia marshaled evidence: Her mother's facial expressions and body language made it clear that she was disgruntled. It was then that her mother said, "Stop paying so much attention to me."

This was maddening to Julia because she knew her mother wanted attention. But the word "attention" has very different meanings in these two contexts. When Julia is preoccupied with her own daughter, her mother is probably thinking something like "I've come all this way, and my visit is so short, yet my daughter doesn't even seem to notice I'm here. I might as well have stayed home." "Attention" in this context means talking to her, doing things with her, making her feel like she's important. In contrast, when Julia's mother says, "Stop paying so much attention to me," she is defending herself against what she perceives as criticism—a negative type of attention. She probably means, "If I didn't *say* I feel neglected, I can't be held responsible for having felt it. It's not fair to blame me for intangibles like body language and facial expression." In this context, "Stop paying so much attention to me" means, in effect, "Stop *scrutinizing* me."

I suspect that Julia's mother felt left out when her daughter focused attention on her own child. It might seem absurd for a grown woman to compete with a child for attention, but hurt that comes with feeling left out is not thought through, not logically justified; that's why the issue never comes up when Julia talks to her mother. It is possible that her mother would not be happy unless she were the focus of attention all the time. But it's also possible that if she had been the focus of attention for a block of time, she might be comfortable receding into the background at other times. Often when a mother visits, the daughter, if she has her own family, is too overburdened with responsibilities to entertain her mother. But it might be worth a try to devote a day or two of the visit exclusively to her.

### DADDY'S GIRL

A family is the first group we encounter in our lives, and in many ways it remains our foundation. If things are going well, a family is a fortress against a hostile world, a place where you find refuge and receive comfort. But if the family itself is making you unhappy, it can feel like you have no place to hide—or like you're falling and there is nothing to hold on to. For a mother, this can translate into close monitoring of the shifting alignments among family members, and bristling when she feels left out. In some families, the mother and daughter have an alignment from which brothers and fathers are excluded. In others, or at other times, the mother perceives that a daughter is aligned with her father, leaving the mother out in the cold. When this rejection becomes a constant in the family's interaction, her resentment can become hardened like a scar where a wound, even an old one, had been.

I was one of those girls who adored my father and was angry at my mother more often than not. My mother could clearly see that I preferred my father, and she always resented it. Even toward the end of their very long lives, when I was no longer angry at her and instead lavished on my mother the lion's share of my attention, frequent gifts, and extravagant expressions of love, this constellation—my alignment with my father and her resentment of it—was never far from the surface. It could rear its head in the simplest interactions. For example, one time I called, and my parents both answered the phone, each on a different extension. As soon as my father heard my mother's voice, he announced, "I'll hang up so you girls can talk." My mother then remarked, "I know you'd rather talk to your father." She was right, and she still resented what she accurately perceived as my preference for him. In contrast, my father had volunteered to get off the phone with no indication he minded in the least that I would spend the next half hour or more talking to my mother and not to him—or that I did so nearly every time I called.

When she was ninety-two and my father ninety-five, my mother and I were in the midst of one of those rambling telephone conversations. We exchanged stories of chance encounters, updated each other on our own lives and the lives of family and friends, and recounted the small frustrations that had arisen since our last conversation. In that spirit, my mother said, "I asked your father to bring me something to drink. An hour later I found him at his desk. I asked him, 'What happened to my drink?' He said he forgot! I got myself something to drink." It was a gentle complaint, not a bitter one. I was supposed to reinforce it by saying something like "That man, what can you do? He's so forgetful." But I provided no chuckling support of her complaint. "Mom!" I chastised. "Daddy can't take a step without his walker, and even with it he has trouble keeping his balance. Besides, he's in pain when he walks. You shouldn't ask him to get you something to drink!" Now my mother's annoyance shifted from my father to me. "I should have known better than to say anything to you," she said. "You always take his side. In your eyes he can do no wrong." I had to admit she had a point.

One predilection my father and I share is a love of writing. As he got old and his physical activities were gradually curtailed, he spent much of his time writing long letters to people, including me. I delighted in these letters, and I responded in kind. I ended one of my letters by telling him how much I loved him—and why. I used the word "adore." The next letter I received from my father implored me never to write him such a letter again. It had so angered my mother that she had made his life miserable in revenge. I thought this dynamic was unique to my family, but a story reported by a student in my class reminded me of it. "My mother gets mad at me when I fight with her and my father takes my side," she said. "I have told him not to stick up for me because it only makes her madder."

Many women I spoke to reported similar patterns in their own families' conversations, as did many of the students in my classes. One student described such an experience when, in connection with a class assignment, she examined a conversation she had had with her mother. Her mother's remarks might seem surprising at first, but they can be explained by the patterns I just described.

Cara was home from college for Thanksgiving. It is a custom in her family that, on the Friday following Thanksgiving, she and her mother go shopping together. As Cara and her mother were talking about other things, Cara mentioned that her father had told her he was not going to work on Friday. "Why not?" her mother asked. "What's he going to do?"

"I don't know," Cara replied. "Stay home I guess."

"To do what," her mother asked, "harass us?"

"I don't know what you mean, 'harass,'" Cara said. "Daddy's a lot of fun to have around."

"Really?" her mother responded.

"Totally," Cara went on. "I think he's really funny."

"Do you?" her mother replied, implying that her daughter's assessment was suspect.

When Cara later asked her mother why she had responded so negatively to the news that her father would stay home Friday, her mother explained that since her husband hates shopping, he would want his daughter to stay home, too, and do something with him. Since she assumed that Cara would choose her father's company over hers, his availability would cut into her mother's precious time with her daughter. Once a mother is convinced that her daughter prefers her father, any praise for him may be met with resistance—subtle or stark—because it reinforces the impression that her daughter and her husband are aligned with each other, leaving the mother out.

## LEFT OUT OF THE JOKE

To explain why she liked spending time with her father, Cara remarked, "Daddy's a lot of fun to have around." I was struck by how often I heard similar comments from women. For example, one woman said of her father, "He is so much fun, he cracks me up." And she added, "I just love hanging out with him. He's so funny." The more "fun" a father is to be around, the more likely it is that the bond between him and his children will create the impression—or the reality—of leaving the mother out. Research has documented that much of the time most fathers spend with their children is devoted to playing rather than to the drudgery of daily care-giving. (There are of course many exceptions.) A particularly poignant account of how this pattern affects the mother is described by a man who found himself in the role of father rather suddenly.

Bob Shacochis and his wife took in their ten-year-old niece, his wife's sister's child, when her mother died of cancer. Describing in an essay the effect this new arrangement had on himself, his wife (whom he calls C), and their relationship, Shacochis illustrates how his tendency to take the role of playmate inadvertently made his wife feel left out.

> That first autumn, our roles and parental identities seemed to curdle into stereotypes. I was the good-time Charlie, the frivolous male, the bystander who could be coopted as a witness for the defense; C was the disciplinarian, the over-extended female, trapped by the solemn duty of blood and betrayed in ways both subtle and overt by her partner. Quickly, C came to believe she was being deliberately excluded, even to the extent of feeling physically deprived, when I tickled the kid. "She gets the playfulness now, instead of me," C lamented one day. It shocked me to realize she was right.

It is clear that in trying to be a good father to his niece, Shacochis did not intend to exclude his wife from their play, nor to deprive her of the humor and attention, the pure enjoyment, that had previously been hers. But that's what happened. There are layers of irony and injustice in this result. The very imbalance in the roles he and his wife took—he getting the fun job of "good-time Charlie" and she getting "overextended" by assuming a disproportionate amount of the caretaking—results in her being punished by being left out of the play.

### MY BROTHER'S KEEPER

If many mothers feel left out because their daughters prefer their fathers, many daughters feel rejected because their mothers prefer their brothers. One woman, for example, was telling me how sad it was that, toward the end of her life, her mother didn't recognize her. Then she added, "But she never stopped recognizing my brother." Another woman had a strikingly similar experience when her mother lay dying. "I was the only one she didn't recognize," the woman said. "She knew perfectly well who my brothers were, but somehow she was convinced that I wasn't her daughter but her daughter's clone—and that I was trying to harm her."

The dismay common among women caused by their mothers' repeated criticism takes on a particularly searing character when a daughter perceives that her mother assumes a less critical stance toward her brother. One woman had occasion to have this impression confirmed. She was standing with her brother at a family reunion when their mother approached and greeted her daughter in the usual way: "What's that on your skin?" "What's with your hair?" "You've put on weight." The daughter noticed nothing unusual—but her brother did. "Does she always do that?" he asked in disbelief. Hearing her brother's surprise, this woman learned that her mother reserved the appearance check for her daughter, not her son.

A woman of sixty-seven wrote me on e-mail, "I still have a problem with my relationship with my mother." The problem was her mother's preference for the woman's brother. "My brother was the apple of my mother's eye," she wrote. "I never measured up to my mother's expectations. It was always 'You shouldn't,' 'Don't,' and 'Why can't you be like . . .' Being myself was a no-no." Her mother's partiality to her brother extended to the brother's family: "Even the gifts she gave to the other grandchildren were better and more expensive than the gifts she gave to my children. She paid their tuition but not my children's. She even gave each of them (my brother and his wife) a $10,000 gift each year, but not to us." As I read all this, I assumed the writer's mother must be long-lived if the daughter is sixty-seven. It wasn't until the end of the message that I read, "Of course she is gone now." But the effects linger: "I can never shake this sadness and I guess I will go to my grave with this unresolved and heavy on my heart." (This woman did feel, though, that she had learned a lesson from her mother's treatment that served her well in raising her own children. The lesson, she explained, was to treat her children equally—but to give her daughter just a slight edge.)

Even when a mother's favoritism is not so obvious or extreme, for many women who have brothers, the pain at their mothers' imperfect love is intensified by the contrast in how their mothers treated a brother. For these women, it is as if their brothers take center stage in the family while they are left in the background, if not consigned to the wings.

## SIGHT UNSEEN

There's another way that many daughters feel shunted to the side in comparison to their brothers, and it too reflects attitudes toward women that are widespread in our society. That is the tendency to expect more of women, and to appreciate their efforts less.

Beth is a family therapist in private practice. One day she got a call from her mother. "I made plane reservations for my visit," her mother said. "I'll be arriving at 2 o'clock; should I look for you in baggage claim or as I come through the gates?"

"That's going to be hard, Mom," Beth replied. "I have appointments all afternoon." Then she added, referring to her brother, "Why don't you ask Ronnie?" Her mother replied, "He works."

Part of the difference in her mother's attitude toward Beth's work and her brother's no doubt resulted from the different settings in which they spent their days: Her brother went to an office in a building downtown, whereas Beth saw patients in an office in her home. But another reason was simply her mother's assumptions about women and men. Her mother always regarded Beth's profession as a kind of hobby: not required to support the family, just something Beth chose to do in her spare time, especially since all she did was sit around and talk to people.

Beth's experience mirrors that of many women who feel that their mothers don't appreciate or recognize their professional accomplishments. But something else is going on here, too. The work women do is often invisible, taken for granted. And this is just as true in the family as in the world outside it. Meals are prepared, the house gets cleaned, children's clothes are purchased and laundered, all on a routine, never-ending basis. Rarely do family members provide significant recognition, though they notice when these things don't get done. Many fathers today do these tasks, too, but when they do, people inside and outside the family tend to notice and applaud; when mothers do them, it is simply part of the landscape.

Both mothers and daughters can come to expect selfless generosity from the other and react with disappointment or anger when they don't get it—or when they can't fulfill the other's expectations. One woman, in telling me why her mother was so important to her, commented, "She has a certain drop everything and run quality." The problem is that family members, including daughters, may protest if their mothers do not drop everything and run to help them out, for example by being available when they visit, meeting them at the airport, or babysitting for their children. And many mothers expect their daughters to help them out in ways they wouldn't think of asking of someone else, including their sons.

## JUST ASK AGAIN

Leah, one of three siblings, was arranging for her eighty-seven-year-old mother to travel from Florida to Milwaukee for a family reunion. She began by sending e-mails to her sister, her brother, and her daughter asking if they could accompany Mom in one direction; Leah would accompany her in the other. All three said they could not, and they all had good reasons. Her daughter Erin, in fact, had two good reasons: First, she couldn't afford to take time off work, and second, her friend was due to give birth right around that time and Erin, a nurse, had promised to be present at the birth. Reluctant to make two round trips herself, Leah repeated her request—but only to her daughter, this time with new information. She told Erin that her uncle had volunteered to reimburse her for the income she'd lose if she took time off work. Would this make it feasible for her to go with Grandma in one direction? Again, Erin explained that she couldn't. Besides the loss of income, there was still the matter of her commitment—and desire—to be available in case her best friend went into labor. A week or so passed, and Leah, feeling her own age at sixty-six, was increasingly desperate to avoid flying between Florida and Wisconsin four times in three days. So she turned to Erin a third time—making sure to preface her request with sincere disclaimers: "I'm sorry to ask you again, I don't want to make you feel guilty; I'm just asking."

Erin explained yet again why she could not do what her mother wanted. But she also went on to protest, "You tell me not to feel guilty, but obviously I do feel guilty when you keep asking me." Leah realized that her daughter was right. She did not go back, again and again, to her sister and brother; she accepted their refusals as nonnegotiable. It was her daughter that her mind kept returning to, her daughter whose reasons she regarded as negotiable—or conveniently forgot. Leah realized that she expected her daughter to help her out in ways she did not expect of others. And she had discounted the metamessage conveyed by the repetition: though her words said, "Don't feel guilty," the fact that she repeated them communicated, "This is something I expect you to do."

In wondering why so many daughters and mothers expect more of each other than they do of their fathers and sons, I thought back to the research I had conducted for my book *Talking from 9 to 5,* about how women and men talk, and are talked to, in the workplace. I had observed this pattern: No matter how highly placed a woman was in the hierarchy, she received less deference than a man in the same role. People seemed to find women more accessible and less intimidating than men in similar positions. I have experienced this myself many times. For example, one Sunday I received a call from a graduate student in our doctoral program who had some questions about the dissertation she was writing. I answered her questions at length, but after a while I remarked that although the advice I had given her reflected my best judgment, she really should be putting these questions to the professor who was directing her dissertation. She explained, "I don't want to bother him at home on Sunday."

As happens with professional women, a mother is often regarded like a secretary: always interruptible, always available. Many mothers take this role by choice. One woman who has two grown daughters commented that she always keeps her cellphone on in case one of her daughters needs her. But being willing, even eager, to help whenever possible does not preclude feeling hurt when family members seem to accept that help as their due. Prominent among complaints I heard from women about their grown daughters was the impression that they were taken for granted, treated with less consideration than others would be. This might take the form of not bothering to make plans in advance, assuming their mothers will be available when needed, changing a date at the last minute without explanation, or simply speaking in a dismissive way ("Oh, Mom, you always say that"). For example, one woman told me that her daughter invited her to join a dinner party because one of the guests had bowed out and the daughter did not want an odd number of people at her table. But when the other guest's plans changed again at the last minute, her daughter simply uninvited her mother. To her daughter, she was both readily available and expendable.

## WHY DON'T YOU JUST SAY IT?

Many daughters, as we saw in the previous chapter, especially resent their mothers' criticism when it is expressed indirectly. The same is true for many daughters' reactions when their mothers make expectations known without requesting outright. But indirectly indicating what you'd like someone to do is common among American women (in many cultures it is common for both women and men), and it works well when both speaker and hearer agree on its use. Daughters who resent their mothers' indirectness are applying to women the conversational ethics and norms more common among men, and this is another way that the family can be a microcosm of the larger society.

Sylvia's mother had a thing about baked potatoes. She liked them, but only if they were very soft, and they seldom were soft enough for her. Whenever she ordered a baked potato in a restaurant, she'd stress to the waiter that she wanted it "well-baked." When it arrived, nine times out of ten she'd cut into it and complain to her dinner companions, "It's hard. I asked for it well-baked." But she'd never send it back, preferring to keep it—and keep complaining about it. When Sylvia was with her mother, she would call the waiter herself and ask for a softer potato. She felt sure that this was what her mother expected and wanted her to do. But there came a time when she decided she wasn't going to do this anymore, because it angered her that her mother expected her to guess what she wanted. Sylvia concluded that her mother deserved to eat hard potatoes as punishment for refusing to say directly what she wanted.

Another woman, Nancy, also told me she is frustrated when her mother doesn't say directly what she wants or thinks. For example, Nancy returned home to help out after her mother broke her wrist in a fall. But when Nancy offered to cook dinner, her mother demurred, explaining that she didn't want the oven to get dirty, since she wouldn't be able to clean it with her broken wrist. Nancy assured her that she would clean the oven if it got dirty. To this, her mother replied that she didn't at all mind cleaning the oven. What Nancy believed to be the message did get through: Her mother did not want Nancy doing anything in her kitchen. She seemed to receive Nancy's gesture of connection as an attempt to wrest control, and she may have thought it kinder to reject the offer for a reason that was out of her control: her broken wrist.

Though both Nancy and Sylvia understood what their mothers wanted, they were frustrated by the way their mothers spoke. Nancy believes it was her mother's refusal to say what she meant that led her to talk in maddening circles. And Sylvia was frustrated because she believes it is wrong to say the opposite of what you want, hoping others will respond to what you didn't say; it seems self-evident to her that stating directly what you want is not only preferable but honest and right. Nancy might be less frustrated by her mother's roundabout reasoning, and Sylvia might feel better about saving the day on her mother's behalf if they thought of directness and indirectness as equally valid ways of communicating. Indeed, indirectness is the norm in many cultural systems.

Haru Yamada, a Japanese linguist, explains in her book *Different Games, Different Rules* that the ability to communicate without putting meaning into words is highly valued by the Japanese, who have a word for it: *haragei,* literally, "belly art." According to Yamada, this term reflects the Japanese belief that talk is suspect and "only the belly speaks the truth." Silent communication, which is regarded as ideal, is an active skill that must be cultivated and practiced, like an art. In the same spirit, the Japanese highly value *sasshi,* which Yamada defines as "anticipatory guesswork"— just the type of gleaning unexpressed meaning that Sylvia feels her mother is wrong to expect.

How could whole cultures have ways of communicating that are flat-out wrong? It's more reasonable to try to understand the logic behind indirectness. Insisting that it is best to state meaning outright is focusing on the message level of talk, as if that is the only level there is. But acknowledging that every utterance has two levels—message and metamessage—means indirectness also makes sense.

## IT GOES WITHOUT SAYING

Recognizing the existence of the metamessage level of talk, I was struck by a contrast in what one woman, Audrey, told me about her mother and about her daughter—comments that came at different times but that, taken together, reveal the logic behind a mother's seemingly illogical way of speaking. Audrey wrote me in an e-mail message that her ten-year-old daughter is like a "soul mate": "She responds to my every emotion and knows what they are even when I try to mask those feelings (and can fool everyone else except her)." This is one of the amazing and unexpected gifts of motherhood: having someone who is so close, so connected, that the tie seems to go directly from your heart to hers.

In a different context, Audrey commented that, although she

loves her mother very much and tries to do all she can to help her, she is irritated when her mother expects her to know what she wants—and provide it—without being asked. For example, when Audrey was getting ready to drive her mother back to her home in another state after a visit, her mother said petulantly, "I had to carry my own luggage out to the car." Audrey knew she was being taken to task for having failed her mother. She asked, "Why didn't you tell me the luggage was ready? I would have carried it out for you." Her mother replied, "You knew I was getting ready, and you must have heard me carrying it downstairs." Audrey's emotional temperature was rising. "I was in the shower," she protested. "How could I have heard you?" At this, her mother changed the ground of the argument: "You're not the same person you used to be." Now her mother's condemnation was not just specific (Audrey's failure to carry her luggage to the car) but general: not being "the same person" clearly meant that Audrey was a worse person than she had been before. Helpless to defend herself against such a damning judgment, Audrey simply retaliated in kind: "Neither are you."

Someone who overheard this interchange might conclude, as Audrey did, that her mother is unreasonable: she was angry at her daughter for not performing a service that she did not request, and that her daughter could not have known she needed. Then, when confronted with the irrationality of her complaint, she shifted to a vague but devastating accusation that her daughter had become a bad person. How to make sense of such maddening behavior? Audrey's comments about her own daughter provide insight into the reasoning that might underlie her mother's apparent irrationality. Audrey exults in the bond she feels with her daughter—a bond that is evidenced when her daughter perceives her unexpressed feelings. After all, anyone can know your emotions and acknowledge your needs if you express them explicitly. Only someone with whom you have a special bond can sense the emotions you don't put into words. This is the precious metamessage of indirectness that many women prize in close relationships.

If the value of being understood without saying what you

mean seems hard to understand, think of the birthday present routine. Anyone can get you exactly what you want for your birthday if you say what you want. But we rarely make such explicit requests. (There are exceptions: one woman told me that after several birthdays on which her husband gave her expensive jewelry she didn't like, she instituted a new regime that pleased them both. When her birthday approached, she bought herself a piece of jewelry and showed her husband the perfect gift he had just given her.) For most of us, hinting is as explicit as we want to get, because what we want is not so much the gift as an object but the gift as evidence that the person knows us well enough to choose something we'd like, and cares enough to take the time to get it. In other words, the gift is the message, and it is nice, but what we really treasure is the metamessage of rapport that comes when someone surprises us with just the right gift.

This is the logic behind indirect styles of communication. And this is the logic that might make Audrey's mother's irrational complaint understandable. If her mother had asked Audrey to carry her luggage to the car, she would have had her luggage carried, but she wouldn't have had the metamessage: evidence that her daughter thinks of her needs and cares enough to fulfill them without being asked. Perhaps Audrey's mother is missing the very kind of "reading" of her emotions that Audrey prizes in her daughter. And perhaps that is exactly what Audrey resists: an interconnection so close that the link between her mother and herself would go directly from one heart to the other. Many women are uncomfortable with this connection when they are adults because they don't feel able to make up for their mothers' unhappiness, whether by providing companionship or by adjusting their own lives to conform to what their mothers expect and approve.

It may also simply be that Audrey and her mother have different conversational styles. Her mother tends to be indirect, especially when it comes to getting her way. Audrey's habitual style is relatively direct. This difference may not be just an unlucky coincidence. Audrey believes that she developed a direct style precisely because she found her mother's use of indirectness frustrating.

## TROUBLES TALK CAN GET YOU IN TROUBLE

The conviction that expressing desires indirectly is slightly under-handed, if not downright manipulative, and that directness is preferable, even more honest, is common among middle-class Americans, but directness represents a style of speaking that is more characteristic of men than women. (This is not to say that men do not use indirectness; it is just that they tend to use it in other contexts, such as admitting fault or ignorance.) We are all inclined to misunderstand and devalue styles of speaking we do not share, but the behaviors widely valued in society at large tend to reflect men's styles more than women's. So a family's disparage-ment of a mother's or daughter's tendency to be indirect when making requests is yet another way that women can find them-selves odd man out in their own homes. And the same can hap-pen with many other ways of speaking that are typical of women, including that fundamental way of using talk to create alliances: exchanging detailed accounts of what happened during your day.

Researchers who study the dinner-table conversation of middle-class American families quickly notice a ritual that some call "telling your day." According to linguist Shoshana Blum-Kulka, this is a common way of initiating conversation at dinner in middle-class American families (though not in the Israeli fami-lies she observed). Elinor Ochs and Carolyn Taylor, anthropolo-gists who also videotaped and analyzed American families around the dinner table, observed that it is usually the mother who en-courages the children to "tell Daddy what happened," and who tells how her own day was. Ochs and Taylor found that mothers' accounts of their days—like many women's conversations with their friends—often include problems that arose, which can be discussed, empathized with, and explored by other family mem-bers. Sociologist Gail Jefferson has dubbed these kinds of conver-sations "troubles talk."

Troubles talk is more common among women than among men. For women, talking about daily experiences is what I call rapport-talk—a way of using talk to establish connections. Troubles talk is a type of rapport-talk, as it invites the other person to express sympathy, display understanding, and recount similar experiences. Many men, however, seem to sense that talking about problems could make them appear weak. Also, and perhaps most important, many men prefer not to talk at home about problems that arose at work, because talking about them would bring back the troubling feelings they aroused. It would, in effect, be dragging the day's dirt into the house, like failing to wipe their feet before entering their home. They'd rather enjoy the comfort of home as a danger-free zone where they don't have to think about problems related to work.

These differing habits with regard to troubles talk lead to an imbalance in many families. If the mother is telling about troubles she confronted during her day but the father is not, the result is that mothers come across as more problem-ridden and insecure than fathers. And many men, because they don't tend to talk in this way, understandably assume that a woman who recounts a problem must be seeking help solving it; why else would she talk about it? That's why they generously provide solutions. So the woman's conversational gambit ends up being refracted through the man's point of view. This misunderstanding of women's rapport-talk often results in mothers appearing to their families as less confident, or even less competent, than their husbands. Just this result was described by a student in an assignment she wrote for my class.

Celia's parents work in similar fields: Her father is a doctor, her mother a nurse. Both work in hospitals, and both encounter many challenging situations daily. But Celia's mother frequently tells her family tales of the cases she handled and issues that arose among her colleagues at work. Celia's father, who presumably grapples with equally interesting and challenging cases, never mentions at home what is going on at work. Celia (and her brother) interpret her mother's work-talk as a sign of insecurity, indication that she needs help confronting the daily challenges of her job or reassurance that she handled them well. This is an in-home version of what I found to be a common source of misjudgment of women's abilities in the workplace: A way of talking that is focused out, to create connection with others, is taken as evidence of the woman's internal state: insecurity or lack of confidence. In this way, many families, like Celia's, replicate the processes—and injustices—of the larger institutions that make up our society: processes and injustices which often result in women feeling—and being—left out. This effect is particularly hurtful to women, since sensitivity to any sign of being left out is part of the legacy most women retain from their childhoods spent playing in groups of girls.

These are some of the ways that relationships between mothers and daughters are shaped by their both being women. And it explains why, if they could make a single request, many mothers would say to their grown daughters, "Don't shut me out."

# 4

# SHE'S JUST LIKE ME, SHE'S NOTHING LIKE ME
## WHERE DO YOU END AND I BEGIN?

M y mother and I are very close." "I wish I were closer to my daughter." "When I started going to Weight Watchers with my mother, I felt closer to her."

When I talked to women about their mothers or their grown daughters, a word that was almost certain to come up was "close." Whether they felt they had it or not, whether they wanted more of it or less, closeness was often the yardstick by which women measured this relationship. They told me that they cherish closeness, that they miss closeness when it's not there; and that too much closeness makes them uncomfortable.

Many women also said that they fear—or seek—the opposite of closeness, distance.

"I had to put more distance between us," a daughter explained. A comment I heard from a mother sounded as if it could have come from this woman's mother, though in fact it came from someone else's: "Distance is painful because there are things in my daughter's life that I can't enjoy because she doesn't tell me about them."

When daughters are small, physical closeness with their mothers is typically a given, even more than it is between mothers and sons. Psychologists have found that mothers tend to have more direct physical contact with their infant daughters than with their infant sons. As children grow older, many mothers who have both sons and daughters notice that their daughters tend to stay physically closer than their sons. For example, a woman who has two sons and two daughters told me (in an e-mail), "The girls want to be really close, most strikingly physically close. I was out clothes shopping with my youngest yesterday (she's almost seven) and I kept stepping on her foot or elbowing her in the face because she needed not just to be holding hands, but to literally have no distance between our bodies at all. Whereas Jimmy suggested we bring our walkie-talkies so we can wander apart and not lose each other."

As daughter and mother grow older and their lives evolve, they keep adjusting and readjusting distance and closeness—both physical closeness, as reflected not only in literal bodily contact but also in where they live, and metaphorical closeness, in how often they talk, how much they tell each other, and the emotional connection they feel. When women told me of the greatest pleasures and the saddest disappointments they experienced with their mothers and their daughters, they often talked in terms of closeness and distance.

The other phrase that was sure to come up when women talked about their daughters and their mothers is "the same," along with its opposite, "different." Nearly all women have had the experience of opening their mouths to speak and hearing their mothers' voices come out, or doing something and then realizing that they did it just as their mothers do—or did. (Mothers have told me of having similar experiences with regard to their grown daughters.) Sometimes this is a pleasant experience. After her mother's death, one woman noticed that she holds a knife, cuts an onion, and wipes down the sink in just the way her mother used to. She found this comforting because it made her feel that her mother was still with her. But there are also times when women catch themselves doing or saying something reminiscent of their mothers, and they recoil, because it is something they did not like when their mothers did it. "I sound just like my mother" is usually said with distaste.

In addition to the closeness-distance yardstick—and inextricable from it—is a yardstick that measures sameness and difference. Hovering at almost any moment is the question, Are my mother and I, my daughter and I, the same or different? And what does that sameness, that difference, mean for me and for my own life?

## REPEAT AFTER ME

Janet takes her three-year-old daughter along to visit her mother, who is recovering at home from surgery. When the grandmother reappears after having retreated to her room for a nap, Janet asks, in a solicitous voice, "Were you able to get some rest, Mom?" Both Janet and her mother burst out laughing when three-year-old Natalie asks, in the same soothing tone, "Grandma, were you able to get some rest?"

Another mother told me that she heard her small daughter talking on her toy telephone. "Hi," the four-year-old said in a treacly voice. "It's so nice of you to call." The mother laughed as she told me this, repeating the little girl's dead-on imitation of her mother's telephone voice—the one she uses when she isn't all that thrilled to hear from the person who called.

When a very small child mimics her mother's voice, it's funny. When a grown daughter's voice echoes her mother's exactly, it can also be amusing to observe, and a source of pleasure to the speakers at the time. A student in a graduate seminar I taught, Jennifer McFadden, captured an example of this on tape. As part of a research project, she tape-recorded telephone conversations with her mother and found that their opening greetings sometimes sounded like a musical duet in which two instruments play the same lines of melody. For example, one exchange began when Jennifer placed a call, her mother answered, and Jennifer then said, "Hellooo, Mommeee," speaking in a high pitch and drawing out the last syllables with a distinctive melody. Her mother replied, "Hellooo, Jenneee," with precisely the same pitch, rhythm, and melodic contour. "How are *you*?" Jennifer then asked, using high pitch again on the end of her phrase. And again her mother's response, "I'm fine, how are *you*?" was a perfect echo of her daughter's phrasing. Finally, Jennifer's answer, "I'm goood," spoken with a unique wavy intonation, was met with her mother's exact rhythmic and intonational copy: "Goood." After that the conversation began. There is something reassuring whenever a greeting proceeds without a hitch, but it is especially delightful when the shared ritual is unique and involves exact repetition, as it did between this mother and daughter.

McFadden's example is striking because her voice and her mother's were like auditory carbon copies. Unusual as this may seem, there are many instances in which mothers and daughters sound alike. This is not surprising, because mothers serve as models for daughters of how to talk, and how to use language to negotiate relationships and the world. As a result, daughters become mirrors for their mothers of how they talk and how they may come across—another facet of the way each feels the other represents her to the world. Sometimes they like what they hear and see; sometimes they don't. In either case, seeing your mother or daughter in yourself, or yourself in her, makes you stop and think about who you are in relation to who she is.

In her memoir *Fierce Attachments,* Vivian Gornick grapples with ways she is like and unlike the woman who raised her. Gornick recounts an occasion when a neighbor hears her say, "That's ridiculous!" and remarks, "You sound just like your mother."

Gornick recalls that as a young girl she "imbibed" her mother's characteristic words. In addition to the response "That's ridiculous," she adopted her mother's habit of dismissing others as "undeveloped"—along with the attitudes and assumptions both expressions convey:

> My father smiled at her when she said "undeveloped," whether out of indulgence or pride I never did know. My brother, on his guard from the age of ten, stared without expression. But I, I absorbed the feel of her words, soaked up every accompanying gesture and expression, every complicated impulse and intent. Mama thinking everyone around was undeveloped, and most of what they said was ridiculous, became imprinted on me like dye on the most receptive of materials.

Gornick was receptive to the impression of her mother's words as her brother was not. And she was not pleased to discover this aspect of her mother in herself. (It is clear from the context that the neighbor did not intend her remark in a spirit of approval.)

Many mothers know or sense that their daughters are less than pleased to discover their mothers in themselves, and this might explain in part why a mother may be less than pleased to discover her daughter doing things differently from the way she did them. The difference may seem to send a metamessage of rejection: "I think the way you do things is wrong." This reaction is not completely irrational. I often heard women say that they made life decisions precisely to be different from their mothers (though they sometimes added that later in life they came to respect their mothers' choices). For example, I heard comments like "When I saw how my mother deferred to my father, I vowed I would never do that" or "All my friends' mothers were professional women, and my mother was at home; I disapproved of her for that and made up my mind I'd have a profession." One woman summed up her impression that her mother prided herself on being different from her own mother by saying, "She thinks of herself as the un-Mommy."

### "I'M THE SAME WAY"

I was talking to a group of women about their mothers and daughters. One woman said about her teenage daughter, "We get along very well on a certain level. The tension comes because we're very different in certain personality things. She's very creative, but she's also very disorganized and messy. And I'm way too organized about everything."

"I have the other issue," another woman said. "My daughter is *very* much like me. . . . The stuff she does is what I did. It drives me crazy. It's like the two same poles of a magnet. They just won't come together."

"My mother's a perfectionist," said a third, "and I'm a recovering perfectionist."

Women I talked to mentioned that they were like or unlike their daughters or their mothers to explain either harmony or discord. One woman, in telling me why she and her daughter got along well, said, "Maybe it's because she's like me. I've been told we walk alike and sound the same on the telephone. We even wear the same size clothes." But another woman said, in explaining why she and her daughter did not get along, "My daughter and I often lock horns because she's like me—complicated." Yet another told me that she is bothered by the ways her daughter is like her: "I see Isabel raising her kids the way I raised her. She's really strict; like she insists they eat everything she puts on their plates. Even though I did that myself, I can't stand to see her do it."

We all compare ourselves to family members: not just to parents but to siblings and cousins as well. Yet the question "Are we the same?" is more fundamental to the social lives of girls and women than it is to the social lives of boys and men, because so much of girls' emotional energy is focused on monitoring and negotiating alliances (who's in, who's out?) in contrast to boys, who are more often focused on negotiating their status in the group (who's up, who's down?). This contrast is evident in a comparison of girls and boys at play included in a video that I made for workplace training.

The camera crew of ChartHouse International, who made the video, recorded children playing in a preschool. Two brief clips capture the pattern that tended to distinguish how the girls and boys talked while they played. In one clip, three boys are talking about who can hit a ball highest; clearly enjoying their verbal competition, they laugh with delight each time one tops another. In a different clip, two girls are sitting at a small table, drawing. Suddenly one girl looks up and says, "Did you know my babysitter, called Amber, has already contacts?" ("Contacts" apparently refers to contact lenses.) The second girl hesitates a moment, then replies, "My mom has already contacts, and my dad does too." They go back to drawing, but after a few seconds, the first girl lifts her head again, lights up with glee, and exclaims, "The same?" She seems as delighted by this matching exchange as the boys are by topping one another. The second little girl even echoed the first one's odd syntax: "has already contacts," another way of showing she's the same. (Repeating another's words with altered syntax or pronunciation can come across as a correction.)

I have heard innumerable stories from parents of how their little girls want to be the same as their friends, and want everyone in their family to be the same, too—especially they and their mothers. One mother, for example, commented in the course of a conversation with her eight-year-old daughter, "We're different people." Her daughter strenuously objected: "No we're not, we're the same." When the mother maintained her claim, the daughter challenged, "How are we different?" "I'm bigger," her mother said. The girl handily dismissed this point: "That's temporary." Her mother then said, "You're bossier." The daughter had a comeback ready: "When you were a kid, you were bossy too." Her mother parried, "But I grew out of it," to which her daughter replied, "I'll grow out of it too." This child was not giving in: She was determined that she and her mother be the same.

When they are adults, women's ways of talking often reflect this valuing of sameness without our thinking about it consciously. One of my students, Mike Lal, had occasion to observe such an instance, and he noticed it because it struck him as odd. Mike entered a campus building with another student, a woman. They walked through a hallway lined with computers that students could use to check e-mail. When Mike and his friend passed a group of students waiting to use the computers, his companion was greeted by a girl she knew, who said, "I have to check my e-mail." His friend replied, "I have to check my e-mail too"—and she kept on walking. Mike asked her why she didn't join her friend in the line, and she said that she didn't really have to check her e-mail. "Then why did you say you did?" he asked. She replied, "I don't know." The reason she didn't know, I would wager, is that she hadn't thought through her response to her friend's greeting, and she didn't mean it literally. Her remark popped out automatically as an appropriate way to show goodwill toward her friend by saying, in effect, "I'm the same." For girls and women, emphasizing sameness is a way of reinforcing connection.

Many conversations that take place between women seem designed to reassure each other of their similarity. If one woman says, for example, "I'm always misplacing things," the other is likely to say, "I'm the same way" and perhaps even add, "Just this morning I spent ten minutes looking for my keys." Knowing that someone you like is similar to you can be a source of satisfaction. The reminder of shared habits and perceptions sends a metamessage that you're a right sort of person and all's well with the world. That's why many women are disconcerted when someone declines to respond "I'm the same." Suppose a woman says, "I'm always misplacing things," and the other person says, "Why don't you pay attention to where you put things down?" The first woman may protest, "Don't give me advice," but the reason this response bothers her may well be that it fails to offer the expected reassurance of sameness.

Here's an example of a woman who was annoyed by her

friend's failure to say "I'm the same" that also illustrates how a daughter may, without thinking about it, adopt her mother's style of speaking. Norma was telling her friend Susan about her mother's visit. "My mother complained the whole time," Norma said. "She came off the plane saying how tiring the trip had been and how crowded the plane was, and that was only the first five minutes." Norma went on to tell other tales of how her mother had gotten on her nerves. She expected Susan to say something like "I know; mothers are like that" or even "My mother did that when she visited, too." So Norma was caught off guard when Susan replied, "Oh, my mother never complains. If it's raining, she'll say 'The sun will be shining tomorrow.' And even if she does say something annoying, I can't hold it against her because I know she means well." This made Norma want to defend her mother and wonder why she had been putting her down.

When I thought about this example, I realized that Norma and Susan were both talking in the ways they were attributing to their mothers. Norma was trying to connect with her friend through complaining, just as Norma's mother was probably trying to do when she complained to her daughter. And Susan was putting a positive spin on everything her mother did, even while acknowledging that there were aspects of her mother's behavior that were annoying—exactly the style of speaking she was attributing to her mother.

## DON'T SAY YOU'RE THE SAME

Though many women expect and appreciate the response "I'm the same way," there are contexts in which a reassuring "I'm the same" may be anything but reassuring, especially coming from a mother. One mother thought she was being a good listener and a supportive parent when she assured her daughter, "I know what you mean," and went on to draw parallels between her own experience and what her daughter was telling her. But one day her daughter cut her off: "Stop saying you know because you've had the same experience. You don't know. This is *my* experience, and the world is different now." The mother could see immediately that this was true. When the world changed less quickly, parents' experience really was more relevant to their children's than it is today. But another part of what irritated her daughter, no doubt, was the feeling that her mother was encroaching upon her, denying the uniqueness of her experience—in other words, offering too much sameness.

There is another circumstance in which a daughter might object to her mother replying with the conventional women's response "I'm the same way." If a woman says something negative about herself, she may expect the other person not to ratify that negative assessment but to deny it. In those cases, the response "I'm the same way" can feel like a put-down. When this type of comfort comes from a mother, it can hurt even more. Barbara recalls remarking to her mother, "I'm sort of good at everything but not especially good at anything. I wish I were especially good at something." Her mother's response seemed to seal her fate: "That's just like me. I know how you feel. I always wanted to be especially good at something, but I wasn't." This response felt to Barbara like a confirmation of her inadequacy, condemning her to an undistinguished life.

Did Barbara's mother truly think she was comforting her daughter by reassuring her that she wasn't particularly good at anything either—thereby reinforcing her daughter's negative self-assessment? Barbara, who went on to have a successful career, felt that her mother really did wish her daughter to be like her—a homemaker with no career to make her stand out as especially good at something. When Barbara's life began to diverge from her mother's (she attended university, earned a Ph.D., became prominent in her field), she felt that her mother saw her daughter's choices as a betrayal. Barbara herself felt in a way that she was rejecting her mother by not repeating her life, as Barbara's sister had done. Her sister's life was similar to their mother's, and her mother made it clear she preferred to talk to Barbara's sister. She once said as much: "Your sister and I are in the same slice of the cake. You're not in the same slice of the cake anymore." It is interesting that Barbara illustrated her mother's acceptance, or lack of it, by reference to whom she prefers to talk to. For her, as for many girls and women, talk is the embrace.

Many women resist their mothers' expectation that they be the same. For a paper written in conjunction with a graduate seminar I taught, Laura Wright interviewed women whose parents had divorced. She cites this comment from a woman she calls Lyn, who was explaining her relationship with her mother: "We're just different people, and for so long she's thought that we were the same and so now it's hard for me to express our differences and for her to even accept that. I think that she's been trying to mold a mini her." In Lyn's view, her mother's assumption that her daughter is like her made it difficult for Lyn to let her mother see who she really is, because who she is differs from her mother, and this puts distance between them. Another woman told me of a pithy way she expressed a similar concern. "With all due respect," she reported telling her mother, "I am not you."

### "DO AS I DIDN'T"

A mother's inclination to see her daughter's life as a referendum on her own does not necessarily lead her to send the message "Do as I did." It may lead her to send the opposite message: "Do as I didn't." Many professional women told me their mothers urged them to find work they were good at and enjoyed, have careers, and make sure they were able to support themselves. All these women said that their mothers had been creative, talented, capable young women who gave up the work or the art they loved when they married—and were frustrated for the rest of their lives. Like nearly all patterns of interaction, this can be interpreted in positive or negative ways. The positive side of this expectation is expressed by Erica Jong, who wrote, "My mother wanted me to be her wings, to fly as she never had the courage to do. I love her for that. I love the fact that she wanted to give birth to her own wings." But I also heard from women who felt a deep sense of guilt because their mothers had sacrificed too much in order to raise them. Some also felt that they were expected to make up for that sacrifice. As one woman put it, "I felt that she lived through me."

If daughters are grappling with what it means that their mothers want them to be like them or different, they also are grappling with whether or not they want to be like their mothers. One mother of two grown children told me she so wanted to be different from her mother that she didn't want to be a mother at all. "I never wanted children," she said, "and then I realized that the reason was that I was afraid I'd be like my mother, who never communicated with me. But then I came to understand that I didn't have to be like her—and I haven't been." (Ironically, having children bridged the communication gap. She told me that she and her mother became "closer" when her mother came to help her out with her first baby.)

In deciding what kinds of mothers they want to be, many women compare themselves to their own mothers and try to be different. Sometimes there is a back-and-forth by which each generation reacts against the one before. If this woman felt that her mother did not communicate enough, another told me that her daughter communicates too much. She commented that sometimes she feels her grown daughter confides too much personal information. "There are some things a mother does not need to know about her daughter's sex life," she said. I mentioned that many daughters had told me their mothers wanted to know too much about their sex lives. At this she said, "Absolutely! My mother was very intrusive. She read my diary, she wanted to know everything. That's why I raised a wall and became a private person."

Here's another example of one generation leapfrogging over the next, as each daughter strives to be different from her mother. When Abby was a teenager, her mother did not want her to use tampons. But Abby couldn't stand having her activity hampered by the bulky pads her mother insisted she wear. When her mother refused to help, she locked herself in the bathroom and figured out by herself—after much trial and error, and many wasted boxes of tampons—how to use them. So when her own daughter reached that stage of her life, Abby naturally encouraged her to use tampons and offered to teach her how. But her daughter refused. No way was she going to use tampons. Period.

### YOU CAN'T TAKE ME WITH YOU

Given these many instances in which daughters are motivated by a desire not to be like their mothers, a mother may be right to see her daughter's different choices as a rebuke. And a mother may seem to reject her daughter's choices simply because she does not understand the life her daughter chose. I think that was the case with my own mother.

My mother came to visit me shortly after I moved to Washington, D.C. I had recently taken up a teaching position at Georgetown University and was eager to show her my new home and introduce her to my new life. My mother had disapproved of me during my rebellious youth, and she had been distraught when my first marriage ended six years before. In those intervening years, I had enrolled in graduate school and earned a Ph.D. Now I was a professor; clearly I had turned out all right. I was sure she'd be proud of me—and she was. When I showed her the Georgetown campus, the office with my name on the door, and my publications on the shelf, she seemed pleased and approving. Then she asked, "Do you think you would have accomplished all this if you had stayed married?"

"Absolutely not," I said. "If I'd stayed married, I never would have gone back to grad school to get my Ph.D."

"Well," she replied, "if you had stayed married, you wouldn't have had to." Ouch. With her casual remark, my mother had reframed all I had achieved as the booby prize.

I have told this story many times, knowing I could count on my listeners to gasp at this proof that my mother belittled my professional accomplishments. But when I think about it now, my best guess is that she was simply reflecting the world she had grown up in, where there was one and only one measure by which women were judged successful or pitiable: marriage. I suspect she was trying to figure out what to make of my life, which was so different from any she could have imagined for herself. I don't think she intended to denigrate what I had done and become, but the lens through which she viewed the world could not encompass the path I had chosen. Although I believe she was not motivated by malice, nonetheless it made me sad that my mother could not appreciate the professional recognition I had received because she had no idea what any of it meant.

Many of the stories women told me were testaments to how their mothers never truly appreciated or even recognized the success they valued in their own lives, especially in the realm of work. Comments or questions that would be welcome in another context can be irritating if they seem to show that your mother focuses on something other than what you value. This explains Leslie's reaction to a question her mother asked. Leslie rolls her eyes as she says, "When I told my mother that I was invited to give a presentation at my company's year-end retreat, and that it went well, she asked, 'What did you wear?' Who cares what I wore?" In fact, Leslie cared. She had given a lot of thought to selecting an outfit that was casual enough for a retreat but not so casual that her colleagues wouldn't take her seriously. But her mother's focus on her clothing seemed to dismiss the honor of being chosen and the achievement of doing well. Her mother's question seemed to undercut that achievement, and Leslie's sense of herself as a successful professional.

June had a similar experience. She was pleased to learn that the academic conference at which she'd be presenting a paper was to be held in the city where her parents lived. She invited them to attend her session, eagerly anticipating how proud they'd be to see their daughter at the lectern, addressing a large and attentive audience. June's parents did attend, and when the session ended, they approached her, beaming. Her father said, "You were wonderful, honey. It's amazing how much you know." Her mother said, "You looked terrific in that black suit." Both her parents' comments were compliments, but somehow her mother's compliment disappointed June.

Leslie's and June's mothers had simply talked in ways that they always had, connecting to their daughters through a shared interest in clothes and attention to their appearance. But it is the very familiarity of these responses that makes them hurtful in these contexts: While Leslie and June were presenting themselves to their mothers in new guises, their mothers were regarding them in the old ones. This is what rankled.

Being complimentary in the old way also explains another woman's annoyance with her mother. Her mother happened to be visiting when Emily got word that a grant proposal she had submitted to a government agency had been funded. This was a major milestone in her career. Emily was glad to be able to announce the good news to her mother. Upon hearing it, her mother said, "Now that deserves a kiss!" Though her mother reacted with approval—a kiss is a reward for a job well done—Emily felt it was inappropriate to the significance and nature of winning a highly competitive grant. A kiss is what a child might get for receiving a star on her homework, not the type of congratulations a distinguished scientist expects for receiving professional recognition. Emily's heart sank; she felt like her mother had diminished the significance of her important news. Her mother probably thought she was showing appreciation and sharing her daughter's pleasure, but the world of scientific peer review was so removed from her experience that she simply did not know the appropriate way to respond. She related to Emily as mother to daughter, in ways that had been formed when Emily was a child.

## GET DOWN HERE THIS MINUTE

Another woman's disappointment at her mother's reaction to her success seemed to stem from a different source—the envy that can come with closeness. Psychologist Abraham Tesser has shown that the closer people are to us, the more likely we are to compare ourselves to them. If we feel that we look worse by comparison, we end up feeling worse about ourselves. One way to avoid that unpleasant feeling is to minimize the difference, which often entails minimizing the other's accomplishments.

Angela is a writer who still recalls her frustration and hurt when her first short story was published in a small literary magazine. The moment the magazine arrived in the mail, she began anticipating the scene when she would show it her mother. As soon as Angela next visited home, she raced to the kitchen, where she found her mother washing dishes. Without waiting for her to dry her hands, Angela held before her mother's eyes the journal opened to the page on which Angela's name was in print. Drying her hands on her apron, her mother took the magazine, examined it, and said, "Where can anyone buy a magazine like this? No one will be able to find it, so who's going to read it?" With that, Angela's excitement dribbled away, like the dishwater down the drain.

Angela figured that her timing had been off; she should not have taken her mother by surprise in the kitchen. She made sure to be more careful the next time she had a publication to present: a collection of her stories, an actual book with her name on the cover. This time, while visiting her parents, she waited for the right moment. She thought she had found it when her parents retired to the living room after dinner, her father reading a book and her mother reading *The Wall Street Journal*. Angela went upstairs (this time she didn't race) to retrieve the book, then returned with it and showed it to her mother. After looking at the book, her mother pointed to the newspaper she had been reading, where a front-page story told of housewives who made gobs of money writing romance novels. "Why don't you write books like that?" she asked. "At least then you'd have something to show for it."

Angela believes that her mother deflated her excitement in these ways because she envied her daughter's accomplishments in the wider world, even though her mother was the one who had encouraged her to pursue them. Vivian Gornick's memoir holds a clue to why some mothers may react this way to their daughters' successes.

Gornick and her mother were walking together the day after her mother had heard her give a rousing and effective speech to a large, receptive audience. "I am properly expectant," Gornick writes.

> She is about to tell me how wonderful I was last night. She opens her mouth to speak.
>
> "Guess who I dreamed about last night," she says to me. "Sophie Schwartzman!"
>
> I am startled, taken off balance. This I had not expected. "Sophie Schwartzman?" I say. But beneath my surprise a kernel of dread begins growing in the bright bright day.

Gornick explains that Sophie, ten years dead, had been a neighbor whose children had achieved considerable success: her son became a famous composer, and her daughter Frances married a rich man. This is how Gornick's mother described her dream:

> "I dreamed I was in Sophie's house," my mother says. . . . "Frances came in. She had written a book. She asked me to read it. I did, and I wasn't so enthusiastic. She became very angry. She screamed at her mother, "Never let her come here again." I felt so bad!

Gornick describes the effect her mother's remarks had on her: "My feet seem to have lead weights in them. I struggle to put one foot in front of the other." Her mother slighted her not only by neglecting to praise her triumphant performance but also by telling her of a dream in which she had disliked a daughter's book, though in her dream it was someone else's daughter. The lead weights in Gornick's feet are heavy with her disappointment at her mother's dismissive response.

Why would Gornick's mother (or Angela's) resist heaping praise and expressing enthusiastic approval of her daughter's success? Early in her memoir, Gornick writes of her mother: "It was, in fact, part of her deprivation litany that if it hadn't been for the children she would have developed into a talented public speaker." It is possible that her mother found it hard to be happy about her daughter's talent and success in the very arena where her own thwarted ambitions lay. Given how close mothers and daughters are, and how likely it is that mothers will see in their daughters reflections, rejections, or refractions of their own lives, it is not surprising that they may at times feel envious if their daughters get what their mothers wanted and could not have.

## THE GREEN-EYED MONSTER IN YOUR LIVING ROOM

"I'm thrilled I can give my daughter things I didn't have," one woman commented. "But sometimes I also resent her. She's only seven, and she's already been to China and Indonesia. I'm glad, of course. But every now and then I catch myself thinking she isn't grateful enough, doesn't realize how lucky she is—and I realize it's because I'm jealous. It's a terrible thing to admit, being jealous of your own daughter, especially such a little one. But sometimes I have to admit, that's how it feels." Some daughters may sense this envy, even if it is never spoken.

Dana called her mother from the Bahamas and described, with excitement, the glory of the sun and the beauty of the sea. "It sounds wonderful," her mother responded. "I would have liked to go to the Bahamas. I guess I'll just have to live vicariously through you." Though her mother never said a word to indicate she begrudged her daughter the exotic vacation, knowing that her mother envies her life (which her mother acknowledged she did, when they discussed it later) made Dana uncomfortable; it was hard enough living her life without feeling that she carried her mother on her back. There is another reason a mother may feel ambivalent about her daughter's adventures. A mother who sees her daughter living a more exciting life than she had might not only feel a touch of envy but also be reminded that she is getting older. The days when she might have taken a romantic trip to the Bahamas are long gone.

Even mothers who encourage their daughters to be all they can be may, at times, want to hold their daughters back, because their daughters' accomplishments make their own seem paltry, and their daughters' interesting lives make their own feel dull. Many women have told me that their mothers' joy at their accomplishments is not unalloyed. This was the case with a writer who has enjoyed considerable popular acclaim. She commented that although her mother had always urged her to do more than just raise children, to continue her education and make something of herself, nonetheless her mother is not entirely thrilled by all the attention her daughter now gets. "She often gives me the impression that she thinks I should be spending more time taking care of my husband and children," the writer says, "and less getting recognition from the outside world. I think in a way she's jealous, because she herself could have accomplished so much more if she had not left school to get married."

There is evidence in psychological research that a daughter's success can make a mother feel worse about herself. Carol Ryff, Pamela Schmutte, and Young Hyun Lee investigated the relationship between how parents evaluate their adult children's achievements and how they evaluate themselves. Based on a survey of 114 mothers and 101 fathers (from different families) with children over the age of twenty-one, they examined (among other questions) how adult children's attainment affected their parents' sense of well-being. The authors were surprised to find that the effect was negative—only for mothers and daughters! In the authors' words, "For fathers, attainment comparisons with sons or daughters did not explain any variance in their rating of themselves"; nor did sons' attainment affect mothers'. But "mothers who perceived that their daughters had done better than themselves in the attainment domain had *lower* well-being." The authors put the word "lower" in italics because this finding was unexpected. Yet it's exactly the effect that so many women, both mothers and daughters, perceive in their own lives—and it reinforces the impression that of the four possible parent-child constellations, the daughter-mother relationship carries a unique emotional load.

## DIFFERENCE EQUALS DISTANCE

Envy and comparison are not the only reasons that a mother, even though she truly wants her daughter to soar higher than she herself has flown, might nonetheless feel a tinge of regret to see her daughter receding in the sky. We can see this fear in the dream that Vivian Gornick's mother had the night after witnessing her daughter's public speaking triumph. In Mrs. Gornick's dream, Frances Schwartzman had screamed, "Never let her come here again." That's what turned the dream into a nightmare. A daughter who moves into worlds her mother doesn't inhabit moves away, creating a distance more unbridgeable than the physical distance of moving to a different city. Here again Gornick's memoir is eloquent. When she began attending college (which her mother did not), Gornick writes, "My sentences got longer within a month of those first classes. Longer, more complicated, formed by words whose meaning she did not always know. I had never before spoken a word she didn't know." This angered her mother, and Gornick was stunned by her mother's anger. "I was going to take her into the new world," she writes. "All she had to do was adore what I was becoming, and here she was refusing."

One reason a mother might not adore what her daughter is becoming is that she cannot accompany her into the new world she is entering. Another woman, Cheryl, who had grown up in a working-class family in New Jersey, tried to show her mother the world she had come to inhabit in Washington, D.C., and to share it with her. For example, Cheryl took her mother to a classical music concert at the Kennedy Center. When the concert ended, she eagerly anticipated her mother's praise for the music and the sumptuous hall in which it had been performed. What her mother said was "When we used to go to the Christmas shows at

Radio City Music Hall, that was really wonderful." Cheryl heard in this remark the implication that her mother had been disappointed by the Kennedy Center concert, and this disappointed Cheryl in return.

When Cheryl tried to introduce her mother to the luxuries and sophisticated pleasures she could now afford and appreciate, her mother accused her of becoming a snob. The truth was, her mother did not feel comfortable in Cheryl's new world. The daughter had taken a path her mother could not traverse, and no amount of enticing, coaxing, or dragging could change that. A gulf had opened between them where before they had stood on the same ground.

It saddened Cheryl that the difference between her new world and her old one created distance between herself and her mother, because when she was young they had been very close. She was close to her own daughter, too, but that closeness didn't take quite the form she had expected it to. "The shock of my life," Cheryl remarked, "was that my daughter didn't come out exactly like me."

Anything that makes a daughter different can be a potential source of distress to her mother. In his book *Mother Father Deaf,* Paul Preston, a hearing child of deaf parents, tells of a conversation he had with a deaf woman about her daughter's birth. The woman recounted how upsetting it was to learn that her newborn baby could hear:

> I was holding her in my arms near the metal food tray. I picked up a spoon and dropped it on the tray. I couldn't believe it! I was really upset. I did it a second time because I just couldn't believe it. I dropped the spoon again, and it was the same thing. I even did it a third time. I thought, Oh, my God, she's hearing! What am I going to do? I have a hearing daughter! My husband came and I said, "My God, our daughter's hearing!" He was just as surprised, but he told me it was fine, it was going to be okay.

The mother explained to Preston that she was upset to learn her daughter could hear because she wanted to be close to her daughter, as she had been close to her parents, who were deaf like her. She went on, "I worried that we would never connect, or that we would drift apart."

This mother's explanation of why she was upset that her daughter was different—that they would "drift apart"—explains how the sameness-difference dimension intersects with the closeness-distance measure. Although it doesn't always turn out that way, it often seems that sameness ensures closeness, and difference leads to distance. And this equation raises the specter that haunts girls' and women's social lives: being left out.

## BODIES TOUCHING

I have been using the terms "distance" and "closeness" as metaphorical ways of talking about conditions that are fundamentally emotional. But sometimes emotional closeness is literally embodied in physical contact, and distance in lack of it. Here too daughters' and mothers' ideas of how much is the right amount often differ. Some women treasure physical connection with their mothers or daughters, others recoil from it, and some just have different ideas about how much and what type of physical connection feels right. Adjusting to differences in how much seems like the right amount is a concrete aspect of negotiating a comfortable relationship with your daughter or your mother.

"One of the things I love about my relationship with my daughter is that we are physical with each other," one woman comments. "She's twenty-three, and she'll still cuddle up to me." This woman is not alone in treasuring physical affection. For the narrator of Sue Monk Kidd's novel *The Secret Life of Bees,* a teenager named Lily, whose mother died when she was four, imagining physical contact with her mother's live body is a poignant reminder of what she has lost. Here she describes the ache of missing the mother she can barely remember—or perhaps of missing *a* mother, an idealized physical mother, which is why readers whose mothers did not die when they were small can also identify with this ache:

> The worst thing was lying there wanting my mother. That's how it had always been; my longing for her nearly always came late at night when my guard was down. I tossed on the sheets, wishing I could crawl into bed with her and smell her skin. . . . My mouth twisted as I pictured myself climbing in beside her and putting my head against her breast. I would put it right over her beating heart and listen. *Mama,* I would say. And she would look down at me and say, *Baby, I'm right here.*

The bodily contact, the feel and smell of her skin, represent all the presences of a mother in her daughter's life. (Never mind that if Lily's mother had been alive, the fourteen-year-old Lily might well have been lying in bed tallying her shortcomings.)

A woman whose mother had died when she was an adult spoke of their physical contact as evidence of how deeply connected they had been: "We used to sit so close and touch each other so much my father would laugh that he could never tell where her body started and my body stopped," she said, recalling this as something precious. But there are women who are distressed when they sense that their mothers lose track of where one's body ends and the other's begins. Rochelle, at thirty-five, was taking a rest as her mother sat companionably on the side of the bed. Suddenly her mother saw something that concerned her—a mark on Rochelle's face. She leaned over to examine the mark more carefully, bringing her face right up to her daughter's and keeping it there until she satisfied herself that the mark was not worrisome. Rochelle squirmed at the intrusion, the proprietary nature of her mother's gaze. It was almost as if her mother were staring at her own face, so closely and steadily did she examine it.

For Carla, too, her mother sometimes gets—or wants to get—literally too close for comfort. "One of the things that makes me uncomfortable when my mother visits," she tells me, "is when she says—and she says it a lot—'I need a hug from you.' Of course I do it because I don't want to hurt her, but it feels terrible inside because I don't really want to, so it makes me feel like a child, having to do things I don't want to do." It's not that Carla doesn't love her mother, or doesn't want to hug her. The point on which they differ is how often. "When I greet her at the airport," Carla says, "I'll give her a hug and kiss, but she wants to hang on when I want to pull away. And I feel like I don't have to do that again until she leaves. For her, it's every morning, every evening, and in between: 'Can I have a hug?'" Back and forth, forth and back. How much is too much, how much is too little—and what happens when daughter and mother have different notions of which is which?

The line between too little and too much closeness can be, as in this example, a physical one or (as we've seen before) a matter of information exchanged. And sometimes it has to do with the way one behaves in the other's home.

## THE COMFORT OF (YOUR) HOME

Many of the anecdotes I heard from women when they talked about their mothers or their daughters had to do with their homes, which can feel like an extension of, or an embodiment of, their selves. In Chapter Two I told of a mother who tried to improve her daughter's home by moving things around—and succeeded only in angering her daughter. In another instance, it was the mother who found herself the object of similar efforts, with similar results. She returned home from work one day and discovered—to her horror—that her furniture had been rearranged to accommodate a new coffee table. Her daughter, who had a key to her house, had bought her the coffee table, which she had been telling her mother for years that she needed, and had redecorated around it as a birthday surprise. Her mother was surprised, all right, but far from pleased. She called a friend and asked him to come over and help her put things back the way they had been. She didn't call her daughter because she was so angry, she didn't even want to talk to her.

In these cases, a mother or daughter behaved in the other's home as she would in her own, and I heard about it because the result was conflict. Yet other women mentioned their daughters' homes in explaining why they got along well. In one case, a mother, while telling me how wonderful a visit to her daughter had been, offered as evidence that her daughter had allowed her to prepare a meal. Letting her mother take over her kitchen was evidence that her daughter had, metaphorically, let her in. In another case, a mother told me that one reason she has excellent relationships with her daughters is that she behaves like a guest in their homes. Although the stances these women took toward their daughters' homes were opposite, the metaphorical meaning of the homes was the same: a stand-in for the woman herself, a locus for finding a comfortable level of connection while avoiding the uncomfortable impression of intrusion—in other words, negotiating how close or distant mother and daughter want to be.

Similar satisfactions and struggles take place over other types of possessions. One mother, for example, said she loves to see her daughter wearing her clothes. Yet another told me, after saying that she almost never says no to her daughter, "The only thing I said no to her about was wearing my clothes." Either practice makes sense, so long as mother and daughter have the same attitude toward sharing clothes or other possessions. When their ideas differ, the result can be disconcerting or worse.

### WHOSE IS IT?

When I was about fourteen I bought a colorful, hand-knitted ski mask in a small shop in Greenwich Village. Made in Peru, it covered the face completely except for openings for the eyes and mouth. I didn't ski, and I didn't wear it. (I wore it once, with disastrous results: I boarded a crowded bus on a bitter cold day and was mocked by passengers who, to make matters worse, mistook me for a boy.) I kept the bright-colored hood in the hall closet with the other hats. One day I discovered it missing and asked my mother if she knew where it was. She did indeed. She had given it to a friend who thought her son might like it. I was outraged. It wasn't that I intended to wear it ever again, though I did still like it and had bought it with money I'd earned working part-time after school. Most of all, I took umbrage because it was mine, and I felt that my mother had no right to give it away.

I was reminded of this incident while visiting New York City with a couple in their seventies, both native New Yorkers who no longer lived there. The sight of a particular building triggered a memory for them. "That's where the CCNY prom was held," the man said with nostalgia. He turned to his wife. "Remember? I gave you a corsage." The woman picked up the story: "And because it was the first corsage you ever gave me, I decided to keep it. I put it in the refrigerator. And the next day it was gone. My mother had given it to a neighbor." At first this sounded inconceivable to me: I asked the woman how on earth her mother could have given her daughter's corsage to a neighbor. She tried to explain what she imagined her mother's motive to be: "She would have shown it to the neighbor in order to boast that her daughter had a boyfriend who bought her a corsage. And then giving it away would earn her points with the neighbor."

Since mothers are judged by their children's success or failure, it stands to reason that evidence of her daughter's romantic success enhances the mother's prestige with her neighbors, the court of public opinion before which she stands every day. Giving away something of her own that she no longer needed would be a generous and appropriate way to keep good relations with neighbors and friends. So why not do the same with something her daughter won't use? That must have been my mother's motivation in giving away the ski mask she knew I never wore. By the same token, the mother who gave away her daughter's corsage must have figured, The prom is over; the corsage has served its purpose.

What harm in now putting it to use to serve another purpose: earning a neighbor's goodwill? Yet what seemed reasonable to the mother seemed outrageous to the daughter because of a small difference in their points of view: The daughter felt that the corsage was hers alone, but her mother felt that she had a right to it as well. The mother's sense of their closeness, and what it entailed, differed from her daughter's.

In all these examples, daughters and mothers are struggling to figure out in what ways they are the same, in what ways they are different, and what to make of their similarities and differences. This struggle is inextricable from their ongoing negotiation of closeness and distance. Does being the same bring you closer or drive you farther apart? Does difference entail distance? And just how much closeness and distance do you want? These dynamics are among many ways that relationships between mothers and daughters resemble all relationships, but with more intensity and more urgency.

# 5

# STOP THIS CONVERSATION,
# I WANT TO GET OFF

Mothers and daughters share a long history—a lifetime, in the daughters' case—and that includes a lifetime of conversations. They may laugh at the same jokes, talk at the same pace, and know just what the other means when she says a word or two. Sharing this conversational universe can be a source of great pleasure. But if there are aspects of the other's ways of talking that irritate, both are well aware of those, too. Like listening to a radio perennially tuned to the same station, each knows what's coming when she hears a certain type of remark, a recognizable tone of voice, a particular lilt. If she expects the remark, the lilt, to be followed by something she's not going to like, her back will be up before it's said. The conversation may suddenly turn tense, or even turn into an argument—the same argument they have had many times before. They are weary of the bad radio drama but feel powerless to change the station: the dial is permanently stuck.

At times it can seem that both daughter and mother are taking part in a mysterious ritual, each playing her part. A man commented to me that when he listens to a friend talking to her grown daughter on the telephone, he hears her raise topics (he calls them "neuralgic points") that he knows will cause their amiable conversation to take an unpleasant turn. Because the two women love each other and have a good relationship overall, they will eventually put this topic aside and return to the congenial tone that had prevailed before the neuralgic point was touched. But the man wonders why, if he can see it coming, his friend can't. I would guess that something prods her to try one more time to get her daughter to see things her way, and something prods her daughter to respond in her accustomed way, too. The reason he can see what's coming is that he is watching from the outside. If mothers and daughters could step outside the loop and watch the process unfold, they too would see clearly what's happening—and also see ways to change the script.

## WE'RE PLAYING OUR SONG

The pattern this man noticed while listening to his friend's telephone conversations is enacted daily between mothers and daughters in homes and over telephones across the country. Here is an example. It takes Tracy an hour and fifteen minutes to drive to her work, but it takes her husband only twenty minutes to drive to his. Since Tracy works longer hours and also does a lot more child care and housekeeping, her mother, Mona, can see clear as day that it would make more sense for Tracy and her family to live closer to her workplace, not his. But whenever she raises the issue with her daughter, they end up in an argument—yet she keeps raising it when they speak on the phone. Mona thinks she is looking out for her daughter, trying to prevent her from taking all the burden on herself. Tracy feels that her mother is unfairly crit-

STOP THIS CONVERSATION, I WANT TO GET OFF *115*

icizing the choices she's made and, even worse, her husband; she hates being caught between them, and disapproval of her husband is, indirectly, disapproval of her.

Let's look at how the conflict develops and escalates. In the course of their talk, Mona comments, "Gee, honey, you sound tired," and Tracy admits, "Yeah, I guess I am." Mona then says, "You know, dear, you wouldn't be so tired if you didn't have such a long commute. Have you looked into finding a house closer to where you work, like we talked about?" Tracy's blood pressure begins to rise as she repeats the point she always makes when her mother brings this up: "Mom, I told you. We did look. We couldn't get as nice a house if we moved closer to the city. And anyway, Marty takes a lot of work home and he needs the time. My job stays at the office." To this Mona replies, "Tracy, it hurts me to see you putting Marty's needs ahead of yours. There are plenty of neighborhoods nearer to your work where I'm sure you could find a nice house you can afford. I was looking in the listings the other day and—" Tracy cuts her off: "I *like* the time I spend in the car driving to and from work. It gives me a chance to unwind, to be alone with my thoughts before I get home and get caught up in all the pressure." Mona then says, "Well, if you didn't have such a long commute, your time at home wouldn't be so pressured." As they talk, Mona becomes increasingly upset by her daughter's refusal to improve her life, and Tracy gets more and more upset as her mother elaborates the criticism. She made her point, Tracy thinks. Why does she have to keep repeating it?

Why, indeed, would Mona keep raising the issue when she knows it will make her daughter angry? And why does Tracy get caught up in it each time? Having been party to similar conversations with my own mother, I wonder this myself. Looking at it from the mother's point of view, I surmise that Mona's path is lit by the radiance of hope: she does not give up in her quest to better her daughter's life, to protect her when she will not protect herself. Looking at the mother's behavior from the daughter's viewpoint, I'd say that Mona is driven by blind stubbornness; she is so certain she is right that she really believes this time her daughter will make a 180-degree turn and see it her mother's way. Furthermore, it certainly seems that Mona is oblivious to the pain her implicit disapproval inflicts; she doesn't seem to notice—or care—that she's making her daughter feel bad. Could it be that she actually wants to have that effect?

Combining these two points of view, I can see that the mother doesn't notice how she is making her daughter feel because she is focused on the message, trying to improve Tracy's life, rather than the metamessage of implicit disapproval. And she is relentless because she feels powerless: It is so obvious what her daughter should do, yet she can't make her do it! The engine is fueled, too, by Tracy's determination to make her mother see that her choices were not wrong, that she is not letting herself be exploited—the insulting assumption implicit in what Mona regards as protection.

There is yet another source of fuel for the engine of this conversational juggernaut, and that is the conversation itself. Each one's reaction to the other's comments sparks ever more irritating comments in response. Working backward, Mona wouldn't have mentioned that Tracy's commute makes life at home more pressured if Tracy hadn't said she needs the drive home as a kind of quiet before the storm. And Tracy only said that to refute her mother's insistence that the commute is a hardship. That's also the reason she said that her husband needs the extra time at home, but this remark is what made Mona think Tracy is putting her husband's needs ahead of her own. Mona thinks she only mentioned the need for Tracy to move because Tracy sounded tired. And Tracy didn't really feel all that tired; she just said she was so as not to contradict her mother's remark "You sound tired." Each comment was a response to what the other said and simultaneously provoked a response in turn, in a self-perpetuating cycle of escalating responses that became provocations.

## A MUTUALLY AGGRAVATING SPIRAL

The term I use for this mutually aggravating spiral is "complementary schismogenesis." A schism is a split, and genesis is creation, so "complementary schismogenesis" means creating a split in a mutually aggravating way. The term was coined by the anthropologist Gregory Bateson to describe what can happen when different cultures come into contact: Each reacts to the other's differing pattern of behavior by ratcheting up the opposing behavior. To exemplify this process, Bateson referred to a hypothetical culture that favors assertiveness, which comes into contact with a culture that exhibits patterns of submissiveness. "It is likely," Bateson wrote, "that submissiveness will promote further assertiveness which in turn will promote further submissiveness."

Bateson also devised the term "symmetrical schismogenesis" to describe what happens when cultures with relatively similar patterns of behavior come into contact: A behavior found in both cultures becomes exaggerated along similar rather than opposing lines. To illustrate this process, Bateson posits a hypothetical situation in which two cultures both exhibit patterns of boasting. Each responds to the other's boasting by intensifying its own. Both cultures' behavior becomes exaggerated, but in similar rather than different ways.

I have adapted Bateson's terms and concepts to describe what happens between speakers in everyday conversation. Symmetrical schismogenesis could refer to a situation where one person becomes annoyed and raises her voice, and the other raises hers in response. In the end they are both shouting, each reacting to the other by intensifying the same behavior: raising voices. In contrast, complementary schismogenesis would describe a situation in which the first person becomes annoyed and raises her voice, and the other lowers hers in order to communicate that a raised voice is unacceptable. This makes the first one angry, because the lowered voice seems to imply a lack of emotional engagement. So she speaks even more loudly, which makes the other speak even more softly. In the end, one is shouting and the other is whispering, or has even retreated into silence. That's complementary schismogenesis, because each one's reaction to the other results in increasingly exaggerated forms of the opposing behavior.

When symmetrical schismogenesis occurs in conversation,

speakers usually know perfectly well what is happening. Both are talking in ways they recognize and understand, although they may be doing more of it than usual. But complementary schismogenesis can be baffling. The other person's ways of speaking make little sense to you, and your own ways of speaking aren't having the effect you intend, yet you can't think of any other way to deal with the situation. It's as if you've been sitting on one end of a seesaw and the other person jumped off her end, sending you plopping to the ground. You certainly know where you landed, but you're not sure how you got there, because it didn't result from anything you did. When complementary schismogenesis takes over a conversation, you hear yourself talking in ways you never set out to do. And you wonder not only Why am I talking this way? but also How did I become this sort of person? These are the conversations that can be maddening, especially when they occur over and over, like a perennially playing tape loop.

### ROUND AND ROUND WE GO

There are many ways that daughters and mothers can get caught up in complementary schismogenesis. It is especially likely to happen as they negotiate closeness and distance. For example, Irene wants to get closer to her daughter Marge. She calls often and tries to start the sort of conversation she assumes they should be having by asking what's going on in Marge's life and by telling about her own concerns: her health, her loneliness. Marge feels that her mother calls too often, that her questions are intrusive, and that she talks too much about herself; she especially resents it when her mother talks about how lonely she is, because Marge hears this not in the spirit of "rapport-talk," to which she might reply "I know how you feel," but rather in the spirit of criticism: I am lonely because you don't spend enough time with me. As a result Marge limits the information she gives in response to her mother's questions and never asks questions of her own so as not to encourage her mother to talk at even greater length. She gets off the phone as quickly as she can, claiming that she's busy, which, after all, she is.

As her daughter recedes from her, Irene intensifies her efforts to get connected by calling more often, asking more questions, and exaggerating her health problems to increase her chances of getting a response. All of this drives Marge to more concerted efforts to keep her distance lest she be overwhelmed by her mother. Neither realizes that the behavior she dislikes is in part a reaction to her own. Irene sees her daughter as distant; it doesn't occur to her that the distancing is partly a response to her efforts to get close. And Marge thinks her mother is intrusive; it doesn't occur to her that this intrusiveness is partly provoked by her own backing off. Each sees herself as reacting and the other as initiating. Neither suspects the culprit: complementary schismogenesis.

Because this process is operating on the metamessage level, it is hard to see, so it's also hard to see a way out. This is yet another force that can make both mother and daughter feel powerless and hence acutely aware of the other's power. Irene feels helpless because she doesn't know what to do to bridge the gulf. Yet Marge reacts as she does in part because she is easily overwhelmed by her mother's power. To a daughter, her mother's ability to bestow or withhold approval is a mighty sword poised over her head. Adult daughters often don't realize how much their own power has swelled: the ability to limit contact, and to control access to grandchildren, has become an equally mighty sword brandished in return.

### IRRECONCILABLE STYLE DIFFERENCES

Sometimes troubling conversations among family members, including mothers and daughters, result from differences in temperament and habit. One is fanatic about neatness; the other is incurably sloppy. One packs for a trip days in advance; the other packs in a panic hours before her flight. One wouldn't go out to the mailbox without her hair, makeup, and clothing in order; the other throws on jeans and a T-shirt, gathers her hair in a ponytail, and heads out to keep a lunch date. Because these differences are known to have led to frustration and harsh words in the past, either mother or daughter (or both) may try to head off an unpleasant response by using indirectness. Ironically, this very indirectness can irritate. Just such a situation was described by a student in one of my classes who based a written assignment on conversations that took place between her mother and grandmother, as reconstructed by her mother, whom I call Sandra.

Sandra frequently faces a challenge: Her mother is punctilious about punctuality—and is also a worrier—while Sandra's family are blithely cavalier about timing. Sandra sometimes gets caught between them, and the conflict can spiral into major frustration for both. Whenever Sandra, her husband, and their teenage children are to drive to her mother's home for a family gathering, her mother gets all worked up about when they will arrive, which depends on when they set out. On one such occasion, Sandra and her family are readying to leave around 11:00 A.M., plenty early since the drive takes about four hours and dinner is likely to begin between five and six. At ten o'clock in the morning, the telephone rings. The entire family knows who it is sure to be: Sandra's mother, calling to find out when they are leaving—and to urge them to leave earlier. Sandra picks up the phone and hears, "Oh, *hi,* Sandy!" Her mother's breezy tone belies the incipient anxiety that Sandra knows has prompted the call. "I have to go out for a while, so I thought I should just call to see if you had left yet." Sandra believes that her mother really wants to say, "What are you still doing at home? Get a move on." This is annoying, as is her mother's using going out as a pretext for calling, as if her being out in the morning is relevant to their afternoon arrival.

The conversation continues in the same mutually frustrating vein. "So when are you leaving?" Sandra's mother asks. Sandra replies, "We're aiming for eleven," though they both know that Sandra's family is unlikely to leave at the hour for which they aim. That's the beauty and utility of the word "aim." Reaching for a definite time as for a lifeline, her mother says, "Oh, okay, so

you'll be here about three." Sandra knows that agreeing to a specific hour is a setup for complaints down the line, so she equivo-
cates: "Well, maybe a little . . . thereabouts. When is dinner?"
Now it is Sandra who is using indirectness. The implication of
her seemingly straightforward question is clear. If dinner isn't
until five or six, it is not crucial that they arrive at three. Knowing this too, her mother replies, "Oh, four or five."

Ah, these subtle pushes and pulls, Sandra pushing the dinner
hour forward toward six, her mother pulling it back toward four.
Just as Sandra resists specifying the time she'll arrive, her mother
resists naming a specific hour for dinner, for fear her daughter's
family will arrive just in time rather than comfortably early. Then
her mother will be a wreck until the moment arrives, apprehensive that her daughter's family will be late and ruin the meal. And
that apprehension will be added to her general uneasiness about
the possibility of an accident—a fear that cannot be allayed until
her beloved daughter and her precious family have safely arrived
at her home.

As Sandra and her mother talked about timing, each became
more indirect in response to the other. If Sandra's mother called
in order to pin down the time her daughter would arrive, she
ended up with less assurance. The more she pressed for a time
commitment, the more her daughter equivocated. Her attempts
to be less intrusive by sounding casual only proved annoying, and
caused Sandra to press her to specify a time for dinner. Though
Sandra felt obligated to stand up for her husband and children by
demonstrating that they did not need to come as early as her
mother wished, her mother's specifying dinnertime could actually
have become justification for Sandra's family arriving even later.
Each one's way of speaking drove the other to more exaggerated
forms of the opposing behavior.

There is probably no way for Sandra to avert friction over
timing, given her mother's and her family's different attitudes
toward punctuality. She will probably never be able to specify a
time of arrival and get her family to stick to it, and her mother
will probably never be able to loosen up, trusting that her daugh-

ter's family will arrive when they can and that dinner will take place one way or another. But less indirectness might be helpful. So might acknowledging each other's perspectives. The mother might say, "I know that you can't completely control your family, and that they don't worry about time the way I do. I'm sorry to pressure you to specify a time when you really can't be sure, but it would help me a lot if you let me know how things are going so I know what to expect." And Sandra might say something like "I know it makes you nervous, Mom, that we tend to run late and can't be specific about what time we'll get there. I'm really sorry, but I just can't get everyone to move faster. We'll call you when we leave, and when we're getting close, so you don't have to be watching the door."

## ANOTHER LAYER: ALIGNMENT

The examples I've given thus far in this chapter are based on conversations I've observed or been told about, but the specific dialogue I presented was my reconstruction or, in the case of Sandra, based on the daughter's recollection. To get a more precise picture of how complementary schismogenesis creeps in and takes over, it's helpful to look closely at conversations that were tape-recorded and transcribed. For the rest of this chapter, I'll uncover the process of complementary schismogenesis by looking in detail at actual conversations, with names changed, that were taped and transcribed by students in my classes. In order to try their hands at analyzing conversations (and to fulfill an assignment), these students tape-recorded interchanges with their mothers that occurred naturally; they didn't set them up or consciously try to direct them. The commentary I offer builds on their insights into what was going on. (Of course, they and their families have seen my analyses and given me permission to use their conversations in this way.)

Several of the students recorded conversations that included not only their mothers but also a sister. Any time three people are involved, things get more complicated than if there were only two.

In addition to whatever else is going on, there are ever-shifting alignments that affect what the speakers say and how they react to what the others say. By "alignment" I mean the focus of attention between two that excludes the third, or the apparent connection that makes two of the three seem like a team. As with complementary schismogenesis, alignments are formed and operate on the metamessage level, so their effects may be palpable yet hard to pin down.

Let's see how alignment and complementary schismogenesis work together in a conversation that involved a mother, father, and daughter. My student recorded the conversation one evening as she, her parents, and her younger sister Joyce were having dinner. At that time in their lives, her mother and seventeen-year-old sister could barely talk to each other without arguing, as is very common between teenage girls and their mothers. (The older sister was just an observer, not a participant, during this part of the conversation.) The teen years can be a hothouse environment that forces seeds of conflict to sprout and burgeon. Although these arguments are in some ways particular to the teen years, they give us a chance to see how small points of contention can turn innocuous conversations into arguments at any stage of life. Watch how subtle the triggers are, and how mutually aggravating the predictable responses.

An ongoing point of contention in this family is the mother's belief that Joyce spends too much money on clothes and makeup, which she buys in upscale stores rather than more economical stores, like Wal-Mart. So when the father, who is scanning a newspaper, remarks, "I see Wal-Mart set a record for sales yesterday," the seed is planted for an argument to sprout. The mere mention of Wal-Mart seems to remind his wife that their daughter refuses to shop there. She responds, "So? We don't shop at Wal-Mart, so what's the point?" (Her husband's remark, a neutral reference to impersonal information as a way of making conversation, is what I call "report-talk." It may strike her as odd, because report-talk is not a conversational gambit common among women.) "Okay," Dad says. But seventeen-year-old Joyce challenges her mother:

"What does that have to do with anything?" Whereas the father let his wife's challenge drop with a noncommittal "Okay," the mother picks up the gauntlet of Joyce's challenge, and Joyce presses forward in her attack:

Mother: I'm just saying—
Joyce:  Saying what?
Mother: Yeah, so what's the point?
Joyce:  What point, Mom?

The alignments are forming, and the effect they have on the conversation is beginning to emerge. By challenging her husband's comment, the mother focuses her attention on him, creating an alignment between them. But Joyce may have sensed that any reference to shopping at Wal-Mart sends a critical metamessage about her; in any case, by challenging her mother's challenge, she takes a protective stance toward her father, aligning herself with him against her mother. This sets the stage for everything that comes after.

As the conversation proceeds, Joyce's and her mother's comments carry metamessages way beyond the literal meaning of their words. When the mother says, "We don't shop at Wal-Mart," the father shows surprise: "You don't shop at Wal-Mart? I thought they had everything." The mother then turns the question back on him: "Do you shop at Wal-Mart?" Laughing, her husband replies, "I don't really shop anywhere." Though the father's tone is light, Joyce's is not: she turns on her mother with the accusation "You don't shop there either, Mom." Her mother protests, "Yes, I do," and tells Joyce, "You could shop there for toiletries." Joyce continues to accuse her mother of not practicing what she preaches: "For clothes you shop there, Mom?" and her mother admits, "No." Joyce takes this as vindication: "See, so why should we go shopping there for toiletries?" Then she adds, "I don't go shopping for toiletries anywhere because you buy them for me." Her mother is not defeated: "No, but you buy makeup." The conversation continued in this vein, mother and daughter trading accusations and self-defenses about the seemingly trivial topic, yet clearly getting each other riled up and feeling attacked in return. In the end, the father defused the argument by humorously summing up, "Well, this year we can do all our Christmas shopping at Wal-Mart."

It was the tone rather than the specific words that characterized these mundane interchanges as an argument. In a sense, the argument was really about Joyce being a teenage girl and all that entails: the critical eye toward her mother that this age often engenders, her mother's frustration at her daughter's behavior, and also her pain at having her daughter turn on her. If Joyce didn't earn her mother's disapproval by shopping too much in too expensive stores, she would probably have done so with some other behavior. And regardless of what provoked it, her mother's disapproval would anger her. Yet it's interesting to see the specific way this argument grew out of Dad's offhand mention of a fact he read in the newspaper. The topic of Wal-Mart reminded both mother and daughter of a point of ongoing contention. As the argument progressed, each found ways to make the other wrong: Joyce challenged her mother's questioning of her father; then her mother implied criticism of Joyce for not shopping at Wal-Mart; then Joyce tried to prove that her mother doesn't shop there either; then her mother pointed out that Joyce could shop there for toiletries and for makeup.

Like the trouble between Sandra and her mother about the difference in their attitudes toward punctuality, this argument had a basis in behavior: a difference in attitudes toward shopping. But the father's casual remark turned into a tense interchange because of a combination of alignment and complementary schismogenesis. The father's comment sparked a conflagration because of Joyce's impulse to defend him and oppose her mother: that's the alignment factor. It was further stoked by the mother's desire to defend herself and remind her daughter of her offending behavior. As each responded to the other's responses, complementary schismogenesis kicked in. Though the focus of tension was the antagonistic alignment between mother and daughter, the father's participation (unintentionally) provided a trigger for the argument and also provided a resolution, by disrupting the antagonistic alignment between mother and daughter, and by introducing a note of humor.

There is another subtle metamessage of alignment that may explain why the mother challenged her husband's statement in the first place, setting the stage for Joyce to take his side and oppose her. In introducing her assignment, my student, the older sister, who recorded the conversation even though she did not speak during the segment she analyzed, explained that she and her father "would strategically place a tape recorder at the dinner table or at breakfast in the morning in hopes of capturing an interaction between mother and daughter" for her to analyze. This collaboration between father and daughter is an alignment that the mother may have perceived. If she did, it could have formed a background to the rest of the interaction.

## HOW DID WE GET HERE?

The next conversation was also taped by an older daughter, and it, too, includes a teenage sister, Michelle, who was at that stage where nothing her mother did was right. But in this case the older sister, Patricia, defends her mother against Michelle's onslaught, making Michelle angrier. The verbal conflict becomes a referendum on the mother's taste in clothes. But that's just the message level. On the metamessage level, it is about Michelle's rejection of her mother, her mother's attempts to win back her daughter's approval, and the extra added layer of an alignment between the mother and her older daughter. As in the previous example, it begins with a casual remark, then escalates as each response provokes a more aggravated response in turn. It is, in a way, a mock fight, in that there is laughter throughout, and it builds to accusations that are so extreme they clearly are not meant literally. Yet the exchange is about points of contention that are of serious concern, and the way the conversation develops illustrates how complementary schismogenesis can turn a small remark into a big argument.

Patricia taped the conversation when her family was having dinner at a restaurant. Whereas the older sister was silent in the previous example, the father is silent in this one, so again we end up with a three-way interchange, even though there were four people present (mother, father, and two daughters). Toward the end of the meal, the mother called attention to the clothing she was wearing, a common way for women to initiate rapport-talk. The expected and usual response from another woman would be a related observation or comment about that article of clothing, or something she herself owns, or clothing in general. It's just a way to establish connection by engaging in friendly conversation. Indeed, many women who told me that they felt close to their daughters or mothers mentioned talk about clothes as a source of shared pleasure. But in this instance, the comment functioned as a setup for Michelle to criticize her mother. Through complementary schismogenesis, the more Michelle criticized, the more her mother defended her style, the more hurtful her daughter's criticism became.

Here's how the conversation started:

Mother: Do you like this jacket?
Patricia: Yeah, is it new?
Mother: No.
Patricia: It's nice.

Had Patricia been the only daughter present at the time, the interchange might have ended there or expanded to more clothes-talk, such as where her mother had bought the jacket, why it was flattering, how well it went with whatever else her mother was wearing, how it resembled a jacket Patricia had seen in a store, and so on. But Patricia was not the only daughter present. Michelle was there, too, and she said something that is unintelligible on the tape but was not a compliment, judging from her sister's and mother's responses:

Patricia:  What, do you not like it?
Mother:  Michelle likes none of my clothes.
Michelle: I like [unintelligible]
Mother:  All she does is comment. I can't believe it. I ac-
tually think I'm quite a stylish mother.

When the mother said, "Michelle likes none of my clothes," the message was a statement, but the metamessage was a complaint: not only had Michelle just criticized the jacket she was wearing but Michelle always criticizes her mother's clothes. And in response to this habitual criticism, the mother defended herself: "I actually think I'm quite a stylish mother." (Patricia agreed: "You're a stylish mother.")

If her mother's remark upped the ante from "You're criticizing this jacket" to "You're always criticizing the way I dress," Michelle's response upped the ante of criticism—and verbal aggression. She said, emphatically, "Are you out of your mind?" The implication of this is pretty clear: To claim you are stylish is so patently false that you must be crazy to say it. Again the mother tried to refute her daughter's accusation:

Mother:  Who's more stylish than I am?
Michelle: Everyone.
Mother:  Who? Tell me whose mother.

Michelle named someone. Then she went on to make her criticism of her mother more specific, addressing her sister:

Michelle: Mom wears like shoulder-paddish like—
Patricia:  Mom doesn't wear shoulder-padded—
Mother:  This has not got shoulder pads.

Here Patricia defended her mother, who also defended herself. Then, as a further self-defense in the form of challenging her daughter's claim, her mother asked for more names: "So wait a minute, who else?" Michelle's reply was unequivocal: "*Everyone,*

Mom!" Then, to support her claim, Michelle mentioned two other women and added, "They just wear normal clothes, like they don't wear like weird things like you."

Faced with this escalated attack, Patricia took her mother's side: "Mom, I think you look nice." At this Michelle turned on her sister: "Patty! Stop sucking up 'cause you want something." The accusation of "sucking up" is a protest against the alignment by which Patricia and her mother formed a team. If a teen's hostility results in part from her feeling that she doesn't measure up, seeing her older sister and mother allied against her reinforces that impression. Younger sisters often feel left out by what seems to them an impregnable alignment between an older sister and their mother—an alignment that is often reinforced by seating arrangements, such as in a car when the older sister gets to sit beside the mother in the front seat while the younger one is relegated to the backseat. There may well be conflicts between the mother and older sister, but the younger one, the outsider, doesn't see them.

The mother continued her self-defense, drawing on her older daughter for support: "Patty doesn't think— I don't know why you think I dress weird." Patricia continued to do repair work: "I like your hairstylist." Michelle tried again to break up their team by undermining her sister: "Mom, she just says that because she wants herself to be the favorite." Her mother, though, was still focused on Michelle's earlier attack: "Do you honestly think that I'm that weird? *Do* you?" Michelle then invited her sister to come over to her side: "Do you think she dresses normally?" but Patricia disappointed her by replying simply "Yes." Soon the family left the restaurant, but the argument was reborn in the car, when Patricia commented that she planned to live at home after graduating from college, and Michelle accused her of saying this, too, "so that Mom likes you better."

At this point the mother asked, logically, "Why would you care who I like better since you're so annoyed at me anyway?" Patricia backed her up: "True true true." Michelle explained, "'Cause I get annoyed at you when you like her better and you show it!" Her mother reiterated, "But *why* because you say to me that I do so many things that are stupid and annoying anyway then what would you care?" Now the tables turned, with Michelle challenging her mother's assertion that she finds her "stupid and annoying." Providing specifics to support her claim, the mother listed ways her daughter had criticized her: for "not knowing stuff" and "being a bad mother" and for (as we saw) being less stylish than her friends' mothers, who also make better milk shakes. (This last complaint, which Michelle no doubt had made in the past, reveals the theater-of-the-absurd quality that arguments often assume. We rarely see the absurdity at the time, as we do later when we have stepped out of the fight frame.)

To counter her mother's list of ways Michelle criticized her, Michelle retorted, referring to a friend, "You make comments about how Krista's a better daughter than I am." This remark touched a nerve. "That is a downright lie!" the mother burst out. "I mean, that is just ridiculous! That is a lie and you know it! I have never in my life ever ever said that. That is really wrong, Michelle, because that's a lie. You're lying!" And Patricia backed her up: "Michelle, you're such a liar! You are the most blatant liar ever! Michelle, you're going to someday be involved in a big scandal 'cause you're such a liar. You're going to commit fraud on the stand. Every other word out of your mouth is a lie."

Whoa. There was laughter as mother and daughters hurled these outrageous accusations at each other; obviously Patricia doesn't literally believe her sister will commit fraud. Nonetheless, it is intriguing to ask how the conversation got from "Do you like this jacket?" to that outburst. The answer could apply to many other arguments, including many between mothers and daughters that are deadly serious: by a combination of alignment and complementary schismogenesis. The teenage daughter is hypercritical of her mother, especially of her mother's taste in clothes (one of the Big Three domains in which mothers often criticize daughters, along with hair and weight). When the mother called attention to the jacket she was wearing, her jacket became a red cape flashed before a bull, and her bullish daughter lunged.

Once the daughter introduced the note of contention, everything each one said raised the stakes of the argument. First the mother generalized that her daughter dislikes all her clothes. Not getting praise from Michelle, she praised herself. In response, Michelle intensified her refusal to approve her mother's style of dress by calling her crazy. Her mother's means of defending herself—challenging her daughter to back up her claim that her mother is not stylish—provoked Michelle to specify rivals. Her mother then used Michelle's answers as evidence that Michelle finds her stupid and annoying. And so it went. Each new insult from the daughter spurred the mother to defend herself, but each defensive move provoked her daughter to intensify her attacks.

Overlaid on this spiraling confrontation was Michelle's mounting anger as Patricia took their mother's side, forming a team against her. And her mother didn't miss the irony that Michelle wants her mother's love even when she acts anything but lovable. When her mother specified how Michelle *showed* she didn't like her, Michelle retorted in a way that makes perfect sense from the point of view of the argument: In effect, "You may be right that I don't like you, but you don't like me, either." A matching accusation is a common move in an argument. But telling a mother she does not like her daughter is one of the worst accusations one could levy, and that's why the mother's response reached new heights of outrage.

Because the final blowup was sparked by the question of whether her mother ever said that she thinks Krista is a better daughter, this point of contention is worth exploration. I'd be willing to bet that metamessages are at the heart of this dispute. The mother is probably right that she never said that she thinks Krista is a better daughter, but I would be surprised if she did not praise Krista at some point, since teenage girls tend to be nicer to their friends' mothers than to their own. Assuming she did, Michelle probably picked up the metamessage "You are not worthy of the praise I am giving Krista." The inclination to feel rejected when someone praises a third party is a common, probably a universal, response. The Turkish language acknowledges this. It has a fixed expression that a speaker can say when praising someone who is not present: *sizden iyi olmasin,* roughly translated "may she or he not be better than you." In other words, "Don't think that my praising this other person means I don't think equally highly of you." So Michelle probably *heard* her mother implying that she thought Krista was a better daughter even though she didn't say it.

Given that each step in the argument followed logically from the one before, how could this escalation have been avoided? Since Michelle is a teenager, I'll focus on what her mother could have done differently. There is no way a mother could avoid saying anything that might spark criticism from her teenage daughter. The challenge is to make sure the opposition doesn't escalate. It's probably best, if she possibly can, to leave it alone rather than widening the theater of battle by generalizing. Sadly, the mother of a teenage daughter may have to give up hearing anything positive about herself from that daughter for a while—at least not reliably, predictably, or often. Any move that seeks a positive response leaves the mother open to rejection and hurt. Thanks to complementary schismogenesis, she'd be more likely to get a positive interaction if she seemed not to be seeking it.

Though in this conversation, Michelle exclaimed "Are you out of your mind?" apparently in jest, it's common for girls to make accusations like that—and worse—in all seriousness. When they do, it would be a good time for a mother to stop the conversation with "You can't talk to me that way." The mother might even say, "You don't have to like me, but you have to treat me with respect." Another option would be to reframe the conversation, perhaps by talking in terms of her own experience: "This conversation is making me feel bad, so let's have a different one instead." If the argument frame is not defused, it might also be helpful, though admittedly very difficult, for a mother to ask an older sister to refrain from taking her side at the time, though there is no reason she should not bask in that support in private.

Anything she can do to head off the process of complementary schismogenesis, and to beware the power of alignments, will give her more control over the conversation and lessen the risk of small conflicts spiraling into big ones.


## HOW DO WE GET OUT?

The conversation among Michelle, Patricia, and their mother, though in some ways unique to families with teenage girls, has much in common with spiraling arguments every one of us has found ourselves caught up in. I think we keep having the same hurtful conversations over and over in part because these are the conversations we know how to have. If we tried other types, we might discover that we know how to have them, too—or that we could learn.

To see how this could be done, let's return to the conversation I described at the beginning of this chapter, the one in which Mona encouraged her daughter Tracy to move closer to where she works in order to shorten her commute. Mona could make up her mind that she is going to bite her tongue: She has made it clear how she feels about Tracy's living arrangements; she can do no more. This would mean not only resisting the urge to say anything outright but also trying to prevent her opinion from leaking. (I was amused when, more than once, a mother told me of something she disapproved of about her daughter but assured me that she never said anything, yet the daughter told me in a separate interview that her mother frequently mentioned that very point. It is likely the mother never "said" anything on the message level, but the daughter "heard" it loud and clear on the metamessage level.)

If Mona finds it too frustrating to say nothing, or if she feels she has not laid out her case fully, or if she is convinced that she has an obligation to remind Tracy of her options, then she could try to find a good time to talk about it and let her daughter know that this is what she intends to discuss. In that way Tracy would not be blindsided when she thinks she's just having a pleasant conversation, and their casual conversations would not unexpectedly, though predictably, become tense. For her part, Tracy could make up her mind that she will not engage in this conversation. If her mother brings up the familiar topic, she could resist the impulse to respond. She might say directly, "Let's not talk about that," or she could accomplish the same result indirectly by changing the subject. She could also suggest that they discuss it another time, whether or not she means to arrange such a time soon.

When what we are doing does not work the way we expected, our response is often to try harder by doing more of the same. The other person will likely try harder by doing more of what she is doing in response. The result, as we have seen, is complementary schismogenesis. Anything a mother (or a daughter, if she is an adult) can do to stop this cycle will be a boon. Often that means doing less of what may seem self-evidently appropriate.

Consider again the situation in which a mother seeks more closeness and the daughter feels her mother is too intrusive, too needy. The solution may be paradoxical: If the mother did not seem to be desperately seeking connection, her daughter might seek more. If the daughter expressed more concern for her mother's health, her mother might dwell on it less. Conversely, if the mother never volunteered information about her health, her daughter might inquire about it. If the daughter volunteered more information about her own life or asked more about her mother's, her mother might ask fewer questions, and so on.

The daughter might also try inviting her mother into her life in ways that are not sensitive, such as accompanying her on an errand across town, or asking advice about what gift to buy for a friend's wedding, even if she thinks she won't take it (though, who knows, she might find one of her mother's suggestions helpful). This will make her mother feel involved in her life and less likely (rather than more) to reach for forms of involvement that irritate. In this way, the "schism" part of complementary schismogenesis can be ameliorated: Instead of growing farther apart, they're getting closer together, and that reduces the temptation to escalate by doing more of the offending behavior.

No matter what the point of contention, daughters and mothers would do well to avoid little digs that leak frustration and resentment. Let's go back to the mother, Irene, who is hurt because her daughter, Marge, won't engage in the kind of rapport-talk she values as a sign of closeness. Let's say they are having one of their brief telephone conversations, planning when the mother might visit. Marge says that late May would be a good time, and Irene says, "I was thinking of scheduling my knee replacement around then." Marge expresses surprise: "Mom, I didn't know you were going to have a knee replaced. Why didn't you tell me?"

It would be tempting for Irene to respond, "Well, I would have told you if you ever stayed on the phone more than two minutes." Irene might find it satisfying to make a remark like this because it would vindicate her experience: She just got evidence of her point of view, so why not call attention to it? The reason why not is complementary schismogenesis. Such a remark would imply criticism of her daughter for not talking longer on the phone, and criticism always hurts. Who wants to talk to someone who might suddenly take a verbal swipe at you? So the result would be just the opposite of what Irene wants: Marge would resolve more firmly to keep their conversations infrequent and short.

An effective way to defuse any conflict is changing the frame to humor. We saw a father do this in the Wal-Mart conversation. It seems to be more common for men than women to use humor in this way. I received an e-mail from a man, Michael Eckenrode, who described such a pattern in his own family. After listing the many ways his mother always criticizes him and his sister—and everyone else—he explained:

> Now, on *Everybody Loves Raymond* or the *Roseanne* show, mothers like that are funny, because there is a laugh track. In real life, it really isn't funny. I found that, at least in my

family, the women always outlive the men. When the last
of the rascals died a couple of years ago, there was no one
to deflate the tension with a bawdy remark or a joke.

Humor, of course, like any verbal strategy, can work well in some
situations but less well in others. Reading this e-mail, I recalled
that my father makes jokes all the time—to everyone's delight
much of the time. But I also recalled my mother's frustration
when she felt that his humor took the place of attention to a complaint she had made. "Go ahead, laugh," she'd say. "Everything is
a joke to you!"

With this caution in mind, women who do sometimes use
humor to deflect conflict could remind themselves to use it more—
and those who rarely use humor in this way could try it out.
Here's an example of how humor worked to deflect an ongoing
disagreement between one mother and daughter. The mother
liked to know far in advance what her schedule would look like,
especially if it required travel, so she could take advantage of discount fares or frequent flyer miles. The daughter tended to put off
firming up her schedule until the last possible moment, often just
in time to make the two-week window for nonrefundable tickets.
One year right after Thanksgiving, the mother said, "I had a nice
Thanksgiving with friends this year, but I was thinking it might be
even nicer to spend the holiday with family next year. How about
if I make Thanksgiving dinner for you, Marv, and his parents?"
Her daughter replied, "You know, Mom, I don't usually make
plans that far in advance. Why don't you call me the week before
Thanksgiving, and we can talk about it?" Rather than stating directly that she thought planning a year in advance was absurd, the
daughter exaggerated her own tendency to leave decisions until
the last moment. The contrast between a year and a week was so
funny that they both laughed—and the mother got the point her
daughter was making.

Humor is just one of the many ways we've seen to stop complementary schismogenesis from taking over conversations. Simply understanding how it works—as well as how alignment can

play a role—is the first step off the merry-go-round (or should we say misery-go-round) that can turn pleasant talk into familiar arguments between mothers and grown daughters. If you don't understand what's driving the conversations that are causing you grief, it's hard to know how to turn them in a different direction. It's easy to blame the other person, and to feel you are reacting in a justified if not inevitable way to an obvious provocation. But I am continually impressed by women who tell me that once they understand the processes, they begin to see the conversations from the other's point of view and to realize they have the power to respond differently. A small change in the way they respond can avoid conflagrations and improve conversations—and consequently relationships—with their daughters or their mothers.

*6*

# WANTED: MOTHER
# A JOB DESCRIPTION

Nearly every mother I talked to said at some point that she worried about ways she had not been a good mother: The divorce that was right for her was not good for her children; she had been so overwhelmed by the demands of small children that she often lost her temper, frightening them with her anger; the many hours she spent at work meant she wasn't home whenever she was needed; because she regretted giving up her work in order to stay home with her children, she encouraged her daughter to pursue a career, but now she sees her daughter struggling to raise children, manage a home, attend to her husband, and work full-time, and she fears she gave her the wrong advice. Because their value as people rests largely (in the eyes of the world as well as in their own) on their success or failure as mothers, many women are troubled throughout their lives by the nagging doubt "Did I do a good job as a mother?" These doubts can never be fully assuaged because the job entails an almost infinite number of tasks, expectations, and requirements, none of which can be performed in a way that everyone will agree is best. Anything a mother says or does can be held against her.

Who would answer an ad for "mother" if the job description were accurate and complete? Let's think about the tasks that might be included in an employment ad entitled "Wanted: Mother."

## COMMUNICATION CENTRAL

I'm talking to my mother on the phone. After we've chatted for a while—a long while—I say that I'd like to talk to my father. "If you're a good girl," my mother says, a smile in her voice. Of course she is joking; she will pass the phone to my father. But her teasing comment reverberates with dynamics from my younger life: Like a switchboard operator, my mother routed communication, deciding who got to talk to whom. And I counted on her to keep track of what my sisters were up to, whether they were out of town and when they'd return, when their children's birthdays were.

Many mothers take the role of family communication specialist. Often this job entails being an intermediary between her children and their father: "What does Daddy think about my breaking up with Paul?" a daughter asks her mother. "Your dad is so happy you're home," a mother tells her daughter. Mothers typically convey fathers' opinions—and, even more, their emotions—to sons as well as daughters. A striking example came up in an interview with John Richardson, who wrote a book about his father's career as a CIA spy. In explaining how his father gradually opened up about his past, Richardson commented, "When I first broached the subject of doing a book, he got really upset," then added, "He didn't *tell* me he got upset, but my mother told me later that he was upset for days."

Being an intermediary often also entails parceling information out. Kathryn Chetkovich describes this in a short story entitled

"All These Gifts." When the protagonist, Dinah, gets involved with a married man, the author writes, the news "fired through the family"—that is, Dinah's sister, brother, and mother. However: "No one told her father, who could not be expected to understand. He got all news of the family through his wife, who broke it into manageable bites, as though she were cutting up a lamb chop for a child." Comparing the father metaphorically to a child captures an aspect of this separation of labor: In contrast to the sheer number of hours most women have spent talking about relationships, most men are relative novices in this domain. And that may be partly why they cede the communication department to their wives.

The vast majority of my students who have two parents living together tell me that when they call home, they ordinarily talk at length to their mothers; if they speak to their fathers at all, those conversations are brief and focused on business. Alison Kelleher, for example, wrote, "Usually, when I speak to my mom at night, my father gets on the phone for a 5 minute conversation about my bank statement or computer problems and ends with 'hope everything is going well. Love you!'" The same was true for me.

For most of my adult life, I called home weekly. Over time I realized that though I thought of myself as calling my parents, in fact I spoke to my mother. If my father answered, he'd say almost immediately "Hold on, I'll get Mother. She'll be so happy to hear from you. *Dorotheeee!*" I'd hear him call out, *"Pick up the phone!"* At first my father would be on one extension, my mother on another, but before long I'd notice a silence on his end and realize he had disappeared, leaving the conversation to my mother and me. I'd always felt disappointed, almost abandoned, when I realized that my father was no longer on the phone. One day I happened to call when my mother was not at home, and I was amazed that my father was able and eager to carry on a lengthy telephone conversation. What I had taken to be his discomfort with the medium was actually his accommodation to what he saw as his wife's prerogative and domain. After that, I made a point of calling, from time to time, when I knew my father would be home alone.

In many families, mothers become the go-betweens, interpreting fathers' and siblings' reactions and impressions. This can work well in many cases, but a go-between can also come between, in the sense of preventing (even if inadvertently) intimacy and direct understanding between children and fathers or among siblings. For an assignment, a student in one of my classes, Varina Winder, compared letters she had received from her parents. In the course of her analysis, Varina noted that "my mom and I talk frequently on the phone, while my father and I, at this point, had never had a phone conversation." It emerged in her father's letter that this was not a situation he was completely happy with. "I get a version of how things are going via your mother," he wrote. "Would rather listen with my own ears."

As I had discovered with my own parents, opening lines of communication to a father sometimes requires special effort. But communication between a daughter and her mother often develops without either consciously setting it up, because communication is the mother's domain.

## HEAD OF THE PR DEPARTMENT

It isn't only internal communication that typically falls to the mother but also external communication: what information gets to the world outside the family, and how that information is presented. Part of a mother's job description is head of public relations.

Deanna Hall and Kristin Langellier tape-recorded conversations with five pairs of daughters and mothers in which they asked for stories about food. In one of the excerpts they present, a daughter is blithely revealing an image of her family that does not cast them in a favorable light, as her mother tries in vain to stop her. The daughter is telling her mother how she had described to the interviewer a typical dinner in their home when the speaker was growing up: "I was telling Deanna how it would start off where we'd get going and you'd end up saying, 'I can't sit here and eat,' and you'd go to your bedroom." Without waiting for her daughter to finish the sentence, the mother interrupts to say,

"Well, don't tell this, this didn't happen all the time." Her daughter continues undeterred: "And then Tom would say, 'I can't eat, I have a stomachache now,' and he'd go into his room and close the door." Now that the story is out, the mother tries to ameliorate the negative impression it might make on the interviewer: "This is only a few occasions now, she's telling you the worst times we've had. We really shouldn't be telling this. . . ."

As head of the family's PR department, this mother was trying to manage the impression the family makes on the outside world, first by preventing information from leaking out and then by modifying how it was presented. When neither of these is possible, a mother may try to control the timing of a public announcement. Thirty years ago one of my sisters and I separated from our first husbands at almost exactly the same time. Shortly after that my other sister announced that her marriage, too, was ending. My mother implored her to keep the news secret. "I've just told everyone about your two sisters," she pleaded. "There's no way I can tell them so soon about you, too." My parents, who were born in Europe, felt keenly their responsibility for unmarried daughters. I can barely imagine the shock and the burden they experienced, going from having three married daughters to having three unmarried ones in so short a time, as if someone had pressed the rewind button and the plot of *Fiddler on the Roof* had quickly unfolded in reverse. But I didn't think about that at the time. Instead I was critical of my mother for focusing on how she would tell other people about my second sister's divorce rather than on how my sister felt.

Many women are angered by their mothers' concern with how their daughters appear to the world. We want to be seen as individuals, not as our mothers' representatives. But how can mothers not be concerned with what they know will be the basis for judgments made about them? In his poem "For Anne Gregory," W. B. Yeats wrote that "only God, my dear, / Could love you for yourself alone / And not your yellow hair." "Yellow hair" could stand for any aspect of appearance by which the world judges us. This line could be adapted to reflect the impossibility of daughters' demands that their mothers ignore the impression they make on the world, because "only God could love you for yourself alone and not how your children appear." That's why many mothers try to manage how their children will be seen by friends, family, and that amorphous conglomeration of members of the jury: neighbors. In his lyrical play *Under Milk Wood,* Dylan Thomas portrays the intertwined lives of people in a small Welsh town. One of the refrains running through the play is the voice of a woman repeating, "What'll the neighbors say, what'll the neighbors . . ." Thomas does not end these sentences with a question mark, because they really aren't questions at all. The answer is implicit; the behavior at issue is not to be contemplated because the neighbors will gossip—that is, they will disapprove.

Gossip plays a similar role in Puerto Rican culture, as described by Esmeralda Santiago, who moved with her family from their native Puerto Rico to New York City at the age of thirteen. Santiago writes that when she was a teenager, her life was circumscribed by her mother's enforcement of social norms. Her mother continually stressed that her daughter must be a *nena puertorriqueña decente,* a "decent Puerto Rican girl," which "meant she was conscious at all times of *'lo que dirá la gente,'* what people would say." Each of her mother's injunctions to behave in a particular way, or not behave in another way, was followed by: *porque si no ¿qué dirán?*—if she doesn't, what will they say? Santiago's mother was not only the spokesperson for this code of conduct but also its enforcer, the in-house FBI. When Santiago goes for a walk in Central Park with a young man, a high school classmate, she writes: "I kept expecting Mami to appear from behind a tree to remind me that *nenas decentes* didn't walk unchaperoned in the park with boys their mothers didn't know."

Most of the gossip-avoiding strictures Santiago describes have to do with maintaining the proper demeanor with respect to sexuality. In many cultures, a woman's sexual purity is the repository of the family's honor.

### CHIEF INTERROGATOR

Santiago's experience was particularly frustrating because her mother expected her daughter, who was living in New York City, to adhere to norms that had applied in the village in Puerto Rico. But every mother faces a daunting challenge when her daughter reaches puberty, develops an interest in sex, and becomes the object of sexual attention from men. Vivian Gornick recalls that, when she reached this age, "Safeguarding my virginity was a major preoccupation" for her mother:

> If I came in at midnight, flushed, disheveled, happy, she'd be waiting just inside the door (she was out of bed as soon as she heard the key in the lock). She'd grasp my upper arm between her thumb and middle finger and demand, "What did he do? Where did he do it?" as though interrogating a collaborator.

The rhythm of those questions—"What did he do? Where did he do it?"—echoes the rhythm of the questions we associate with the Watergate cover-up: "What did he know? When did he know it?" In the context of family, a daughter's sexual activity often becomes the topic of a full-scale investigation, with mother as chief interrogator.

Though far fewer mothers today share Mrs. Gornick's goal of ensuring that her daughter remains a virgin until she marries, every mother of a daughter is concerned about the timing and nature of her daughter's sexual activity. A mother of daughters commented that one of the most difficult aspects of mothering occurs when a daughter becomes sexually active—and that the time always comes sooner than the mother thinks best. A dilemma is almost invariably posed at this challenging time. In order to protect her daughter and guide her, a mother needs to know what her daughter is up to. But sometimes she will think that what her daughter is up to is not wise. If she expresses this view, her daughter may regard her mother's reaction as disapproval, and will therefore be inclined to withhold such information in the future. One mother told me that she confronted this dilemma by refraining, as much as possible, from offering advice; instead, she asked a lot of questions. She took the approach, Don't tell, ask.

Questioning need not be in the spirit of interrogation, which presupposes a hierarchical relationship with the asker holding the power. Questions may also be asked in a spirit of connection, as happens when women are friends.

### BEST FRIEND

In her book *Raising America,* Ann Hulbert notes that child-rearing advice over the last century has veered between emphasizing bonding or intimacy and emphasizing authority or discipline. This is another way of talking about the paradox of connection and control. Dealing with a daughter's emerging sexuality is a part of a mother's job that sets her squarely at the center of this paradox. She is most likely to learn details of her daughter's life if she takes the footing of a friend. And indeed, many American mothers and daughters speak of each other as their best friends. But a mother who takes this role as part of her job description faces an inevitable conflict of interest. A best friend is not also charged with protecting you, whereas a mother is. The role of best friend is at odds with the authority that comes with being a parent.

A woman now in her fifties recalls how her mother learned that she was no longer a virgin—and her experience shows how connection and control dovetail when a mother veers between the roles of best friend and interrogator. Home on vacation from college, the young woman told her parents that she now had a boyfriend. Later, when they were alone, her mother questioned her about this relationship, especially with regard to sex. "You can tell me," her mother encouraged. "I want you to think of me as a friend." Finding her mother so calm and reasonable, the girl confided that she had slept with her boyfriend. At this her mother's composure disintegrated: distraught, she implored her daughter to swear she would not resume this sinful behavior when she returned to college. The girl felt that her mother had used the pretense of friendship as bait to snare her in a trap—a sneaky form of interrogation.

It is not only with regard to sexuality that a mother's role as friend conflicts with her parental responsibilities. Alla Tovares begins a study of mother-daughter conversation with an example from a television sitcom. In one scene, a mother encounters her teenage daughter and her friends at the mall and does her best to be one of the girls. Later, at home, her daughter complains that her mother had embarrassed her. "Don't act like my friend!" she admonishes. "You're my mother." "Okay," her mother accedes, then says, "Go to your room!" The daughter then changes her tack: "Hey," she says, "I thought we were friends." This scene dramatizes in a condensed and comical way the paradoxical interplay of intimacy and authority between daughters and mothers.

When daughters are young, the best-friend role goes only one way: daughters tell mothers their problems, but mothers don't tell daughters their own. Indeed, many women whose mothers used them as confidantes before they were fully grown—for example, following the parents' divorce or, as the poet Anne Sexton did with her daughter Linda, regarding her love affairs—perceived this as a burden they were ill prepared to shoulder. But when a daughter becomes an adult, exchanging mutual confidences signals friendship. And if it doesn't, one or the other may feel disappointed. A woman in her seventies, for example, had assumed that her daughter would be the one she'd turn to when she felt lonely or worried about her health or finances. Her daughter's reluctance to take that role is a source of pain. It seems likely that her daughter resists playing her part in the best-friend script because she doesn't want to feel responsible for—and therefore obligated to dispel—her mother's sorrows. In other words, at this stage in their relationship, the daughter is struggling to reconcile the intimacy of friendship with the obligations that connection entails.

For all these reasons, the role of best friend, the source of much satisfaction and comfort between mothers and daughters, can also cause confusion and conflict.

## PROFESSOR OF MOTHERING

Another life stage which places some mothers and daughters at the intersection of intimacy and authority occurs when a daughter has a child of her own. A daughter who gives birth shares a perspective with her mother that she did not have before. But this does not put them on an equal footing. Her mother has more experience in this arena, so in many cases they both assume that the mother will teach her daughter how to mother.

Sherry's mother came to help when her child was born. Sherry told me that she regarded her mother as a "senior supervisor," someone who "knows the ropes." She went on, "We both knew I didn't know what I was doing," so she would often ask her mother, "What do I do now?" Another woman, Renee, told me that when her baby was born, her mother came to help and stayed three months. Renee quoted her mother: "She said, 'I'm not leaving you with a baby for at least three months because you're not going to know what to do with a baby.' I was mother-in-training." Renee added that her mother taught her how to do things the right way: "and Mom's like, 'Okay, now you've got to bathe him. Let me show you how to do this. You get the towel first, you line this up, you do this, you do that . . .' And she has trained us to do that." It was clear from the way Renee spoke that she was grateful to her mother for her help and her lessons.

Many mothers help their daughters in this way, but there are also many ways for them to fail. When Theresa's first child was born, her mother came to help out. Theresa appreciated this, but she felt that her mother was taking over. When the baby cried, her mother rushed to pick him up, often getting there before her. Theresa began to feel like she was competing in a race as she'd try to get there first. And she found that her mother's constant advice about how to take care of the baby was making her feel incompetent. Her mother's help was a job too well done.

If Theresa resented her mother for telling her how to take care of her baby, Penny resented her mother because she didn't. When Penny's first child was born and her mother came to help, Penny felt that her mother was telling her to do things she didn't know anything about, because when Penny and her siblings were small, her mother had had paid help. Her mother felt strongly, for example, that babies must be bathed every day, at the same time each day. But she had never actually bathed a baby. She also felt that the house must be kept clean and uncluttered, which is easy when someone is being paid to keep it that way but unrealistic for Penny, who performed all these tasks herself. You might say that Penny felt her mother had let her down because she could not fulfill the role of professor of mothering.

Mothers are almost bound to fail as professors of mothering, because assumptions about how to care for children are sure to have changed in the years since they gained experience. Even Sherry, who so valued her mother's help and greater wisdom, recalled an occasion when her mother's advice wasn't the best and she was glad she hadn't taken it: "Jason had a fever," Sherry said, "and my mother was saying, 'Wrap him and make him really hot. He has to sweat the fever out.' So we had him swaddled up in all these blankets, and he was looking like a little tomato, and I said, 'I'm going to call the doctor.' And the doctor said, 'Oh no! That used to kill babies. Put him in the bathtub, put him in tepid water, chill him down a little bit.' And my mother said, 'Well, that's not how we did it.' And I said, 'Well yeah, but we're trying not to kill this one; he's the only one I've got.'"

## PERENNIAL C STUDENT OF MOTHERING

Though Sherry's mother was mostly successful in fulfilling one requirement of a mother's job description by teaching her adult daughter how to take care of children, in the matter of how to treat a baby's high fever, her advice was wrong. Medical treatment is only one aspect of child care that changes from one generation to the next. A young mother's job description requires that at times she step aside in favor of child-rearing experts who presumably know better. But this expectation is coupled with the contradictory one that she should know what to do instinctively. In *The Mask of Motherhood,* Susan Maushart points out this irony: Child-rearing experts like Dr. Spock and Penelope Leach begin by telling mothers to trust their instincts, but then proceed to offer books full of advice, thereby implying that their readers can't trust their instincts after all.

To make matters worse, expert advice keeps changing, so doing exactly what the experts tell you ensures that you will soon be told that what you did was wrong. It was not all that long ago that experts warned American parents against any displays of physical affection, thereby providing a subsequent generation of adults with damning evidence of their parents' failure to express love. Experts also told mothers to feed infants on a rigid schedule, regardless of how much they cried—until another generation of experts devised a revolutionary new method called "feeding on demand." This new method instructed mothers to adopt the innovative practice of letting their babies eat when they were hungry. Doctors today encourage mothers to breast-feed their babies, because they now know that mothers' milk provides antibodies that cannot be replicated in infant formula. Yet my own mother was asked by her doctor when she said she intended to breast-feed her first child, "What are you, a cow?"

Mothers don't have to wait a generation to learn that their efforts to do what's best for their children can result in putting them at risk. One mother whose children are still young recalls the care with which she followed expert advice and put her first baby to sleep on his stomach. Only three years later, when her second child was born, she was told she had endangered her first: Babies, the experts now agreed, must be put to sleep on their sides.

The existence of so many books, magazine articles, and radio and TV shows giving parents advice on how to care for their children sends mothers the metamessage "You're doing a job that you are unqualified for." The message level is even more disturbing. As sociologist Frank Furedi shows in *Paranoid Parenting,* American experts' child-rearing advice is designed to give mothers an overwhelming—and exaggerated—sense of the ubiquitous dangers threatening their children. So the very thing they are doing to make sure they fulfill this job well—following expert advice—is guaranteed to reinforce mothers' insecurity about how well they are doing their job.

### CHIEF ADVISER—ON EVERYTHING

I was in third grade, and I was late for school. As I rushed out the door, I realized, in panic, that I had nothing to take to class for show-and-tell. My mother helped me out. She told me a bit of news she had just heard on the radio: Nat King Cole had died. Later that day, I stood up in front of my class and offered my information—and discovered that my mother had gotten it wrong. Nat King Cole was very much alive. My teacher was kind; I can still feel her comforting arm around my shoulder, so I must have looked stricken when she pointed out my error. But I remember the depth of my humiliation, for which I bitterly blamed my mother.

In another memory I am in sixth grade, twelve years old. Because of redistricting I, alone among my friends, have been forced to attend a new school. Deeply insecure about my new friendships, I am excited and nervous: I have been invited to Rosellen's birthday party. My mother walks with me to a warehouse-type discount store on Coney Island Avenue to buy Rosellen a gift. We survey the aisles for something my family can afford. On my mother's recommendation, I buy a game of tiddlywinks. Days later, at the party, Rosellen is opening her gifts with all the girls gathered round. When she opens mine, I can see immediately that I made a disastrous choice. Later Rosellen admits to me that a game of tiddlywinks is kind of young for her. Once again, trusting my mother has caused me public humiliation—and I feel betrayed, unforgiving.

At the time they occurred, these and countless other misjudgments that caused me distress seemed evidence of my mother's failure. As I look back now, her offenses seem not only minor but completely understandable. How many times have I, as an adult, only half-listened to the radio and misheard a bit of news, or bought an inappropriate gift? I can see this now, but when I was a child, I expected my mother to be all-knowing, all-giving, without human faults. From my point of view at the time, this was not an entirely unreasonable expectation, because my mother was responsible for so much of my world. (My father, like many others, worked long hours and was rarely home.) But from the point of view of a mother who is just a human being, it's an expectation impossible to fulfill.

As adults, many women continue to look to their mothers as experts on everything. My husband was doing some last-minute shopping for Thanksgiving dinner. In the seasoning section, he was looking for sage. Striking up a conversation with another shopper who was looking for the same item, he wondered whether poultry seasoning might not do the trick. "No," the woman declared with finality. Her cellular phone still in her hand, she said, "I just spoke to my mom. It has to be sage."

Many of us depend on our mothers for the last word on cooking. Here's an example of a daughter who depended on her mother's judgment in a very different domain. In 2003 Polly York looked back on a time when she found herself implicated in international affairs. In 1988 Polly's ten-year-old daughter, Sarah, had written a letter to Manuel Noriega, who was at the time the ruthless dictator of Panama. Noriega not only answered the girl's letter but invited her and her mother to visit him in Panama, all expenses paid. Polly was uncertain whether it was wise to accept the invitation. Her brother thought it was not. His reaction had been "He's a bad guy and you should have nothing to do with him." But Polly still wasn't sure, so she consulted—not the State

Department but her mother. After thinking it over, Polly's mother told her, "I really don't think that there should be any kind of problem with Sarah going. I think it'll be a great experience for her." Polly decided to go to Panama with her daughter as guests of Noriega because, as she explained years later in a radio interview, "I had my mother's blessing and I just thought, you know, 'That's all I need.'"

Polly York is not unusual in valuing her mother's judgment. Renee, who valued her mother's parenting lessons, also treasures her mother's advice in other domains. When her mother sees Renee behaving in a way that she feels isn't in her daughter's best interests, she will take Renee aside and say, "Come here; let me put your head on straight." For example, during a visit, her mother noticed that when Renee arrived home from work she rushed immediately to relieve her husband of child-care duties. Taking her aside, her mother cautioned, "Let me put your head on straight. You work just as hard as he does, and your commute is longer. Take care of yourself first. Change your clothes, take a shower. He can watch the baby for a few more minutes." In this as in many other domains, Renee feels grateful that her mother is there to give her advice.

But another woman told me that, even though she values her mother's advice, she wearies of it when it overwhelms other types of communication. Much of the advice Ruby's mother gave was good, and she took it: "You must be the financial force in the family. You control the money." ("My poor husband." Ruby laughed. "He has no credit rating on his own.") "Thank-you notes must go out within twenty-four hours, so when your children have a party, have them address their thank-you notes before the party." "Never start to eat until everyone is served." And the one-inch rule: "When you set a table, the bottom of the silverware should be one inch from the edge of the table." But sometimes her mother keeps repeating a lesson long after Ruby has learned it. How many times does she have to be asked, "Are you sure you turned the Christmas tree lights off so the house won't burn down?" And not all of her mother's advice is sound. Ruby commented, "She's convinced that if you put sterling silver knives in the dishwasher, the handles will separate from the blades. I've been testing this hypothesis for twenty years; the knives are still attached." In the end, Ruby feels that the constant stream of advice crowds out other types of talk. "Our conversations during her visits often circle around advice," she says. "I don't take care of myself. I put the kids and my husband first. I never shop." And, as we've seen, advice easily morphs into criticism.

Many women resist taking their mothers' advice even in areas where the mothers truly are experts. A well-known interior designer mentioned that her daughter refuses to get decorating tips from her, even as everyone else in town is trying to do just that. The young woman doesn't want anyone to think that her home is attractive because of her mother's eye rather than her own. It was frustrating to the mother, not because there was anything wrong with the results of her daughter's decorating but because an avenue by which she could help her daughter was closed to her. In other words, not only is chief adviser a part of the job that is difficult to fulfill but if you fulfill it particularly well, you might find one day that you have been summarily fired.

## EMOTIONAL LIGHTNING ROD

I was forty years old, and I was arguing with my parents. I was trying to explain why I had been hurt by a remark my father had made. My mother defended my father, justifying what he had said. Soon I found myself berating her. I stopped midargument and asked out loud, "Why am I yelling at you, Mom, when it's Daddy I'm angry at?" "Yeah," she said. "Why are you?" By arguing my father's position, she had become his rhetorical surrogate. But why did my anger *shift* to her rather than including her? I realized that I never yelled at my father—nor for that matter at anyone but my mother. I used to think it was because she made me angrier than anyone else, but I wonder now whether there weren't other reasons: Was I just used to being angry at her and unused to being angry at him? Maybe it was because I knew she would forgive me and still love me no matter how I spoke to her, whereas my father could carry a grudge forever and probably would. Or—and this explanation is the one I feel most guilty about—did I see her as an easier target?

I am not alone in having made my mother the prime target of my anger. A student in one of my classes wrote this:

> Four hours before Thanksgiving I sat down to peel sweet potatoes for my special sweet potato dish. As the first strip of skin dropped into the sink, I realized that the root's flesh was light yellow instead of reddish-orange: my mom had bought the wrong kind of sweet potato! I was so mad that my dish would be ruined, and my immediate reaction was exclaiming, "How could you do this? I guess I just can't make the dish now!" to my mother. After a larger argument ensued my older brother said to me, "You are meaner to Mom than you would be to anyone else." I regret to admit that when reflecting on this statement, it is quite accurate. I am less hesitant to talk in a disrespectful and contemptible way to my mother than I am to anyone else I respect and care for as much as I do my mom.

According to the research of sociologist Samuel Vuchinich, this student and I are not unusual. Vuchinich audio- and videotaped sixty-four dinner-table conversations that took place in fifty-two American families. Examining how conflicts arose and were resolved, he found that children were much more likely to initiate conflict against mothers than against fathers.

It is as if mothers are emotional lightning rods, absorbing and grounding the emotions—both negative and positive—that are swirling around the family. This may be partly because mothers are usually around more, so they are more likely to step on toes. And it may be because women are expected to be more expressive of and comfortable with emotions. But I suspect it is also because, as I discovered in myself with regard to my mother, women are easier targets, either because they seem more vulnerable or because they seem less likely to retaliate.

## FAIR GAME FOR JUDGMENT

As if it were not bad enough to be the in-house targets of family anger, mothers also are the ones most likely to absorb disapproval, hostility, or aggression from the world outside the family. Many women express disapproval to other women they don't know far more freely than they would to a man. A woman whose children are now in their thirties still smarts to recall an incident that took place when her daughter was five. The little girl had caused her mother and two siblings to leave an ice cream parlor prematurely because of her misbehavior, and then, on the way out, she had turned and hit her brother on a flimsy pretext. At her wits' end, the mother slapped her daughter—and became the target of a passing stranger's impromptu harangue: "Stop abusing your daughter! I was an abused child and I can't bear to watch!"

Another young mother was chastised by a stranger in a supermarket checkout line. Her small child had been chatting away with the woman behind them about the puppy awaiting them in the car. The woman turned to lecture the child's mother: "You shouldn't leave a dog in a car. Animals can asphyxiate in hot weather like this." The mother assured the stranger that there was no such danger. The puppy they had left in the locked car was the child's stuffed animal. This mother later laughed at the incident, because it was the stranger who ended up looking foolish. But mothers whose children misbehave in public as a result of physical or psychological conditions beyond the mothers' control see nothing amusing when strangers chide them for their children's antisocial behavior.

The mother of a three-and-a-half-year-old child with autism suffered not only from the challenge of managing her little boy's meltdown on a crowded public street but also from strangers' open expression of disapproval. As the mother, Marie Lee, explains in an essay, her child, like others with autism, has only limited speech and is hypersensitive to sensory stimuli, so he easily descends into what she calls "the 'point of no return,' where his brain short-circuits into an unstoppable outburst"—an uncontrollable tantrum which is far easier for him to fall into than for his mother to pull him out of. On one occasion she was struggling to lift her screaming child off the ground and protect his head from injury, when she heard a man sitting at an outdoor table call out to her, "Bring him over here!" Convinced she had simply failed to discipline her child properly, he was offering to do it for her.

I don't doubt that people often feel critical of a father's treatment of his child in public, but they are less likely to berate a man they don't know lest they spark an angry—if not violent—reaction. So fathers are not often subjected to such rebuke, even as they are less often seen in public caring for children. For mothers, however, verbal sniper attacks from strangers are ready reminders that their parenting is perennially under scrutiny.

## PERFECT ROLE MODEL

Strangers who critique the mothering of women they do not know expect these women to be model mothers every moment of the day. And as we've seen, the same expectation is placed on mothers by their own children. It is obvious that being judged and found wanting is painful. But so is being judged a winner, if it comes with the expectation that you have to wear the crown on your head all day, every day. Being the object of idealization is no doubt preferable to being demonized, but this too can become a burden for a mother who is, after all, just a human being trying to do her job.

If a daughter is not looking at her mother and thinking, *I don't want to end up like her*, she may well be looking at her and thinking, I want to be just like her—and I don't know if I can. This can put them both in a difficult position. Betty recalls of her mother, "It just seemed like she just had it all together, you know, she seemed to me like the perfect housewife, the perfect mom, the perfect career woman, and everything seemed to be clean all the time." But Betty gradually realized that she and her mother were two different people. She explained, "And the big wake-up call for me was to realize, Betty, you are trying to be your mother. You're not your mother. You're going to have to come up with *you*. And so I had to find me."

Another woman expressed a similar view: "I remember watching my mother dress, particularly in adolescence, and thinking, She never sweats. She always looks so good. And you know in adolescence you feel like your whole body is in rebellion, and your zits, and your breath smells, and she just seemed to always be so put together and I thought, Wow! I can't wait to be like that." Any mother who is put on a pedestal will have a hard time keeping her balance—and a long way to fall when her daughter starts seeing her faults.

Seeing a mother as perfect places unrealistic demands on the daughter, too. "My mother's opinion is very important to me," said a woman, Alma. "If she was disappointed in me, if she raised her voice, I'd be devastated, so I was very keen on making sure that I modeled the behavior that was to her liking. Any passing comment she made might make me restructure my life and attitude." Alma realized years later that she had modeled her actions on a remark her mother had not meant in the way she took it. Alma had mentioned to her mother that she thought she'd stay home for a few years when she had children. Her mother responded, "How boring." Looking back, Alma was pretty sure that this remark had played a large role in her decision to put off having children for a long time. When she mentioned to her mother years later how she had interpreted that remark and implemented its implications, her mother said, "Oh, I didn't mean it that way. It was just a passing impression, not a reason to avoid staying home with children." It's a heavy burden to know that a chance word from you may alter the course of your daughter's life, or that someone is watching every move you make and may try to emulate it.

## THE JOB OF YOUR LIFE

Because most mothers' sense of themselves as worthy human beings depends on how well they perform as mothers, many women find themselves competing with other mothers. When a caller to a radio talk show complained of "competitive mothering," the guest, Susan Douglas, concurred, calling it the "ultimate female Olympics." The one whose child brings the most elaborate homemade dessert to the bake sale wins; the one whose child brings Pepperidge Farm loses. The one whose child wears the most labor-intensive homemade costume on Halloween wins; the one whose child, poor soul, has to wear a store-bought costume loses. Observing with humor this impulse in herself, one mother remarked to her daughter that she writes to her daily when the girl is away at summer camp because she is vying for the title Mother of the Year. With matching humor, her daughter reminded her that this award is unwinnable: "Stacey's mother writes every day too," she quipped, "and she writes in poetry."

For her book *A Potent Spell* psychotherapist Janna Malamud Smith interviewed many women and found not one who felt certain she had done things right. In Smith's words, mothers today face "criticisms and demands so diverse and contradictory as to make Catch-22 seem straightforward by comparison. Mothers are left feeling off balance, uncertain, uneasy about themselves and how they are doing."

In her book *Of Woman Born,* the poet Adrienne Rich writes that until she became a mother herself, she did not grasp the enormous sense of guilt that comes with that role:

> Soon I would begin to understand the full weight and burden of maternal guilt, that daily, nightly, hourly, *Am*

*I doing what is right? Am I doing enough? Am I doing too much?* The institution of motherhood finds all mothers more or less guilty of having failed their children.

According to Rich, her own mother's burden came not only from society in general but from her father, who expected his wife to raise perfect children. But when fathers don't place that burden on mothers, mothers can place it on themselves—and at the same time, perhaps unwittingly, place it on their children as well. If the measure of a mother's success is the perfection observable in her children, then the children bear a burden equal to her own: Whenever they are less than perfect, they are letting their mothers down.

If mothers ask themselves "daily, nightly, hourly" whether what they've done is right, then self-questioning reaches a crescendo when something goes drastically wrong in a child's life. Mary Gordon portrays such inner questioning in her novel *Pearl*. At the start of the novel, a mother, Maria, learns that her daughter, who she thought was studying the Irish language in Dublin, has chained herself to the flagpole outside the American Embassy and is near death from self-starvation. Maria falls into paroxysms of self-blame, without having any way of knowing what error on her part drove her daughter to such a self-destructive act:

> What had she done wrong? Was she too indulgent? Not indulgent enough? Was she too much the animal mother, thinking all her child needed was warmth and food and a place under her arm, near the warmth of her side, that licks and nips and hugs would take the place of something else, something she needed more, some kind of knowledge, some kind of discernment or attention? Had she had too much faith that this overwhelming, drowning love, as natural as breathing, as sleeping, was the thing that would get her daughter through? Or was she not enough the animal mother; was she too judgmental, not

accepting enough, did she fail to cook enough, did she assert her own opinion too vehemently, too often? Did she spend too much time at work? Should she have only worked part time, should she have been more available? Or was she too intrusive, not giving her daughter enough distance, not keeping the space between them inviolate, pristine? . . . What did I do wrong, *what did I do wrong?*

While she is certain that she is to blame for her daughter's disastrous deed, Maria has no idea in which direction she erred.

Although the situation that provides the premise for Gordon's novel is an extreme one, all mothers confront similar dilemmas as they raise their children and, in retrospect, as they (and the people around them) assign blame after their children are grown: What is the right mix of connection and control? How much attention, caring, independence, and physical affection is the right amount between mothers and daughters? Even in our experts-driven culture—especially in our experts-driven culture—there is no right answer. Any amount can be judged too much or too little—by the experts, by family and friends, by her children, and by her own self-scrutiny.

The very topic of this book entails an irony: The term "mother" implies a companion term, "child." But this book is about mothers and children who are adults. One of the oddest aspects of a mother's job description is that, once hired, she cannot be fired. She's stuck in this job for the rest of her life—like it or not (though, happily, most do like it). One woman I spoke to whose daughters are entering middle age explained how this aspect of the job surprised her: "Most young mothers think that there's a time frame on mothering," she said. "We think that at a certain age your kids are launched. My friends and I often laugh about this. It was such a naïve concept. Your relationships are interlaced all your lives."

But to say that your lives are interlaced forever is not to say that the forms those connections take are constant. Perhaps the hardest part of this overwhelming job is that it constantly changes. Anna

Quindlen, for example, wrote of her sadness on seeing her two oldest children go off to college, knowing the third would soon follow. She grieves not only the loss of her specific children as full-time residents, she explains, but also the loss of who she was when they were there: "the general to their battalion, the president to their cabinet." With her older children's departure, she is "demoted to part-time work. Soon I will attain emerita status," she writes. And she writes what she thinks of it: "This stinks."

Though a mother is never out of a job, her job description continually changes. Adjusting to these changes, for both mother and daughter, is a challenge of this complex lifelong relationship.

# 7

## BEST FRIENDS, WORST ENEMIES
## A WALK ON THE DARK SIDE

I was talking to two friends. When one recounted a grievance against her mother, I began to suggest that the impression of malice might not have reflected her mother's intentions. The other friend interrupted me, saying, "Maybe there is a side of her mother that doesn't wish her well." I stopped in my verbal tracks. She was right. Much as many of us (myself included—myself especially) prefer not to think that mothers may hurt daughters intentionally, that they may not wish their daughters well, there is a dark side to relationships between mothers and daughters. Although I have tried throughout this book to avoid the trap of demonizing mothers, I don't want to fall into the trap of romanticizing them either. To do so would be to deny the very real experiences of many women.

Laura Dern, an actor whose parents were also actors, was asked in an interview to describe what it was like to appear in films together with her mother, Diane Ladd. Ms. Dern responded that it gave them a chance to enact both aspects of their relationship. In the movie *Rambling Rose,* Diane Ladd played a character called, simply, "Mother." She was the one person in the movie who really understood her daughter, played by Laura Dern. This mother saw her daughter's best qualities and accepted her weaknesses; she was the perfect mother all women long for, whether or not their actual mothers fulfilled that yearning. In another film, *Wild at Heart,* there is a scene in which Ms. Dern looks out a window and sees her mother in the role of a witch riding a broomstick. This, too, is a mother many women recognize. As the talk-show host Diane Rehm put it in her memoir *Finding My Voice,* "When I was a child, the sound of my mother's voice could fill me with joy or make me cringe." Witch or comforter? The one who soothes our pain or the one who causes it? Or the one who does both at once?

We are inclined to see good and bad, angels and witches, as fundamentally separate, like the wicked stepmother and the fairy godmother: The true mother can be only good. But that's not how it happens in life, nor, it turns out, in fairy tales either. In commenting on the Grimms' fairy tale "Snow White," folklorist Maria Tatar notes that, although details of this tale differed in versions that were handed down orally in disparate cultures, the "stable core" of the tale was "the conflict between mother and daughter." In the version we all know, Snow White is tormented by her stepmother, but, Tatar explains, "In many versions of the tale, the evil queen is the girl's biological mother, not a stepmother. (The Grimms, in an effort to preserve the sanctity of motherhood, were forever turning biological mothers into stepmothers.)"

To restore the original spirit of these tales, and to reflect the experience of real-life daughters and mothers, we need to take a short walk on the dark side.

## "YOU LEAP UPON US AND DEVOUR US"

Nowadays people use the word "witch" to refer colloquially to a woman with a disagreeable personality—or one they don't like. Historically, however, "witch" wasn't just a casual term thrown into conversation; when applied to a woman, it was grounds for torture and execution. In her book *Reflections on Gender and Science,* Evelyn Fox Keller quotes a character in a play published in 1659, Walter Charleton's *Ephesian Matron,* who rails against women. Keller quotes lines from this play in order to explain the obsession with witches that was common in Charleton's time: "You are the true *Hiena's,* that allure us with the fairness of your skins; and when folly hath brought us within your reach, you leap upon us and devour us."

This accusation pinpoints what drove the belief in witches: men's fear of—and exaggeration of—women's power. I'd paraphrase it this way: When a man is sexually attracted to a woman, he feels that the woman has power over him. She can get him to do things; she can cause him misery; she can use this power, Delilah-like, to destroy him. Though sexual power is very different from the maternal kind, understanding that the fear of witches is a fear of women's power holds a key to our rage at our mothers. The control they had over us when we were small was overwhelming, and we still feel bound by their power after we're grown. Because we are so close to our mothers, we fear that they will devour us.

Sometimes animosity between mothers and daughters leads to physical abuse. When a daughter is an adult and her mother is physically weak, this can take the form of elder abuse. Better known, and probably more frequent, is the reverse, when the child is small and the mother is in complete control of her world. Many women have documented such abuse in memoirs; perhaps the best known is Christina Crawford's *Mommie Dearest.* It is easy for anyone to understand that abiding anger results from physical attacks. But in many cases, someone outside the family would not understand the depth of a daughter's anger at her mother. Here's an example from my own life.

My mother believed that an important event must be honored by the purchase of a new dress. It was unthinkable to her that a woman might attend a significant celebration wearing a dress that she'd worn before. I couldn't have been more different: I dislike shopping; I have far less interest in clothes than my mother had; I am often too busy to shop; and I see no harm in wearing a dress I've worn before, if it's in good condition and suits the occasion. This difference between our perspectives was a frequent source of discord between us, as it was the year I was living in California and my two sisters and I planned a party to celebrate my parents' sixtieth wedding anniversary. I felt I was honoring this important anniversary by cohosting the party and flying across the country to attend it. But my mother had a different view. She began asking, weeks in advance, whether I had bought something new to wear. Each time I confessed I had not, she got more upset. I absorbed her distress even as I rejected its cause.

One day I made a mad dash to a series of department stores where I tried on innumerable outfits, but the ones that fit I didn't like, and the ones I liked didn't fit. Another day I came home with a pile of dresses to try on for my husband, who confirmed that none of them suited me, so I lost yet more time returning them. I began to feel desperate: I had several writing deadlines looming, and I couldn't spare any more time to troll the stores. The more time I spent shopping, or worrying about disappointing my mother, the angrier I got. I was convinced that her demand was illogical, but I didn't see how I could let her down, either. I felt almost as if my blood supply would be cut off if I crossed her, and this dilemma made me feel like a cornered animal. I remember thinking that there would be no escape until my mother died and set me free.

Saying this now makes me deeply ashamed. Wish my mother dead because she wants me to wear a new dress to her anniversary party? It sounds mad. How could I have had such an inexplicable impulse? I think now that it was because I felt utterly bound by her wishes, and because those wishes seemed to me utterly senseless. I was also incensed—and underneath that, hurt—that my mother apparently discounted all that I was doing to celebrate the anniversary and was focusing only on the one thing she wanted that I was not doing. (I have since heard just that complaint from mothers: their daughters ignore all their mothers are doing for them and focus on the ways they believe their mothers have fallen short.) I discussed my dilemma at length with friends. (These are the kinds of troubles-talk conversations that women so value and men often find puzzling.) With my friends' help I determined that I'd be strong, stick to my guns, and resist my mother: I'd wear a perfectly acceptable dress I had in my closet, and if that upset her, it wasn't my fault. Making this decision made me feel much better. Then I went to one more store and bought a new dress.

In this instance, I ended up doing what my mother wished in order to please her and avoid her wrath. It was, after all, her anniversary, and pleasing her was the point of the whole affair. On other occasions, though, I did not accede to her wishes. I'll describe one, which I was reminded of while writing this book. Looking for an old computer file, I came across one labeled "mother." Thinking it probably contained notes on the topic, I pulled the file up—and was caught off guard to find a letter I had composed (and never sent) to my mother in 1991. As I read the letter, saved on my computer at 5:30 A.M. because my anger had kept me awake, the context came back to me, though without the emotional charge. As with the dress, it now seems a mystery to me that I could have been so upset about a matter so small.

I had taken a one-year leave from Georgetown University to accept a visiting position at Princeton University. My parents were in Florida, where they spent winters. My mother told me, excitedly, that a new friend of hers, Susan Brown, had a son who was a doctor in Princeton, and that she had told Susan I would call her son. But as my time in Princeton began to tick away, I did not make the call. I was more than busy with the people connected with the university whom my husband and I had known or were meeting through my visiting appointments in two departments. Furthermore, I regarded Princeton as a cocoon in which to hide during my year's leave. Finally, and probably most important, I felt foolish calling someone I didn't know when there was no obvious point of shared interest and no reason to think he would welcome my call.

Each time I spoke to my mother on the phone, she asked me whether I'd called her friend's son. And each time I said I hadn't, her insistence that I do so became more urgent. "Susan keeps asking if you called her son," she'd say. "It's embarrassing to have to keep saying no." One day she intensified her pleas; she reminded me how little she asked of me and exhorted me to do this one thing for her, as a favor. Early the next morning, unable to sleep, I composed a letter that included these lines:

> You have brought up the matter of my calling your friend's son at least six times. The first time you tell me, it is a suggestion. The second it is a reminder. The third is nudging. When you get past four, five times, this is badgering. Last night you reached a new level of emotional blackmail, asking me for "a favor" (i.e. implying it's a small thing), telling me how much it means to you and how little you ask of me, etc. . . . It is astounding to me that you would rather cause me pain than disappoint your friend Susan Brown. I don't know who Susan Brown is or why or when she became so important to you, but I know that I am your daughter and I have gone to great lengths to please you.

The mystery, as I reread the unsent letter a dozen years later, is why my mother's request caused me such grief. Why didn't I brush off her requests rather than let myself be torn apart by them? A different mother might have refrained from repeating her request so many times, but a different daughter might have simply held the phone away from her ear when her mother sang this refrain. The reason I could not do that was the opposite of what my mother thought. She took my refusal to do as she asked as evidence that I didn't care enough about what she wanted. In fact, I cared too much.

It's clear from the letter I wrote early that morning that what upset me most about my mother's demand was her assumption that she could decide what I should do and make me do it. My use of the phrase "emotional blackmail" is interesting. Blackmail is a threat that someone will harm you if you do not do what she demands, but my mother was not threatening anything, so why did I use that term? Because it was making me feel awful to know that I was causing my mother distress and failing to please her. I later came to understand that Susan Brown was the linchpin in a new group of friends my mother was hoping to join, much as I had been eager to please my new friend Rosellen, who had invited me to her birthday party in sixth grade. Perhaps it is that knowledge that makes me now think I should have made the call to please my mother. At the time, though, I felt that if I acceded to her pressure I would lose a part of my self—as if she had been trying, in the words of Walter Charleton, to "leap upon" and "devour" me.

If I regarded my mother's insistence as emotional blackmail because her wishes had so much power, I surmise that my intransigence was driving my mother crazy because she believed that she should have the power to get me to make a phone call, and apparently she believed that her friend Susan Brown thought so too. Or maybe it was because she thought our connection should mean I'd want to do it because she wanted me to. It's hard to know which, because connection and control are intertwined and entail each other.

The way that connection becomes control and threatens to engulf is captured by Phyllis Chesler, a pioneering feminist psychologist, in her book *Woman's Inhumanity to Woman*. Chesler traces her frustration with her mother to her mother's desire to control her: "No matter what I did to try to gain her love and approval," Chesler writes, "it was never enough, because all she wanted was me for herself, me, merged, me as her shadow, me, devoured." The sequence of adjectives reflects the way closeness threatens her very self: in "me for herself" her mother uses her; in "me, merged," there are two people, though together they make one; in "me as her shadow," Chesler fades and her mother alone retains personhood; and in "me, devoured" she ceases to exist.

Though Chesler's descriptions seem extreme, almost mythic, it nonetheless reflects a danger many women perceive. Another psychologist, Jeanette Witter, told me that she encounters women who, much as they would like to be close to their mothers, keep their distance, because they too feel they would be "devoured." Dr. Witter quoted a woman who said, "My mother has a back door into my head. I have to stay away because she takes me over."

## MOTHER LOVE: BOTH SIDES NOW

If daughters at times fear being "taken over" or "devoured" by their mothers, mothers at times have exactly the same fear with regard to their children—and this can lead them to fear they are becoming the monsters their children may later perceive them to be. Adrienne Rich describes these impulses and fears in her book *Of Woman Born*. She identifies the "psychic crisis of bearing a first child," which results from the "sense of confused power and powerlessness, of being taken over on the one hand and of touching new physical and psychic potentialities on the other." To illustrate this ambivalence, Rich quotes from a journal she kept when her children were small:

> My children cause me the most exquisite suffering of which I have any experience. It is the suffering of ambivalence: the murderous alternation between bitter resentment and raw-edged nerves, and blissful gratification and tenderness. Sometimes I seem to myself, in my feelings toward these tiny guiltless beings, a monster of selfishness and intolerance. Their voices wear away at my nerves, their constant needs, above all their need for simplicity and patience, fill me with despair at my own failures, de-

spair too at my fate, which is to serve a function for which
I was not fitted. And I am weak sometimes from held-in
rage. There are times when I feel only death will free us
from one another.

Reading this, I felt almost exonerated for my shameful and irrational thought that only death would free me from my mother.

Five years later, in another journal entry, Rich again described
the suffering "with and for and against a child":

To be caught up in waves of love and hate, jealousy even
of the child's childhood; hope and fear for its maturity;
longing to be free of responsibility, tied by every fibre of
one's being.

Rich explains that this overwhelming ambivalence results "because that child is a piece of oneself." In other words, she, as a
mother, is aware of the "me, merged" that Chesler referred to, but
she does not necessarily seek it; she too finds it frightening. The
ambivalence Rich describes parallels the ambivalence felt by
daughters who both adore and detest their mothers, perceive
them to be both essential for and threatening to their lives, simultaneously a guardian angel and a witch.

Rich writes of her "held-in rage" against her small children.
But there are mothers who do not hold in their rage. The poet
Anne Sexton was one who did not. A psychologically unstable
woman as well as a masterful poet, she found the demands of caring for her babies overwhelming. When her daughter Linda was
an infant, according to Sexton's biographer Diane Middlebrook,
Sexton was often overcome by "episodes of blinding rage in which
she would seize Linda and begin choking or slapping her." Once
she even "picked her up and threw her across the room." Many
new mothers—all, if authors such as Susan Maushart and Carol
Dix are right—feel such impulses, although relatively few act on
them in such extreme ways.

## THE TEEN YEARS: MUTUAL MONSTERS

Adrienne Rich, with eloquence and rare honesty, described her fear that because she had murderous as well as tender impulses toward her babies, she was a monster. Many daughters suddenly see their mothers as monsters—and become monsters in their mothers' eyes—when they enter their teen years. The singer and songwriter Peggy Seeger portrays this painful time in a song, "Different Tunes," which interweaves and juxtaposes the voices of a mother and her teenage daughter. The mother's part expresses anguish as her daughter suddenly turns on her and shuts her out ("Looks at me so blank and cold, a look that cuts me to the heart"), mixed with a touch of envy ("I wish that I had looked so pretty, wish that I had had your style") and admiration ("She copes with the world much better than I did, she knows things I'll never know"). For a daughter, too, the song shows, the demand that her mother stop treating her like a child, and the yearning to break free from a mother who "wants to hold me, wants to keep me, wants me in by half-past ten" is mixed with admiration, as represented in the mother's recollection of her own bohemian mother ("Sometimes I wished I had a mother like the rest / Sometimes she was so lovely that it took away my breath").

I talked to Peggy Seeger about the story behind this song. She explained that she wrote it when her own daughter, Kitty, was a teenager, and she based it not only on their relationship but also on interviews she conducted (separately) with four of her daughters' friends and their mothers. Seeger found the interviews both illuminating and tragic. It was clear that each loved the other but didn't know how to communicate that love. Indeed, all the girls she interviewed used the same words: "My mother's a cow," "My mother's a bitch." In retrospect, Seeger commented, they all said the same thing not only (not even mostly) because they necessarily felt the same way but because they had picked up from each other what they should say.

This impression was reinforced by a conversation Seeger had

with her daughter during that painful time. She asked directly, "Kitty, do you even like me?" Her daughter replied, "You're not supposed to like your mother." Seeger next asked, "Do you like Charlotte's mother?" Kitty said she did. "Do you like Sarah's mother?" Yes. Seeger went through all her friends' mothers, and Kitty liked them all. In the end, Kitty said, "But all my friends like you." So the problem with each girl's mother was something inherent not in her character but in her relationship with her teenage daughter.

The end of the story behind this song is poignant. After crafting the words of these mothers and daughters into the song, Seeger invited Kitty to record it with her. She was stunned when her daughter said, "I'm not going to sing that."

"But I wrote it for you and me," Seeger protested.

"But you never asked me," her daughter replied. Seeger realized that her daughter was right—and that her resistance reflected the very transformation of their relationship portrayed in the song. A prolific songwriter who performed professionally with her life partner, Ewan MacColl, Seeger had in the past recorded many songs with their two sons as well as their daughter without asking them in advance. Having written the song for Kitty meant not only that she had tried to reflect her daughter's perspective but also that she had composed it musically with the way Kitty sings in mind. But Kitty stood her ground. Seeger had to find another teenage girl to sing that part, and she had to work intensively with her to achieve something approaching the sound she had in mind. When they recorded the song, Seeger recalled, Kitty was in the studio, having come to lend her voice to other songs on the album. One of her brothers told their mother later that when she and Kitty's replacement were recording "Different Tunes," he had leaned over to his sister and said, "You could have sung that better." And Kitty had smiled and said, "I know."

How telling is this ending. If Kitty was chafing under the power that her mother had over her, the ability to refuse to record the song gave her power over her mother—to cause her dismay, to give her more work, to weaken her song. But there was also a kind of wake-up call in her refusal: it implied, "You can't get me to do whatever you want; I'm not just an extension of you." This message wasn't lost on her mother. Just as I was told by so many women who wrote to me about their mothers, "I'm crying as I write," when Peggy Seeger told me about the history of this song, she said, "When I play it I want to cry." (An encouraging postscript for mothers of teens: On a CD recorded seventeen years later, *Love Call Me Home,* Kitty sings with her mother, who writes in the liner notes, "I love singing with my daughter Kitty," and adds, "What a pleasure when she comes in and the two voices get to work, each filling in the crevices of the other.")

Here's another source of encouragement for mothers whose daughters are hypercritical of them: In explaining why she gets along extremely well with her mother, a woman commented (on e-mail), "One reason why my relationship with my mother feels so easy is that she was never on a pedestal. The opposite in fact: I used to make fun of her when I was a child. (Something I regret and feel bad about now.) With my mother, I didn't have to go through that phase of realizing that she wasn't perfect or all knowing, the way I did with my father. Once I realized my father was fallible, I was angry at him for several years." So not only is there hope that your relationship will improve when your daughter gets older, but the criticism you are absorbing now may actually lay the groundwork for that improvement.

### "WHEN YOU'RE DANCING, JUST SCRUNCH"

Among the complaints sung by the daughter in Peggy Seeger's song "Different Tunes" is that her mother "wants to run my life"; she asks, "Why can't Mum leave me alone?" The reason why mothers can't leave their teenage daughters alone—and also why teenage girls often turn on their mothers—is that the mothers must at times keep them from doing what they want to do. In many cases, what the daughters want to do is unwise if not downright dangerous. But sometimes daughters sense that their mothers want to hold them back in more general, not always necessary, ways.

A woman told me that when she reached high school age and grew taller than the boys in her class, her mother gave her a piece of advice: "Bend your knees a little, dear. When you're dancing, just scrunch." This must have seemed reasonable to her mother; if one assumes that a girl should date boys who are taller than she is, a tall girl must conceal her height or she will have no dates. But height is kind of hard to hide. The image of a tall young woman trying to scrunch to appear shorter is a physical analog to ways that some daughters have cut themselves down to size at their mothers' behest—or feel that their mothers wanted them to.

The Lebanese poet Kahlil Gibran wrote in *The Prophet* that even as love "is for your growth," so too is it "for your pruning." In other words, love gives and it takes away; it makes you more than you were before, but it also makes you less. Gibran's poem was referring to romantic love, but the same is true for love between daughters and mothers. Ideally, a mother has chosen the trade-off, and believes that whatever she gives up (her pruning) is outweighed by what she is gaining (her growth). In reality, though, many women, even those who genuinely want the children they have, may not foresee, or may not be all that happy about, the ways their children will limit them—that is, be for their pruning.

A daughter has no memory of her mother's life before she was born, so she cannot fully appreciate how her birth was for her mother's pruning. And children, for their part, did not choose to lose as well as to gain in their own lives, so they may well believe that their mothers should be only for their growth—that is, give them things and encourage them—and never for their pruning, never hold them back. Yet no matter how much a mother encourages her daughter to soar, there are ways she will pull her back down to earth.

### "A HEAP OF 'IFS'"

Psychotherapist Janna Malamud Smith writes in her book *A Potent Spell* of a fundamental way that children are for their mothers' pruning: having a child condemns a woman to lifelong debilitating worry for her child's safety. Smith shows that because of the pervasive fear of losing a child and of harm coming to the child, "In becoming a mother one becomes a hostage to fortune." A mother also becomes a hostage to a man if she is dependent on him for support; to an endless parade of child-rearing experts who (implicitly or explicitly) tell her she will harm her child unless she follows their (ever-shifting) advice; and to marketers who tell her she must buy not only these books but also a slew of devices, such as car seats and baby monitors, to keep her children safe.

Some of these means of instilling fear are products of our modern world, but the fear itself is not new. I encountered a description of it in a novel written by a modern Greek writer, Lilika Nakou, in the 1920s. Here is my translation of how Nakou expresses her protagonist's fears for the safety of her little boy, Petros:

> Is that what they call "Motherhood"? Is it this uneasy love, all agony which I feel for my Petros? Everywhere, wherever I am, my thoughts are elsewhere. With my child. I tremble when it's cold. When he goes out, lest he fall. If he eats custard, that it might spoil his stomach. A heap of "ifs" drive me mad.

In the novel, this mother is subject not only to this emotional bondage but also to a more literal one: She must hold down two jobs to support her son. And it is the need to support him that keeps her trapped in her native, impoverished Greece, preventing her from returning to her beloved Paris, the cosmopolitan city where she had lived before.

## MY MOTHER'S KEEPER

Many women writers have documented their fears that caring for their children, much as they love them, will prevent them from exercising and developing their own talents and creativity. And a similar "pruning" results when women are required—or choose—

to abandon careers in order to care for their parents, usually their mothers. Several women told me that their mothers' lifelong unhappiness stemmed from having forsaken their education or their work because their own mothers had become sick and the daughters had to return home to become caretakers. For example, one woman told me this story to explain why her mother always had an air of disappointment about her: Her mother had been studying on scholarship at Juilliard to become a concert pianist when she had to return home to take care of her mother, who had come down with a serious illness. That was the end of that. She never knew how far she could have gone with her music if she'd been able to stay at Juilliard.

The expectation that a daughter will devote her life to caring for her mother was the central theme of the novel and film *Like Water for Chocolate*. These were set in Mexico early in the last century, but many women I talked to felt that they too had been expected to put aside their own aspirations in order to care for their mothers. One was Edith, now in her seventies, who felt she had been slated, as a child, to be her mother's caretaker, just as her mother had been designated by her family to care for her own mother—and had done so. Edith had also been tracked into a vocational high school program, while her sister, identified as the smart one, had taken the academic track and attended college. Edith tried to escape this fate; together with her husband and two small children, she had moved, at thirty, to California, a land that promised fresh starts. There her sense of herself and her possibilities began to emerge. Encouraged by her husband, she enrolled in courses at a community college and was thrilled—and surprised—to discover that she did well. But everything changed precipitously when her parents decided to move to California, too. Her mother never told Edith directly that she should quit school, abandon her friends, and take up the caretaker role instead, but she kept saying things like "You can't trust strangers" and "Why would anyone waste their time with friends when they have their family?" Edith got the message: she began seeing less of her friends and more of her mother, and she stopped taking college courses. Edith's connection to her mother was for her pruning.

Shannon has a well-paying and secure position in a government agency, but she often wonders how her life would have turned out if her mother had given a different answer to a caller. Shannon studied broadcast journalism in college, and her goal had been to find a position in radio or television news. After graduation, she lived with her parents while she applied for every newscasting position she could find. After months of sending out countless résumés, she took a government job in Washington, D.C., while continuing to send a blizzard of résumés to news stations. Six months into this holding pattern, she was talking to her parents on the phone when her mother mentioned, "Oh, I forgot to tell you. A couple of months ago a radio station in Buffalo called. They had an opening and said your qualifications were what they were looking for, but I told them that you had already taken another position." Was this innocent or calculating? Did her mother truly not know that Shannon was still desperately hoping to break into broadcast journalism? Or did she know and not care, since she herself thought a secure government position was a better bet? Whatever her mother's motive, Shannon always wondered whether she might have had the life she had wanted if her mother had simply given the caller her daughter's new phone number or passed the message on. From Shannon's point of view, her mother had been for her pruning.

There is a second part to this story that might hold a clue to how frustrations like this can be addressed. Shannon was devastated when her mother told her about the missed opportunity, but she said nothing, because it seemed too late to make a difference, and she was not in the habit of openly challenging her mother. Imagine how she felt when several months later the incident was repeated exactly. Again her mother mentioned casually that the Buffalo radio station had called (another position had come open), and she had handled the second call exactly as she had the first—including allowing a significant amount of time to pass before telling Shannon about it. Had Shannon expressed her disappointment to her mother the first time and stressed that in the future she should pass on messages immediately or tell the caller how to contact her, she might actually have gotten a second chance at the broadcasting career she had wanted and trained for.

## CLOSE COMPETITORS

There is no reason to think that Shannon's mother had anything other than her daughter's best interests at heart (though one could certainly argue that anyone who receives a call meant for another should let the other person speak for herself). There are many instances in which a harmful effect is clearly the unintended result of good intentions. For example, a doctoral student at Georgetown University, Najma Al Zidjaly, was extremely tired at the final event necessary for her to receive a Ph.D.: the public "defense" of her doctoral dissertation. Najma felt that she had not done her best because she had slept only two hours the night before. The reason for her sleep deprivation was that her mother had called from her native Oman to wish her daughter luck—at three o'clock in the morning, Washington time. Though Najma was usually up at that hour, she had gone to bed earlier than usual precisely to ensure she was well-rested for this crucial performance. Her mother's call had hampered her (though she did an excellent job), but Najma was not angry because she knew her mother's intentions had been good. Najma told me (on e-mail) that she had been glad to see how happy her mother was that her daughter was receiving a doctorate. (In fact, her mother was so pleased, she told Najma, that as a thank-you gesture to God, when her daughter returned home she would slaughter a cow and distribute the meat to the poor.)

There are times, however, that mothers really do wish to hold their daughters back, in the spirit of competition. Phyllis Chesler, for example, writes that each time she published another book, her mother would remark, "Don't think you're so special. *I* could write a book too." Under some circumstances, competition can spur effort, inspiring you to try harder, but it can also inspire an impulse to cut a rival down. Because it is inevitable that mothers and daughters at times feel competitive no matter how much they love each other, it is also inevitable that there will be times when some mothers and daughters experience the impulse—which they may or may not act on—to impede the other's success.

Competition between mothers and daughters can also result from others' inclination to compare them. For example, Anne Sexton's father told her and her sisters, "None of you girls are as brilliant as your mother." Sexton felt competition emanating directly from her mother as well. When Sexton was in high school, her mother did not believe her daughter could have written the poems she claimed as her own: To verify that they were not plagiarized, she sent a packet of Anne's poems to a college professor she knew. According to her biographer Diane Middlebrook, Sexton understood her mother's suspicion as "evidence of a desire to keep 'top billing.'" In a similar spirit, a college student told me that she sensed her mother, too, wanted to come out on top. At a time when the young woman was struggling to lose weight, her mother informed her, "When I got married I weighed only 110 pounds." And on learning her daughter's scores, she announced that her own scores had been higher.

These examples are fairly obvious evidence of competitive impulses, but sometimes seemingly trivial remarks can lead to competition, too. A college student told me that she bristles when her mother tells her things she already knows. "For example," the student explained, "on the phone she will tell me how important it is that I take my medicine every day because I have a cough, while I've already taken my medicine that day and she knows that I'm very diligent about those things and always have been. And so to compensate I try to preemptively tell her all the things I think she'll comment on later in the conversation. It turns into a competition as to who can do the right thing first."

Competition can be hard to distinguish from envy, an emotion mothers and daughters often feel toward each other, as I mentioned in Chapter Four. A woman who married her first

boyfriend might well feel envious of—or competitive with—
a daughter who, having grown up in freer times, has had several
boyfriends and is not even thinking of marriage. When this
mother cautions her daughter that her relationships with boys
are getting in the way of her studies, is she motivated entirely by
concern for her daughter's education, or are these concerns a way
to discourage her daughter from having relationships that her
mother never had? A mother who feels judgmental because her
daughter is "hanging out" with friends when she herself is working so hard—working, in part, to pay for her daughter's college
expenses—may be motivated by a complex of emotions, one of
which may be envy. The mother doesn't get to hang out with
friends, and she isn't at that moment hanging out with her daughter, either. She may envy her daughter for having friends, or she
may feel competitive with the friends for her daughter's attention.

When my mother spoke of her own mother, she often commented that her mother had been jealous of her friends and made
them feel unwelcome in her home. This always struck me as
ironic, because I often felt that my mother was jealous of my
friends—especially if I chose to spend time with them rather than
her when my time was limited. A particular memory comes to
mind. After graduating from college, I taught English in Greece.
When I returned home for a visit after a year away, my parents
met me at Kennedy Airport. So did four of my friends, three of
whom were musicians—and they had prepared a short concert to
welcome me home. This scene is one of my most precious memories: As I walked with my parents in the international arrivals
building, my friends spotted me and excitedly gathered together.
The three men took up the instruments they had brought, and
the fourth, a woman, held the music in front of them. Right there
in the crowded metropolitan airport, they played a welcome-
home concert for my benefit. Seldom have I felt more loved and
cherished, more honored by friendship, than I did then. But the
glory of the moment was marred by my mother's ill-concealed resentment that after she hadn't seen me for so long, I was paying

little attention to her and so much attention to my friends. She showed no pleasure at this private performance, only annoyance that these young people were distracting me, and eagerness to lure me away from them to take me home, where she felt I belonged. She seemed to feel that every moment of attention I focused on my friends was stolen from her, that every drop of love I felt for them was siphoned off the cup that was rightly hers.

### COMPETING FOR THE BIGGEST PRIZE: FATHER

In the end, I did leave my friends at the airport and go home with my parents. But once there, my mother had that other rival, the one she could not tear me from: my father. In Chapter Three I described the bond connecting many fathers and daughters as an alignment that can exclude the mother. From another perspective, it is a form of competition between mother and daughter. This perspective came into focus as I observed a family other than my own.

My husband and I were dinner guests at the home of friends. As we sat around the table after dinner, our friends' teenage daughter came into the room and headed straight for her father. Standing beside him, she affectionately tousled his hair—and continued to run her fingers over his head long after I expected her to leave off. As I watched, I felt a pang of jealousy on behalf of my friend, the young woman's mother. Suddenly I understood, in a more visceral way than I had before, why my mother so resented my adoration of my father. It is hard to witness any alignment— between sisters, perhaps, or between a father and son—that locks you out. But surely there is a special pain a woman feels at the specter of the man she loves receiving lavish attention from—and lavishing his loving attention on—a younger woman, even if that young woman is her daughter. (It can be even more painful if the young woman is not her daughter, as happens when a man has a daughter from a previous marriage.)

The mother-daughter constellation taps into a pervasive competition that cannot be evaded. As Phyllis Chesler notes, daughters are simply one instantiation of a threat from younger women that all older women perceive:

> In addition, the overemphasis on female appearance, the early age at which female children are eroticized, the aging male's preference for ever-younger women, and the consequent female terror of aging, together lead to a non-stop, all-female competition for the "fairest of them all" prize.

Here too a memory comes to mind: After my first marriage ended, I dated a man named Tom. One day I was visiting my parents in their home and noticed fresh flowers in a vase. When I admired them, my mother told me that my father had brought them. "Was there a special occasion?" I asked. "No," she said. Her voice assumed a tone that reminded me of a taunting teen as she continued, "just because he loves me." Then she added, "Tell that to your friend Tom." I am willing to bet that if asked, my mother would have said she was motivated by a desire to see her daughter treated well. But I suspect her tone leaked a trace of triumph at having won that round of competition for my father's affection.

Competition for a father's attention is the most poignant but not the only beauty-contest aspect of the mother-daughter relationship. A woman, Jackie, told me of an experience she had when she was in her forties that reminded her of her teen years. As she and her mother were walking down a city street together, her mother began to complain that it wasn't fair that her daughter, a strikingly attractive woman, was turning heads, and no one was looking at her. "She used to do this to me when I was fifteen," Jackie told me. "She used to say, 'It's just not fair.' And it made me feel guilty. I did want to look cute for the guys, but I wasn't trying to diminish her. I eventually started to think maybe I did want to diminish her because I didn't want to stop looking good, which is what she wanted me to do."

I almost added that in a competition between a middle-aged woman and a fifteen-year-old girl, the younger will always win.

But then I stopped myself. It isn't always and only daughters who have the upper hand in this competition. Just as an accomplished mother can seem a daunting rival, so can a mother who is strikingly attractive. When someone remarks, "Gee, I could have sworn you were sisters," the mother is flattered by the implication that she looks as young as her daughter, but her daughter may be offended by the implication that she looks as old as her mother. A journalist interviewing the novelist Marilynne Robinson observed, on spying photographs of the author's mother on her refrigerator, that her mother appeared "inordinately poised." Robinson responded, "There should be a support group for the regally mothered." In fact a mother can score points in the physical attractiveness arena whether or not her appearance would be judged regal by outsiders. The Australian historian Jill Ker Conway writes in her memoir *The Road from Coorain* that her mother "wondered out loud how someone whose ankles were as elegantly slim as hers could have produced a daughter" whose ankles "puffed and swelled by the end of a hot day."

## A LIFELONG LEGACY

Jackie, the woman whose mother resented her attracting attention from men, felt that her mother wanted her to stop looking good so as not to outshine her. But many mothers discourage their daughters from dressing in ways that attract men because they want to prevent the young women from putting themselves in danger, from attracting the wrong sorts of men, or from violating the norms of appropriate behavior. In other domains as well, many women feel that their mothers clipped their wings in order to make them more acceptable to society. For example, one woman said, "My mother was very concerned that I present myself well. And she didn't want me to ever rock the boat professionally." This, after all, is how society works: Parents, especially mothers, teach their children the customs and expectations of the group into which the child is born. But conforming to a group's expectations often precludes excelling.

Sometimes mothers' responsibility to enforce society's expectations on their daughters takes the form of physical abuse that is widely sanctioned in a given culture but is no less abusive for being generally accepted. During the centuries that foot binding was practiced in China, it was mothers who bound their little girls' feet, an excruciatingly painful process that entailed breaking the toes and arch, and wrapping the tiny feet in progressively tighter bandages which cut off circulation and often led to dangerous infections. In African countries where female genital mutilation is practiced, it is mothers who make sure that their daughters undergo the procedure, by which their external genitalia are cut off and the edges sewn together—without anesthesia.

These mothers are motivated, we have no reason to doubt, by a desire to ensure their daughters' futures: such disfigurements, despite the physical torment and lifelong handicaps they entail, were deemed necessary to secure husbands, and marriage was the only way a woman and her children could be supported. (The mothers may also be motivated by the impulse toward sameness that we explored in Chapter Four. Dr. Nawal M. Nour, a Sudanese-born physician who founded and directs the African Women's Health Center at Brigham and Women's Hospital in Boston, treats and counsels women who underwent female genital mutilation as children in Africa. When she encounters a patient who intends to subject her own daughter to the procedure, Dr. Nour tries to dissuade her. In an interview, she said that among the counterarguments she hears, one of the hardest to answer is a mother's explanation "I want her to look like me.")

If foot binding and female genital mutilation are forms of physical abuse that are accepted in societies in which they are the norm, there are also instances of mothers physically abusing their children in ways that society does not condone. Although the term "domestic violence" typically refers to men beating women, many of the women I spoke to—far more than I had expected— had been beaten by their mothers. And, according to psychologists Beverly Ogilvie and Judith Daniluk, of the relatively rare instances in which mothers sexually abuse their children, a majority of their victims are daughters, not sons. Interviewing three women who had experienced incestuous sexual abuse by their mothers, Ogilvie and Daniluk learned that the effects of this abuse on the daughters were made worse by the fact that others simply don't believe them. This is an aspect of maternal abuse—not only sexual but also the more common physical kind—that is perhaps most damaging, and not limited to women whose mothers were physically abusive: a mother's power to define what really happened, what it means, and who her daughter really is.

Jessica was beaten by her mother. When she was a child, her mother would wake her from a sound sleep in the middle of the night, force her to sit motionless and silent on the living room floor, and hurl at her both verbal invective and physical objects. Jessica's mother would scream, for example, that her daughter was a monster like her father (from whom the mother was divorced), and that she was a liar who had fooled the world into thinking she was charming and good while her mother knew the truth. At the same time she would throw at the child whatever objects she could easily lay her hands on—silverware, knickknacks, ashtrays. Even if an object struck her and drew blood, the little girl was forbidden to move or speak. Given the unpredictability of being awakened from the safety of sleep, and her mother's absolute power over her, the term "domestic violence" seems inadequate to describe these attacks. A more apt term for this mother's behavior is "domestic terrorism."

An aspect of this heartbreaking account—and it is one that I heard in all the accounts daughters told me of being terrorized by their mothers—is her mother's damning judgment of Jessica's character. The repercussions of such judgment can pervade a daughter's life long after she has grown into adulthood and her mother can no longer physically harm her.

In her memoir, *Finding My Voice,* the NPR talk-show host Diane Rehm describes growing up with a mother who beat her, and she explains how her mother's judgment became part of her legacy. Rehm was beaten "with a belt, a metal pancake turner, a large wooden spoon, or a hard-soled shoe," all weapons readily available in the home, especially the kitchen. She recalls that she kept these beatings secret, because she felt "I deserved to be treated badly because I'd disappointed my parents. . . . There was no way to separate myself from my feelings of self-hatred for having behaved so badly." Years later, as Rehm struggled in her marriage and in her career, she found herself plagued by the same self-hatred. A tape was running in her head, telling her, "You can't do it. You're a failure." In therapy, Rehm came to understand:

> Much of this dialogue had to do with my mother. The more I allowed myself to realize how conflicted I was in my feelings toward her, the sadder and angrier I became. I could scarcely think of her without feeling both desolate and hostile, as though she were still a constant and active part of my life. In fact, my mother had been dead more than forty years now, but the feelings of childhood helplessness I experienced in her presence have remained with me to this day.

A mother's damning judgment is set on her daughter's psyche like the fossilized imprint of a leaf on a stone.

Another woman, Alice, also told me that her mother's accusations have remained with her into adulthood, long after her mother's death. While beating her, Alice's mother would scream, "There is something radically wrong with you!" "These words seem to appear over and over like a negative mantra," Alice wrote in an e-mail. And their power endures. Whenever she has a fight with her partner, Alice finds herself thinking, My mother was right. There *is* something radically wrong with me.

Perhaps most destructive of all, Alice's mother held the power to determine how Alice remembered and interpreted her own life. This emerged in a story Alice told me of an experience, still vivid in her mind, that had taken place more than two decades earlier. She had business in the city where her mother then lived with her second husband, Alice's stepfather. Since she'd be so close, Alice decided to pay her mother a visit. Her mother and stepfather would be returning from a cruise the day after Alice arrived, so she arranged with her stepfather to get a key from a neighbor, sleep in the guest room, and surprise her mother the next day. Everything seemed fine until (as Alice wrote in an e-mail):

> The next morning I woke up and had what I can best describe as a terrible anxiety attack. I started scrubbing the bathroom I had used; ate some breakfast and began scrubbing the kitchen. I freaked out that nothing was clean enough and I would get in "trouble." I called my sister, sobbing. She calmed me down. They arrived that afternoon and my mother was genuinely glad to see me. I told her that I had eaten out, just had a little breakfast, cleaned up after myself and done the bathroom. I burst into tears (which I am doing now as I write this).

When this happened, Alice was no longer a helpless child at the mercy of her mother's irrational and unpredictable anger. But the experience of that helplessness, that anger, remained within her, ready to be resurrected.

This incident had a relatively happy ending. Her mother told Alice that the house looked fine and she shouldn't have worried. Then she added, "I guess I can understand why you worried. I really used to lower the boom quite a bit when you were small." The memory of this acknowledgment is precious to Alice, who explained,

> That was the only time in my entire relationship with her, childhood and adulthood, where she ever saw something from my point of view, even hinted how devastating to me her responses had been or used a euphemism which indicated that she had been out of control pretty frequently. It meant so much to me and I was struck by the fact that it would have meant so much more many many years before. When I was a young adult and tried to discuss these kinds of issues she always denied any examples

and taunted me by saying that I made up these stories to entertain my therapist.

Alice went on, "Although it was very late in both our lives, it still means the world to me that she said it at all" because "I would often doubt my own perceptions and memories."

This, in the end, may be the crux of a parent's power over a child: not only to create the world the child lives in but also to dictate how that world is to be interpreted. As bad as the experience of being abused as a child is, what is most damaging—and most tenacious—is having her own perceptions cast in doubt. It breaks my heart to think of Alice (and Jessica and Diane) as a child being tormented in this way. But even for women who, like me, were never physically assaulted, the desire to have a mother see things from our point of view, to acknowledge the world we lived in as we experienced it, is poignant and real.

One of the most startling aspects of this story is that Alice was in her late thirties when this occurred, and nearly sixty when she cried as she recounted it to me. Our relationships with our mothers go on way beyond their lifetimes, no matter what age we are when we lose them.

### AFTER SHE'S GONE

I was talking to two sisters about ways their mother had caused them pain. "We'd better not talk like this," one sister said. "She'll hear us and be mad." "She's dead!" the other said. The first replied, "That's what you think!"

For many women, a mother's death is a loss from which they never recover. Many women told me, "I miss her every day." One woman, telling me that her mother had died a decade before, said, "A part of me died that day." Another commented, "The hardest thing about my divorce was that she wasn't there to talk to." Yet another said that ever since her mother's death, she has felt as if the sky were slightly overcast: never again can she feel as if it is a totally sunny day.

In the same spirit, for many women, their mothers' enduring presence after death is a comfort. One woman described her mother as a guardian angel watching over her: "Like when I've lost something, I'll ask her to help me find it." Another said, "At times when things are difficult, I imagine my mother there. Because she was the one who was always there for me—the one who worried, who protected, who scolded, who believed I deserved better." The most unusual means I encountered by which a woman kept her mother close was told to me by a photographer: For years after her mother's death and cremation, she kept a small film canister filled with her mother's ashes and took it with her whenever she traveled. Having a small part of her mother with her on trips was precious because it reminded her of actual trips they had taken together: times she had treasured for their special closeness.

For most women, keeping their mothers with them is less literal, more spiritual. Donna Brazile, who managed Al Gore's 2000 election campaign, was being interviewed in 2004 shortly after the publication of her memoir, *Cooking with Grease,* about how she grew up in a poor African-American community and advanced to the highest ranks of the Democratic party. The interviewer asked her to talk about how she approached the challenge of addressing a large gathering of distinguished journalists, members of the exclusive Gridiron Club, at the equally exclusive Greenbrier resort outside Washington. Brazile replied, "Whenever I'm nervous, I look around the room, and I look for my mother." Then she added, "My mother passed away in 1988."

But there can also be a dark side to feeling a mother's presence. An Australian woman, Gayle, experienced what she calls "visitations" from her mother after her death. Walking on the beach, for example, she sensed her mother walking beside her, just outside her line of vision but unmistakably there. When Gayle told me about this experience, I assumed that her mother's presence must have been comforting. But she said it wasn't, not at all. Her mother's presence was menacing: critical and thick with envy. The visitations climaxed one day when Gayle, in a hurry to get to work, spied a paw paw ripening high up in a tree in her yard. Thinking she'd better take it down lest a possum get it before she returned home late that night, she quickly placed a ladder against the trunk, climbed up, and reached for the fruit. Suddenly, the ladder gave way beneath her. Gayle threw her arms around the tree trunk and slid to the ground. She had managed to save herself, but not her skin, much of which had been sheared off by the rough trunk.

Gayle knows it is most reasonable to assume that she simply lost her footing in her rush; people fall off ladders all the time. But there was—and remains—no doubt in her mind that her mother had pushed the ladder out from under her. Furious, she raged to her mother's presence: "This has got to stop! You have to leave and go to wherever you belong now." And that was her mother's last visitation. Whether or not it was her dead mother who pushed the ladder, what is indisputable is the meaning the experience had for Gayle: her conviction that her mother's presence was malevolent, that her mother did not wish her well, indeed, that her mother wished to take away the foundation on which she stood.

Gayle was relieved when she succeeded in banishing her mother's ghost. The same emotion is expressed by Kathryn Harrison in her memoir, *The Mother Knot*. But relief was not the only emotion Harrison experienced. At the same time that she wished to be free from her mother's malevolent presence, she also wanted to keep her mother with her. Harrison writes of her struggle to forgive her long-dead mother for having abandoned her to be raised by her grandparents, and for having treated her cruelly when they were together. (Even her therapist, forsaking the neutrality required by her trade, exclaimed, "Your mother was a sadist.")

During the time Harrison describes in her memoir, her son had become dangerously ill with asthma, and even though he recovered, she couldn't shake an inchoate conviction that something poisonous inside her had sickened her child. With the therapist's help, Harrison identified the source of that dreadful feeling as rage at her mother. "It's been years, so many years since she died," Harrison writes, "and all that time I've embraced her. Remade her. Inside myself. Refused to let her go." You might say, from this description, that Harrison had "devoured" and digested her mother. "Dead," she writes, "a citizen of the underworld, endowed with its privileges and powers, my mother had become not less but more of a presence."

When Harrison finally finds a way to free herself from that presence, that anger, and from her longing to win her mother's love, she writes, "How sad it was—it didn't seem bearable—letting my mother go without having had her." This remark reminded me of a comment a friend had made when my own mother died: "Losing a mother at any age is hard. You mourn the mother you had and the loss of hope for the mother you wish you'd had." On some level, so long as her mother is alive, a daughter can hope that her mother will become the one her daughter wanted her to be. Keeping her alive inside you after she's gone is another way of keeping that hope alive.

To expose the dark side of relationships between daughters and mothers is not to demonize mothers—or daughters. A psychologist I know once commented, "Every relationship is an ambivalent one." The contradictory aspects of all human relationships—the ways they are enriching and the ways they are limiting, the struggles to maintain connection without giving up control or losing yourself—are amplified in the mother-daughter relationship, the fundamental constellation that sets the stage for all those that come after.

# 8

## "OH MOM . . . BRB"
## HOW E-MAIL AND INSTANT MESSAGING
## ARE CHANGING RELATIONSHIPS

My father was born in 1908 in Warsaw, Poland. In 1920 he emigrated to the United States with his mother and sister. (His father had died when he was four.) As my father tells it, when the time came for their departure, his grandfather, in whose house he had lived, took him on his knee to say good-bye. Tears ran down the old man's cheeks and onto his long white beard. He knew he would never see his grandson again. Even if the Holocaust had not taken his grandfather's life, the journey back to Poland for a visit was far too expensive and time-consuming to be undertaken or even contemplated. From then on their only means of communication would be letters, which would have to make the same arduous journey over land and sea that my father was about to undertake—and which would take a month or more to arrive. Though telephones existed, the possibility of a trans-atlantic call did not. Telegrams could be sent if a message was truly urgent, but they were cryptic and rare.

In 1966 I graduated from college, worked for six months, saved all the money I earned, and flew to Europe on a one-way ticket. I ended up in Greece, where I found a job teaching English. During that time I communicated with my parents by writing letters on thin blue aerograms, which traveled faster than the letters my father had exchanged with his grandfather, though they still could take up to a week to bring news. And letters were not the only way to keep in touch. If I wanted to talk to my parents, I could. I would go to the main post office downtown, fill out a form, and wait until someone called my name and indicated in which booth my parents' voices would materialize. Sometimes I waited hours for the call to be put through, until my planned evening call became a terrifying, sleep-destroying one. "Do me a favor," my mother once said. "If it's after midnight, don't call." (I remember because I was surprised and slightly hurt; I had assumed she would be thrilled to hear my voice, regardless of the time.)

In 1996 my sister went to Israel for a year. Within a few weeks she subscribed to CompuServe and learned to use e-mail. Soon my other sister and my sisters' daughters got on e-mail as well. Within a month we were all in daily communication—much more frequent contact than our weekly (or biweekly or monthly) telephone calls had afforded when my sister was home in the United States. My mother never learned to use e-mail, but in 1998, at the age of ninety, my father did. E-mail became a way for me to tell him I loved him without hurting my mother's feelings, as I had when I replied to my father's letters to me with letters addressed to him that my mother inevitably read. And e-mail now allows me to communicate quickly with friends in Greece. If I want to hear their voices, I pick up the phone and call them at home, or on their cellphones.

When my father was a child in Warsaw, families had two means of communicating: People could talk to others who were in the same room or send a written letter or note. (Shops had telephones, but few people had them in their homes.) Face-to-face communication was by far the most common. Weekend entertainment consisted of visiting relatives, who always lived within a few blocks of each other. People also wrote notes on occasion. My father recalls one of his uncles sending him, a child of seven, to deliver notes to the uncle's girlfriends.

In my father's lifetime a slew of new technologies have transformed the way people communicate. First the telephone was added to face-to-face conversation as a channel for talk. My friend Pete Becker, who grew up in the thirties in a small town in Michigan, recalls that his mother talked to her mother every day on the phone even though they lived only a few blocks apart. (Indeed, Pete wrote me in an e-mail, "It was before dial phones so I could call Mercedes, the operator, and ask where my mommy was. 'She's at your grandma's.'") Today we still have letters and telephones, but we also have answering machines, voice mail, cellphones, e-mail, Instant Messaging, and text messages.

Sometimes a new medium just substitutes a new form for an old function. For example, women my age received newspaper clippings from our mothers giving advice, reinforcing points made in conversation, or just calling attention to something of interest. Mothers today still send clippings, but they also forward electronic versions of newspaper articles or send their daughters electronic links to websites that function in the same way—and adult daughters do the same with their mothers. But each new medium also enlarges and fundamentally changes the very nature of communication and relationships.

### NEW GIFTS, NEW RISKS

Even two seemingly similar modes of communication can have vastly different capabilities and resulting implications for relationships. I'll focus on two types of electronic communication, e-mail and Instant Messaging (IM), because these are the ones I most often heard about when I talked to women about communication with their mothers and daughters, though many also mentioned other media, such as cellphones and text messages that appear on handheld devices such as BlackBerries, Treos, or cellphones.

An e-mail message is much like a letter, only faster. It is written when the sender has time and inclination, just as a letter is, and it can easily include bits of other documents "pasted" in much as pieces of paper can be added to an envelope containing a letter. Although an e-mail message arrives at its destination almost immediately, the person to whom it's addressed does not necessarily read it right away. It might be read within minutes if the recipient happens to be logged on when it arrives, but it also might wait days or weeks to be "opened," like a letter. And like a letter, it can go astray, having been delivered to the wrong address or having fallen into the black hole that sometimes devours e-mail. Most important, like written letters and voice mail messages, e-mail is one-way communication: The writer is alone when composing it, developing ideas and trains of thought with no response from the addressee before the message is completed and sent. For all these reasons, it is not by chance that the vocabulary with which we talk about e-mail is metaphorically based on written letters, starting with the name itself, "e-*mail*." We also "open" and "close" messages, and "cut" and "paste" bits of them as if we were dealing with paper. (The same is true for voice "mail," which is typically represented by the icon of an envelope, since this too is one-way communication.)

Instant Messaging seems similar to e-mail on the surface: like e-mail it is typed on a computer screen and sent electronically. Yet it is fundamentally different because it is two-way communication. In this it resembles conversations held over the phone or face-to-face more than letters. IM exchanges take place in real time, when both conversationalists are logged on. Messages appear on the addressee's screen as they are written, so each gets the other's reaction before developing a train of thought. Instant Messaging is often used much like sitting in a room with someone, each engaged in a separate activity, intermittently talking. If two people are logged on to their computers and linked by IM, they are in an open state of communication, whether or not they are exchanging messages at any given moment. The computer screen is like a conversational floor, ready for whoever gets the urge to say something. Young people expect their friends to be at their computer screens and available for IM interaction unless they leave an "away" message announcing that they are not. In other words, the default case is being in a continuing state of communication, in contrast to e-mail, where the default case is not being logged on. It is hard to overemphasize the revolutionary change that this entails for friendships: Individuals alone in their rooms are no longer fundamentally alone; they are, in an existential sense, "with" friends who are on IM and have not posted an away message.

Throughout this book I have shown how mothers and daughters continually integrate the desire to feel connected with the simultaneous desire to feel unencumbered and in control of their lives. Electronic communication transforms the balance of connection and control. A telephone call makes a connection, but it is also an intrusion, and the control is lopsided. The caller initiates contact; the person called can answer the phone or not, but in either case, she is reacting. E-mail apportions control more evenly: One person initiates a message, but it does not intrude into the other person's life until the recipient decides to get it. The words we use to talk about e-mail capture this difference. A person to whom an e-mail is sent does not *receive* it—a passive act—but rather *retrieves* it, an act of volition that she controls. Even if her computer announces intrusively "you've got mail" when a message arrives, it does so only because she set it to function in this way; the volition still resides with her.

We don't give up familiar means of communicating when we discover new ones; we choose among all the available media to suit the context and what we want to say. Imagine a daughter who uses her cellphone to call her mother while traveling to work, leaves a spoken message on her voice mail, sends an e-mail when she gets to work, and in the evening either talks to her mother on the telephone or exchanges real-time written messages using IM. She could write and send a letter on paper, but she probably wouldn't. One young woman, in explaining—on e-mail—why she uses that medium to communicate with her mother, ended by saying, "I suppose these things could have been done through snail mail also, but it would be ridiculous to write her paper letters!" The very term "snail mail," which was coined and has meaning in contrast to e-mail, makes clear why paper letters strike this young woman as ridiculous: They move too slowly. Daughters and mothers can use all these communication technologies to create and negotiate the interplay of connection and control that constitutes their relationship.

Let's look at how some actual daughters and mothers do this with e-mail and IM.

### I LOVE YOU—SEND

Though many mothers and daughters who have excellent relationships use only the telephone to communicate, and others use e-mail infrequently, I encountered many daughters and mothers who send each other e-mails daily, or many times a day, just keeping in touch, letting the other know what she is up to. For some this provides another medium for exchanging the same information they could exchange in person or over the phone. But for others it is a type of communication—and a type of closeness—that did not exist before e-mail made it possible.

A woman in her fifties, replying to my (e-mailed) query, wrote,

The relationship with my daughter has blossomed like I never thought possible. When she was in high school she hardly talked to me. When she went off to college the change started. She would call at least twice a day. Now, it's constant e-mails about sweet little nothings. . . . and I don't disrupt the baby's nap, or when she's busy.

I particularly like this woman's choice of the verb "blossom" to describe how her relationship with her daughter developed thanks to e-mail. The change in communication with her daughter began when the girl went away to college, and the physical distance between them made it necessary to create the connection that was a given when they lived in the same house. Grandchildren introduce new possibilities for connection and caring (though also for criticism), as the daughter and mother (now grandmother) share love and concern for the children. E-mail becomes fertile earth in which this seed of shared love and concern can grow and blossom, because it apportions control evenly: the mother is free to send messages as often as she likes because her daughter can control when she retrieves them, and the daughter, too, can send messages—and baby pictures—throughout the day, knowing that her mother will retrieve them when it's convenient for her. (No doubt the frequency with which this daughter and mother exchange e-mails is increased because neither works outside her home.)

The way e-mail provides connection between a college student and her mother was explained to me by Julie Dougherty, a Georgetown student. Answering my question about the role that electronic communication plays between mothers and daughters, Julie wrote, "My mom sends me an email every day while I'm at school, just to say hi. She knows that I love getting emails and getting an email from her guarantees that I'll always have at least one real letter in my inbox." By "real letter," Julie clearly means a communication that conveys personal information, providing the connection side of the mother-daughter relationship that has to be reinforced when the daughter attends college in a distant city. Julie's description shows how e-mail can be an electronic extension of the "How was your day?" intimacy that many women cherish:

> My mom and I are very close and talking about my day with her, and vice versa, has always been important. If we

are unable to talk much during the day (which is the case when I'm at school or work), email is great because I can just write out some insignificant part of my day before I forget to tell her about it and she'll do the same. We both have a general idea about what's going on. . . . We both love it for quick little notes, jokes, and random things we feel the other needs to know about.

Every reminder that the other is interested in the insignificant details of her life lets Julie and her mother know that they are not alone as each goes through her day, even though they are in different cities and inhabiting very different lives.

E-mail can also create closeness between mother and daughter by reinforcing the impression of their similarity, another element that many women mention when they define closeness. Julie wrote, "Email made me realize how similar my mom and I are. We write in the same way and our sense of humor is identical. Our jokes are obvious to the two of us and I can always tell when she's writing something in jest." The reminder that they share a sense of humor is particularly eloquent given the cryptic nature of e-mail communication, so the metamessage of intimacy and rapport that is created when a listener gets a joke is enhanced when the joke was conveyed by e-mail. This may be, moreover, why such a large percentage of e-mail that people send around consists of jokes. Several women I spoke to told me that most of their communication with their mothers takes place on the phone but that they use e-mail to send each other jokes.

There is another way that e-mail is particularly suited to enhance connection to their mothers when daughters are away at college, and that is its one-way nature. Earlier generations discovered this advantage in writing letters. One woman recalls that she became closer to her mother when she went to college. This might seem surprising; how can going farther away make you closer? The answer was, letters. By exchanging weekly letters, each got to know the other in ways she had not, perhaps could not, when they communicated face-to-face. The one-way nature of letters was crucial. In a letter, each could say at length what was on her mind, and the other had to "listen." How many mothers in their busy lives regularly schedule time just to sit and listen to their daughters tell, at length and at leisure, what's happening in their lives? Writing letters allowed each to show herself and view the other in new ways. The same function can be served now by e-mail.

Another advantage of e-mail is that it gives every child in a family equal access, whereas with face-to-face communication, more talkative children tend to fill the conversational space before the quieter ones can get the floor. Providing a way into the conversation can be especially precious to daughters who were previously overshadowed by brothers. (One woman commented that when her son went off to college, she discovered her daughter could talk.)

With e-mail, mothers and daughters can extend their rapport long after the daughter graduates from college. Perhaps the most dramatic example of this I encountered in interviewing women for this book was the experience of a deaf woman, Amanda, whose mother is hearing. At the time that Amanda was born and grew up, experts in education for the deaf believed that deaf children could and should be taught to read lips and speak. (It has since become clear that this is impossible for all but a very few deaf children.) These experts advised parents not to learn sign language, the medium that would make it possible for them to communicate with their deaf children, because, the experts cautioned, that would impede the children's learning to talk. Amanda's mother followed this advice. As a result, Amanda had been unable to communicate with her mother throughout her childhood. When she went to college, she began exchanging letters with her mother. Only then did she get to know her, and feel close to her. Now, like many other mothers and daughters, they continue this exchange through e-mail. It gives them, literally, a language in which to communicate.

## A VIRTUAL FAMILY GATHERING

When daughters have children, the relationship between their children and their parents can create an enlarged and enriched family. One way they share enjoyment of the (grand)children is relating the surprising and amusing things that the children—especially small children—do and say. (Yiddish has a word for such repeatable clever sayings: *hokhmes*.) Using e-mail, young mothers are able not only to share snippets of incidents involving their children but also to expand the snippets into stories.

I'll give an example from the e-mail correspondence between a young mother, Eileen, and her parents, in order to show how she crafted her two-year-old's antics into a well-told story, and also to compare how her mother and father responded to her account:

> Bobby's days of confinement are over. Tonight I put Bob to bed at 8:00. Emily [his older sister] and I were sitting on the couch looking for pictures of animals in the dictionary. I heard some bar rattling from the kids' room and suspected what was up. Sure enough, a few seconds later Bob came striding into the living room, diaperless, saying, "Mine pee in a bed, Mommy." He is also combining diaper removal with crib escape for the "So, there, Mommy!" double whammy. I let him sit with Emily and me. Later, when I put them both to bed, he started explaining his behavior. "Mine crying, Mommy" (meaning "I was crying in the bed before"). I asked him why he was crying. "Not want a bed, Mommy" (meaning "I didn't want to go to bed"). I'm stumped. He will probably stay in his crib if Emily goes to bed at the same time he does, but that doesn't seem fair to Emily. What to do?

Eileen's father responded, "As a culprit rather than a culpree, I have no idea what to say except Nice going Bob. . . . I never got that far with my iron bed." To this his daughter replied, "I expected you would identify more with Bob than with me in this struggle." Then she went on to show that she shared her father's point of view: "Even when I'm frustrated, it is pretty cute. His triumphant striding into the living room last night was endearing. He looked so pleased with himself." Eileen's mother replied to the same message by writing, "Oh my. This is a pickle! Can you have the same bedtime for both kids? Later than he's been going to bed? I know it is a real drag, but the story is still quite endearing."

Both parents' responses are loving; both are appropriate and appreciated. But they are also different. The father playfully posited a competition between himself and the two-year-old, with the child winning. This was a humorous way to say the same thing that the two women were saying: The child had accomplished something impressive by climbing out of his crib at the age of two. But the mother also expressed her understanding of Eileen's experience ("I know it is a real drag") and made a suggestion ("Can you have the same bedtime for both kids?"). Each parent was able to express and develop the type of response that came naturally, because e-mail provides an uninterrupted conversational floor, whereas the directions taken by face-to-face or phone conversations are typically shaped by one speaker more than another.

Eileen and her mother have a terrific relationship, and exchanging e-mails plays a role in it. (She also has an excellent relationship with her father.) Though she talks to her mother on the phone every two or three weeks, Eileen can use e-mail to tell about incidents involving her son as they occur, and to expand them into more developed narratives. And, thanks to e-mail, Eileen can "tell" the story to both parents at the same time. This not only saves her time but also reinforces the sense of family among her and her parents and children; you might say that telling the same story simultaneously to both parents sends a metamessage of family rapport.

The ability to send the same message to both parents at once is particularly precious when the possibility of talking to them at the same time does not otherwise exist. This was the case with Maggie, a young woman whose parents were divorced and whose father had long since remarried and had a child with his second wife. Maggie was facing a difficult decision in her life. Having finished law school and passed the bar exam, she was questioning whether she really wanted to pursue a career in the law. Instead, she was considering joining AmeriCorps. This is how Maggie explained to me (on e-mail) the special gift provided by e-mail:

> I was really torn about this decision, and I guess that's the kind of conversation you want to have with both parents together, after investing so much time and money and energy into a law degree. So I sent an email to my mom and dad asking them if they'd be terribly disappointed if I became "just" an elementary school teacher in an inner-city neighborhood. They both (separately) wrote an "of course I'll love you no matter what, do what your heart tells you" kind of message. It was reassuring to have them both respond to the same message in the same way. I think I especially appreciated it because I have no conscious memory of my parents being married. I also have never had a conversation with just me and both of my parents as far as I can remember in my whole life (sister/half-sister/dad's wife or someone else is always present). So I kind of felt like email allowed the three of us, in a way, to share a conversation just the three of us, and that was important to me because I was upset and doubting my future.

Maggie is lucky to have two such supportive parents. What she describes as an "'of course I'll love you no matter what, do what your heart tells you' kind of message" would be precious to any child of any age. But e-mail created for Maggie something that was not otherwise possible, given her parents' divorce: a poignant and precious virtual family gathering.

## A LANGUAGE ALL OUR OWN

Let's return to Julie Dougherty, who exchanges rapport-talk e-mails with her mother telling details of their day. In explaining why her mother sends frequent e-mails, Julie commented, "I think another reason she emails me on a regular basis is because I just taught her how to use email and Instant Messenger, so she likes to practice." By learning to use e-mail and IM, Julie's mother learned her daughter's language, and that in itself sends a meta-message of intimacy.

In the early days of e-mail, many of us who used it regarded it as a private and intimate medium. When I first began using e-mail in 1980 on a precursor to the Internet called "bitnet," the medium was not widely used. I exchanged e-mail with a few close friends: the one other person in my department who used it and two others who were professors at distant universities. Over the next dozen years, a few more academic colleagues began using e-mail. In 1993 I returned to my university from a research leave and was horrified to discover that my private domain had exploded into the public sphere. Everyone in my department was using this medium to exchange messages and, worst of all, to conduct department business. I felt invaded, almost as if my home had been broken into. I don't think I've ever completely gotten over that feeling of resentment at getting business messages through the medium that I had regarded as private.

Even now, when e-mail is ubiquitous, it can still function as a very personal domain in which correspondents reinforce closeness by using a private language. For example, one mother and daughter who communicate frequently by e-mail are both deaf and use as their primary language ASL—American Sign Language. Like many others, they cherish keeping in touch this way, but for them e-mail has a special dimension. Because ASL words are formed by hand shapes, they cannot be written as English words can. So when this mother and daughter write e-mail messages to each other, they use written English words in place of ASL signed words, but they slot them into ASL sentences. Since word order is different in ASL than in English, the result is a blend of the two languages. In addition to being more efficient than writing to each other in English, using this private language reinforces their feeling of closeness and of the uniqueness of their rapport.

Any two people can devise a private language, and many who are close do. (This is one of the reasons it is painful when a romantic relationship ends: you're left with a repertoire of words and expressions that you can't use anymore because no one else understands them.) One of my students, Madeline McGrane, also shares a private language with her mother, and theirs is a unique one. For an assignment, Madeline analyzed an exchange of conversations that shows how their private language works. It also shows how mother and daughter use different modes of communication to find a balance between connection and control.

In her assignment Madeline wrote that, now that she's twenty-one, her relationship with her mother has evolved into a friendship. But her mother still "feels the need to parent me," which Madeline defines this way: to "tell me what to do, and tell me when I did something wrong" and "try to give me advice." Madeline comments, wryly, "This, of course, drives me insane." Their private language helps to resolve this paradox. Madeline notes that when her mother uses their shared language to say things that would otherwise annoy her, the private language makes her laugh. It's funny because it sounds a lot like baby talk. Perhaps by exaggerating the mother-child dynamic, as if Madeline were not only a child but a baby, this language shows that she and her mother recognize the absurd dimension to her being treated as a child. At the same time, taking these roles, even while mocking them, reminds them of the intimacy of their relationship.

Madeline recounted a specific exchange that shows how closeness and hierarchy intertwine in communication with her mother. One day she was feeling sick, so she turned to her mother for comfort. Using their private language, Madeline e-mailed her mother, "I miss howm. I is sickie today, but has to go to all mai cyasses." Her mother responded by e-mail, using the same language: "I miss you, too. Pwetty soon you cown howm." Her mother then added a reprimand; the reason Madeline had to go to classes despite being sick was that she had recently missed classes because she was hungover following a night of revelry to celebrate her twenty-first birthday. After chiding her daughter in standard language, her mother returned to their private language to close the e-mail: "Yuv you, Mommy."

Later that day, her mother called on the phone and left a voice mail message asking if Madeline was feeling any better but also taking the opportunity to chastise her yet again, this time for having snapped at her mother on the phone the night before. The voice mail began, "Hey, girlie girl, I was just calling to see how you were feeling and see if you were still sick." But the message also said, "See, that's what happens to bad puhsons they get sickie when they yell at their mommies." Madeline reports that even though a reprimand was the last thing she wanted to hear when she was feeling sick, her mother's use of their private language ("puhsons," "sickie," "mommies") made her laugh. Indeed, her mother slipped into the private language for just the part of her message in which she was saying something negative, exercising her maternal right to scold her child.

Madeline and her mother moved between different modes of communication to accomplish different goals. E-mail was the medium in which Madeline first sought and received her mother's comfort. But her mother followed up with a phone call to convey her continuing concern. Had Madeline answered the phone, her mother would have heard her daughter's voice, to better gauge how sick she was. In leaving a voice mail message, she took the opportunity to chide her daughter for having been snappish on the phone, something that may be easier to do in a voice mail message because it is one-way communication and therefore does not allow for an immediate response. At the same time, using their private language conveyed goodwill. So did the casual, friendly opening, "Hey, girlie girl." In analyzing these exchanges for her assignment, Madeline observed that, whereas reprimanding her daughter places her mother in the role of authority figure, using their private language undercuts that power relation: When she and her daughter both speak in this funny way, Madeline feels that her mother is taking the alignment of a peer.

Though Madeline's mother addressed her daughter "Hey, girlie girl" in a voice mail message, many mothers use more elaborate terms of endearment and explicit expressions of love on e-mail. A graduate student at Georgetown, Rachael Allbritten, generously gave me copies of e-mails she had exchanged with her mother, Wanda Carswell. In her cover letter, Rachael mentioned that her mother uses more terms of endearment in e-mail than in person. I saw this clearly when I read them. Wanda's e-mails began, variously: "Hey," "Hey, sweetheart," "Hey, lady," "Hey ladybug," "Hello, ladybug," "Hey prettie-prettie," and "Okay, darling." The way she closed her e-mails was even more striking: "Love you," "I love you," "I love you very much," "I love you bunches!!," "Remember, I love you bunches and bunches and bunches!!!," and "MUWAAAAAH! <BIG MOMMY KISS>."

That these expressions of love come in openings and closings may hold a key to why they are more abundant in e-mail than over the phone or in person. Everyday conversations have no slots for such elaborate expressions of affection. In-person and on-the-phone greetings and leave-takings are pretty much provided by custom and therefore more understated. They sound rather like Rachael's own e-mail openings and closings. Her e-mails began with either "Hey mom," or "Hi Mom," and ended: "Love," "Love, Rach," "Love you!," "Rachael," and "Yikes." Perhaps this contrast reflects the difference that e-mail is a more routine means of communication for Rachael than it is for her mother. Or it may simply reflect the depth of love that many mothers have for their children, which children may take for granted when they are young (just as I assumed my mother would always love to hear from me even if it meant being jolted awake by the telephone in the middle of the night).

## A COMMUNICATION TAPESTRY

The way Madeline McGrane and her mother shifted between telephone and e-mail is typical of how family members mingle new media with old to create a communication tapestry.

A British woman, Alison, who lives in the United States, uses e-mail, telephone, and text messaging to communicate with her mother, who lives in London. Here is an example of how they combined the various modes to negotiate and settle a dispute that erupted when Alison disapproved of something her mother did.

Alison was upset to learn that her mother had participated in a march held in London to oppose a ban on foxhunting. Alison expressed her dismay on the phone. She reminded her mother that she had always been against cruelty to animals; concluded therefore that her mother had been unduly influenced by her boyfriend; and generally argued in favor of the ban and against the countermovement supporting blood sports. Her mother did not mount a significant self-defense during this telephone conversation. That she did in a subsequent e-mail, defending her decision to take part in the march and telling her daughter she had misunderstood it. Before responding, Alison did research on the Web, then e-mailed her mother information she had uncovered that supported her negative assessment of the march, its goals, and the organization that had sponsored it. Mother and daughter then settled the dispute over the phone: Her mother acknowledged that she had not had the full picture about the march but defended her right to participate in it without being subjected to her daughter's critical judgment—a right that Alison acknowledged and accepted.

Though Alison and her mother could well have conducted and settled this dispute in one medium alone, using a mix of media allowed each to make her best case. After Alison presented her opposition over the phone, her mother was able to gather her thoughts and mount her defense using e-mail. Alison then exploited the Web as a research tool to strengthen her case and used e-mail to forward her findings. Had Alison not had access to the

Web and e-mail, she would probably not have been able to conduct such research, and if she had, sending her findings to England would have taken much more time and effort. The two-way nature of telephone conversations was better suited to resolving their differences as each made concessions and both could feel assured that the issue had been laid to rest.

Alison and her mother did not use text messaging in this exchange, because the information they were conveying was rather long, whereas text messages, which are typed using the keypads on cellphones, tend to be brief. That technology is useful in entirely different contexts. For example, they send each other text messages when they are traveling, and each appreciates knowing where the other is, what she's up to, and that she's safe and well.

In another interchange, Alison was surprised that her mother used e-mail to convey important information, but it is easy to see why her mother preferred it. Alison thought that her mother had agreed to move to the United States part-time, so she could spend more time with Alison and her new baby, since her boyfriend was willing to move part-time with her. But when Alison found a perfect condominium, which she was ready to buy, her mother informed her—on e-mail—that she had changed her mind. Alison believes that such important information should be conveyed in person or at least voice to voice, but her mother explained—on the phone—that it was "too awful" to turn down her daughter's generous offer on the phone. It is hard to disappoint a loved one. When you have to do it, the one-way nature of e-mail can be a boon: you won't have to hear the disappointment in her voice. And it may also be a boon that you won't have to hear her counterarguments—at least not right away.

My student Kathryn Ann Harrison wrote an assignment about an IM exchange with her mother which also showed how they use this mode of communication to find the right balance between connection and control. Kathryn was up early finishing a term paper when her mother came online. Noticing that her daughter was also online and therefore in the open state of communication created by IM, she greeted her: "hey Kate! What are you doing up?" Kathryn explained that she was editing a paper she was about to hand in. Her reply included the remarks, "I'm tired. But everything will get done." The words "I'm tired" were like a clarion call to the protective mother, who replied, "well that doesn't sound very good. . . . Have you been sleeping? Why are you awake? Did you stay up all night? . . . I don't want you getting sick." With this, Kathryn noted, the "friend" footing that had characterized the opening exchange gave way to a "parenting" footing. As a result, Kathryn stopped volunteering information and shifted to a minimalist reassurance: "no mom don't worry everything is fine." Her purpose was to "placate" her mother, "so that she will refrain from asking nagging questions," and to show her mother that she does not want to be treated like a child; she can take care of herself.

The IM interchange then turned to other topics. At one point, Kathryn's mother wrote, "Are you alright you seem a little down? I could call you." She apparently regards the telephone as a more appropriate medium for offering comfort, just as Madeline's mother called on the phone to find out how her daughter was doing when she felt sick. Kathryn quickly rejected her mother's offer: "I'm fine no no." Soon she told her mother, "I really want to talk to you I've just gotta get this done before my brain stops working." Of course her mother reacted to this in the same maternal spirit: "brain stops working . . . kathryn that doesn't sound very good when is it due? you need to get this stuff done ahead of time I dont like this one bit." Kathryn replied, "oh mom . . . brb." Her mother then asked, "brb what does that mean?" And herein lies another aspect of electronic communication across the generations.

## BRB: A BRIDGE OVER THE GENERATION GAP

When daughters in college communicate with their mothers through e-mail and IM, the daughters are almost always more comfortable with and skilled in using these new media than their mothers are. Indeed, it's often the daughter who, like Julie Dougherty in the earlier example, taught her mother to use them. Electronic communication is an integral part of most young people's lives, and has been as far back as they can remember; their parents began using it, if they use it at all, in middle age, when it's harder to learn new things and their habits for managing relationships are already set. Exchanging messages by e-mail and IM is in itself a way of bridging the divide between generations, but the difference in familiarity with the media constitutes a reminder of the generations' differing perspectives and life experience.

Just as a mother has to teach a small child the proper way of answering the phone, young adult children need to teach their parents the conventions of IM. So when Kathryn typed the IM message "oh mom . . . brb," her mother had to ask, "brb what does that mean?" Nine minutes later (IM messages are preceded by the exact time at which they were sent) Kathryn wrote, "ok I'm back . . . see that didn't even take ten minutes. brb= be right back."

Since speed and casualness are the defining characteristics of IM, the young people for whom it is a second language have developed standardized acronyms; others include LOL for "laugh out loud," TTYL for "talk to you later," ic for "I see," and j/k for "just kidding." (Novelist and writing teacher Robert Bausch calls this style of writing "license-plate sentences." He doesn't like it.) The fact that Kathryn has to teach her mother these conventions in itself equalizes the balance of power between them. This is one arena in which the mother's greater age and life experience do not give her more expertise as compared to her daughter; on the contrary, they give her less.

It is not merely the conventions of IM and e-mail that separate the generations. The different technologies represent different worlds that are referenced by the conventions, and each world comes with contrasting assumptions about what's appropriate once the references are understood. One young woman, Alexandra, was caught in a misunderstanding that arose out of such differences.

Many people attach a "signature" to their e-mails, a message or quotation that automatically gets appended to every message they send. Alexandra's mother was upset by her daughter's signature, which read, "When you're there I sleep lengthwise, when you're gone I sleep diagonal across the bed." She sent her daughter an e-mail telling her to change the signature because she regarded it as improper. Alexandra switched media to resolve this conflict. She used IM to ask her mother what the problem was. After a few exchanges, it became clear that her mother thought Alexandra had composed the signature lines herself, announcing to the world details of a personal relationship. In fact the lines are the lyrics—and the only lyrics—to a song by the group called Phish; the song consists of repeating these lines over and over. Alexandra used them in her signature simply to reference the song that she and her friends like. The source of the lines and the reason for attaching them to her signature would be obvious to Alexandra's friends but was opaque to her mother. Alexandra thought that once she had cleared up the misunderstanding, the signature could stay. But even though her mother was relieved to learn the lines were song lyrics, she still considered them inappropriate, since others could make the same mistake she had. Alexandra heeded her mother's caution and changed her signature.

The conflict between Alexandra and her mother arose from and was settled through electronic communication. Sometimes e-mail can be a useful tool to settle disagreements regardless of the medium in which they occurred. Let's return to the example from Chapter Three in which a woman, Leah, repeatedly asked her daughter Erin to help her mother out by accompanying her grandmother, Leah's mother, from Florida to a family reunion in Milwaukee. Although Leah had said explicitly, "I don't want to make you feel guilty; I'm just asking," Erin had protested, "Obviously I do feel guilty when you keep asking me." E-mail played a role in resolving this conflict. Leah sent Erin an e-mail message in which she apologized, admitting she had been wrong to ask three times (though also mentioning that she had forgotten how many times she'd asked, and that maybe her forgetting was related to her own aging—the same reason she was reluctant to fly between

Milwaukee and Florida four times in three days). In response, Erin sent a message thanking her mother for apologizing and not being defensive, though she lamented, with irony, "Now I can't chew you out." Leah, sufficiently chastened, replied, "Sure, chew me out if you want to." The episode ended with Erin's generous reply, "Now I don't want to."

Leah and Erin could have had this interchange either face-to-face or on the telephone, but it seems not entirely by chance that the resolution took place in an e-mail exchange. I suspect it was easier for Leah to apologize, admit fault, and invite a "chewing out" when she was not directly facing her daughter or hearing her voice in real time on the phone. For one thing, many people are likely to snap and get defensive when first accused. They are more likely to see the other's point of view after recovering from the initial surprise and hurt. And many also find it hard to apologize, because admitting they were at fault feels like a public humiliation; e-mail reduces that aspect of the apology: When you are sitting alone at your computer, the embarrassment of apologizing feels less public. Moreover, since e-mail is one-way communication, the writer has time to organize her thoughts and present them in a way that she feels fully expresses—and therefore helps justify—her point of view.

In all these examples, mothers and daughters used new electronic media to communicate. There are many, though, who communicate mostly, or exclusively, by an older technology: the telephone. Some mothers and daughters prefer to talk by phone instead of, or in addition to, online, but in some cases one or the other (usually the parent) prefers the phone, or simply assumes that this is the main or even the only appropriate means of communication. Differing habits regarding use of these media can result in cross-cultural (in the sense of cross-generational) misunderstanding.

Here's an example from a student, Laura Palmer, who compares her telephone communication with her parents to the communication she has with her sister on AIM (the acronym for AOL's Instant Messenger system).

Both of my parents call me on Sunday afternoon as they drive home from their respective golf games. Since I am rarely up before noon I usually receive their voice mails and make a note to call them when I have free time. Therefore it usually isn't until Monday afternoon or evening until I return their phone calls. On the other hand I am in close contact with my two sisters, Sara and Lindsay. Sara and I both attend Georgetown so it is only expected that we will run into each other on campus and be able to stay in contact. However, Lindsay is still living at home with my parents in California and we never talk on the phone! AIM has allowed my sister and me to stay close even though we generally only talk on the phone when I call home to speak with my parents and she answers.

The reason Laura is able to stay in closer contact with her sister Lindsay than with her parents is a by-product of the differing ways that these technologies are used:

It is a lot easier for me to talk online with my sister since I am frequently at my computer writing papers and checking email. On the other hand I feel that I must have nothing going on in order for me to call my parents since I can't double task on the phone.

Because of the open state of communication that IM creates, Laura is available for conversation with her sister when she is doing her schoolwork or checking her e-mail. She doesn't have to clear the decks to open a dedicated conversational floor, as she does to make a telephone call.

But what are Laura's parents to make of the fact that their daughter keeps in closer contact with her sister than she does with them? Laura explains that they often think she is screening their phone calls, choosing not to talk to them: "In their minds if I have time to talk to Lindsay online then I most definitely have time to talk on the phone." Her parents' conclusion seems to me perfectly logical, assuming they tend to use electronic communication more or less the way people who did not grow up with it tend to do: as an extension of the way we use the phone. We sit down to communicate electronically in the same way that we sit down to make a phone call, so if we have time for one, we also have time for the other. We aren't in the habit of keeping an IM screen open to exchange messages while we are primarily doing something else, as young people do. That's the sense in which their suspicion that Laura is screening their calls is a cross-cultural misunderstanding.

Laura's example, and her comment on it, made me think that parents who want more frequent communication with their children might find that switching from phone to IM, or adding IM to the mix of media by which they communicate, might open more lines of communication. E-mail and IM can become a bridge over the generation gap.

## INTO THE FUTURE

Every medium offers unique opportunities for human communication and relationships, as well as unique risks. New technologies entail new ways of staying in touch, reinforcing closeness, and resolving conflicts. But they also provide new ways of expressing anger, hurting feelings, and risking misunderstandings. Electronic media such as e-mail and IM facilitate more frequent communication without entailing more intrusiveness in the form of unannounced visits and jangling phones. E-mail also provides the extra time (of which daughters and mothers may or may not take advantage) to recover from the initial flash of emotion that a remark or request might spark.

But electronic communication also entails liabilities. First, there is an added risk of misinterpretation because, as with any written medium, metamessages cannot be clarified by tone of voice and facial expression. To make up for this failing, e-mailers can use "emoticons": representations of facial expressions created by combinations of punctuation marks and parentheses, such as

":)" for a smile and ":(" for a frown. (If you don't immediately see a facial expression in these markings, rotate the image in your mind ninety degrees, so the colon becomes two dots for eyes and the parentheses become an upturned mouth for a smile or a down-turned mouth for a frown.) Emoticons help signal how a statement is meant, but they can do only so much :(.

E-mail is also heir to the liability of any one-way communication. As with written memos, letters, and spoken voice mail, senders lack feedback, so they cannot know when their words are being taken badly. If you know that something you said has inadvertently offended the person you're talking to, you can move quickly to correct the misunderstanding. You are far more likely to get immediate evidence of such a response when a person is facing you or responding in real time on the phone. Without that feedback, you may dig yourself deeper into a hole, oblivious of the effect you're having. Another risk of one-way communication is that many people become more vituperative, working themselves up into greater expressions of anger or hostility, than they would if the object of their anger were looking right at them or listening at the other end of a telephone line.

A risk unique to electronic communication is also a function of its greatest asset: the speed and ease of sending messages and of copying and forwarding them. Speed can be wonderful, but it can also be dangerous. Once you press SEND, you can't change your mind, as you could decide not to mail a letter. And speed means that when you don't have much time, you may express yourself in an e-mail too cryptically and send it too precipitously.

Even riskier is the ease of copying and forwarding messages. A message forwarded is a message transformed. Every utterance gets meaning not only from the words spoken but from the context, so if the context is changed, the meaning is changed as well. Reading a message that was written to someone else can be like overhearing a conversation not intended for you. You may listen with interest, but you may also be offended by tones or implications that would not have been there had the message been sculpted with you in mind. Disastrously, e-mails often come trailing a long history of correspondence. A person forwarding a current message or sending a copy of a reply to a third party may forget what was written several messages back, where a bit of information or a nuance may be hurtful—or worse—to the recipient who becomes an overhearer to an earlier exchange, one not intended for her ears.

New communication technologies are being introduced at an ever-quickening pace. It is too early to understand fully how e-mail, IM, and other electronic means of communicating such as text messaging will transform relationships between daughters and mothers. We do know, and have seen, that they expand all the possibilities of face-to-face conversation: the precious connection that comes of keeping in frequent touch and of exchanging small details of daily life, the chance to seek and provide comfort, to express love and caring. But they also amplify the possibilities of misunderstandings and hurt feelings, and of creating problems by forwarding or copying messages to people who were not addressees. E-mail provides rich opportunities for going back over troublesome conversations, figuring out what caused trouble, and offering explanations and apologies. But sometimes it will be more efficient and effective to pick up the phone to resolve a problem, or wait to discuss it face-to-face. Understanding the benefits and risks of each communication technology makes it easier to take advantage of the opportunities and minimize the liabilities that come with each medium.

*9*

# BLENDING INTIMACY AND INDEPENDENCE
## NEW WAYS OF TALKING

As my mother got progressively weaker from lung disease, I visited her and my father more and more often. The weaker she got, the more time I spent helping her, caring for her. One afternoon, during a visit, I lay down on the couch to take a brief nap. Before succumbing to the plunge into sleep, I felt a movement at my legs. Briefly opening my eyes, I saw my mother, one hand on her cane, the other carrying a small blanket she had brought from the foot of her bed. Still gripping her cane, she used the other hand to spread the blanket over my legs. I can't tell this story without tearing up. It is one of my most precious memories from the last years of my mother's life.

But it's easy to imagine a teenage girl (even me when I was one) reacting very differently in the same situation. She might even snap, "For crying out loud, Mom, I'm not a baby anymore. I can figure out for myself if my legs are cold!" Any gesture or remark that is comforting in one context can be cloying or annoying in another. And this is especially true for remarks or gestures that a mother makes in order to help or protect her child. That is what was so precious to me about my mother bringing a blanket to cover my legs as I napped: In that gesture, she was still watching over me, protecting me. But protection is a two-edged sword, and this accounts for many mismatches between daughters' and mothers' perspectives. Where a mother sees protection and connection, a daughter may see a limit to her freedom and invasion of her privacy. It is hard for daughters to understand the depth of their mothers' desire to protect them, and it is hard for mothers to understand that their expressions of concern can undermine their daughters' confidence and seem like criticism rather than caring.

I have tried in this book to explain why conversations between mothers and grown daughters can be among the most comforting but also the most hurtful we'll ever have. I have tried, too, to show how understanding why this is so, and seeing conversations from the other's point of view, can minimize the hurt and maximize the healing. Although what works for one mother-daughter pair may not work for another, there are principles that can provide guidance for all. In this last chapter I'll show how women have found that new ways of talking can improve their relationships with their daughters and mothers.

### HOW MUCH CONNECTION IS RIGHT?

"I talk to my mother three or four times a day," a woman tells me, explaining that they have a wonderful relationship. "I call her first thing in the morning, or she calls me. If someone hasn't called by nine o'clock, it's unusual."

Another woman says, "My mother is not one to be on the phone every day. And she will tell you in a heartbeat, like 'What would anybody have to say to somebody every single day? Puh-lease!'"

A woman was recounting to her brother a telephone conversation she had had with their mother. At one point he asked, "How often do you call her?" She replied, *"Every day!"* in a tone which implied that her answer was obvious. Then she asked, "Don't you?" "No," he said. "I call her once a week." In telling me on e-mail about this exchange, the man remarked, "I think we were each appalled, with me thinking that they were too intertwined and her thinking I was negligent."

How much is the right amount of contact between mothers and daughters? How frequently should you visit? How often should you call? There's no right answer: Any amount of contact can be prized as a sign of connection or resented as an intrusion, because connection and control are created and expressed by the same words and acts. On one hand, telephone calls enact and reinforce connection. That's the spirit in which the daughters and mothers who value frequent phone calls told me about them. On the other hand, a daughter who decides to scale back her phone calls to her mother, or who resents her mother's frequent calls to her, is focusing on the freedom-limiting aspect of connection. We all confront this double meaning daily. It forms the core of relationships between daughters and mothers.

## WHO NEEDS YOU?

Along with the impulse to protect a daughter comes an impulse to be helpful and to feel needed. The strength of a mother's desire to feel needed is eloquently captured in *Brown Girl, Brownstones,* Paule Marshall's classic coming-of-age novel set in Brooklyn in the 1940s. The novel ends optimistically as the protagonist, Selina, the daughter of parents from Barbados, realizes her dream of escaping the immigrant community in which she was raised—and the dull fate of a respectable marriage, which her older sister has recently chosen. But Selina's announcement of her impending departure is not a triumph for her mother, Silla, whose response is poignantly expressed in her Barbadian dialect: "Going 'way. One call sheself getting married and the other going 'way. Gone so!

They ain't got no more uses for me and they gone." Having loved ones tell you they are going away is painful under any circumstances. But Silla's disappointment is more searing: it is the particular pain of a mother who sees that her daughters are leaving because they no longer need her.

Selina needs to leave, and her mother needs to be needed. Fulfilling the needs of one thwarts those of the other, much as satisfying a mother's desire to help can collide with a daughter's desire to feel that she doesn't need any help. The conflict can lead a woman to reject help from her mother even when she could benefit from it. Is there a solution to this dilemma? Daughters might find ways to involve their mothers in their lives without compromising their independence, and mothers might find ways to be helpful other than giving advice and protection. Here is a way that one daughter found.

Pam's mother is a talented seamstress who never worked outside the home. When Pam and her brothers were growing up, their mother's dressmaking talent especially shone at Halloween: the elaborate costumes she had made were the envy of their friends. When Pam had a child of her own, she had neither time nor talent to make Halloween costumes for her daughter, so she bought costumes ready-made. One year her mother offered to make a costume for Pam's daughter. Pam refused her mother's offer because it felt like an accusation: "You can't be a proper mother so I'll just have to do it for you." But then Pam decided to reframe her way of thinking about this. Resisting the impulse to interpret her mother's offer as sending a metamessage of her incompetence, she embraced it instead. Letting her mother make a Halloween costume for her daughter was a win-win-win situation: The child gets a fabulous costume, Pam is relieved of the task, and her mother feels involved in the lives of her daughter and grandchild. It worked so well that the next time her mother offered to sew, Pam didn't hesitate to accept. When Pam was expecting a second child, her mother made curtains, sheets, and a dust ruffle—all matching—for the new baby's room. Pam's mother was happy to be involved in the excitement of anticipating the new baby's arrival, and Pam appreciated the enhancement of the infant's room.

## A STAMP OF APPROVAL

Not all women are expert seamstresses, nor do they all have time to sew Halloween costumes or curtains and sheets. But there are gifts that mothers can offer daughters which take no time at all, such as understanding, acceptance, and approval. Recognizing this can dispel the frustration that results when the help or advice you offer is rejected.

Bea Lewis writes a column entitled "Day and Age" that appears weekly in the *Palm Beach Post*. One of her columns featured a letter from a frustrated reader whose daughter had recently bought her first home. The mother had offered advice about insurance, mortgages, and other matters of concern to a first-time property owner. Her daughter took offense and assured her mother that she knew what she was doing. But shortly thereafter her daughter told her how helpful a friend had been in making recommendations—the very same ones that she had rejected when they came from her mother. The mother commented, "I would expect this kind of response from a sixteen-year-old, but why at age thirty-five? I am perplexed."

It is easy to see why this mother feels perplexed. But she can take heart that advice on insurance and mortgages is, after all, something her daughter can get elsewhere, as in fact she did. What only a mother can give is reassurance that she is proud of her daughter for having attained this rite of passage to adulthood and that she trusts her to handle the responsibility that comes with it. From this point of view, it should be comforting for the mother to know that her approval continues to be important to her daughter—not only at age thirty-five but so long as they both shall live.

Another woman found that this insight helped improve her relationship with her two daughters. In the past, if she took literally their requests for advice—especially if it differed from what they had already done or said—she might hear a withering response like "I did not call you to get critiqued!" She realized that what they really wanted—even if they seemed to be asking for advice—was her stamp of approval on what they had done. Her relationships with her daughters improved immeasurably when she adopted a policy of withholding her opinion when she disagreed (except in matters of health and safety).

Sometimes it is tempting to add advice to an expression of praise. One woman, Toby, told me that learning to resist such temptation helped her relationship with her daughter. For example, if her daughter said, "I went to Weight Watchers and lost three pounds the first week," Toby would previously have replied, "That's great," then gone on to offer encouragement: "You have to keep it up." And she'd be surprised that her daughter was annoyed. Eventually she realized that the second part undercut the first: Rather than offering encouragement, it seemed to diminish the praise, as if to imply, "What you've done so far is meaningless." So now when her daughter makes an announcement like that, Toby says, "That's great"—and stops there.

A woman I spoke to shortly after her mother passed away commented, "I wrote a eulogy for my father when he died, but when my mother died I didn't write a eulogy for her, because she wasn't there to hear it, to say 'You did a good job.'" This comment reflects what many of us seek from our mothers—and as daughters get older, what mothers seek from their daughters: a stamp of approval.

### PLEASE SEE ME

"I don't think my mother ever saw me," a woman commented. I was struck by how often women I spoke to made remarks like this. What could they mean, their mothers didn't see them? I came across an answer in an essay by Anndee Hochman about telling her mother that she is a lesbian. Hochman too begins, "I don't think my mother ever really saw me." Then she goes on: "I wanted to be known, and seen, in the ways I had come to know and see myself." In this spirit, when women told me their mothers didn't see them, they meant their mothers didn't see them as they saw themselves, didn't see—and hence didn't value—the qualities they most valued in themselves. Why should this matter so much? Why is it a disappointment worth mentioning to me when I asked women about their mothers? Because, for many of us, our mothers are the measure of the world; if they don't see us for who we think we are, we wonder whether we're right about who we are. We look to our mothers as a reality check.

Vivian Gornick's memoir *Fierce Attachments* is eloquent on this point. One of the conversations Gornick recounts dramatizes the deflating effect of a mother's seeming not to "see" her daughter. It also suggests that the impulse to protect may explain in part why mothers often seem to look right past their daughters. Gornick describes an incident that took place on one of those glorious days when everything seems to expand, and anything seems possible: "I taste the air, feel the light I breathe evenly and slowly. I am peaceful and excited, beyond influence or threat. Nothing can touch me. I'm safe. I'm free." In this exalted mood, she goes to meet her mother. "I'm flying," she writes. "Flying! I want to give her some of this shiningness bursting in me, siphon into her my immense happiness at being alive." But what happens is the reverse:

> "Oh, Ma! What a day I've had," I say.
>
> "Tell me," she says. "Do you have the rent this month?"
>
> "Ma, listen . . ." I say.
>
> "That review you wrote for the *Times*," she says. "It's for sure they'll pay you?"
>
> "Ma, stop it. Let me tell you what I've been feeling," I say.
>
> "Why aren't you wearing something warmer?" she cries. "It's nearly winter."

The space inside begins to shimmer. The walls collapse inward. I feel breathless. Swallow slowly, I say to myself, slowly. To my mother I say, "You do know how to say the right thing at the right time. It's remarkable, this gift of yours. It quite takes my breath away."

But she doesn't get it. She doesn't know I'm being ironic. Nor does she know she's wiping me out. She doesn't know I take her anxiety personally, feel annihilated by her depression. How can she know this? She doesn't even know I'm there. Were I to tell her that it's death to me, her not knowing I'm there, she would stare at me out of her eyes crowding up with puzzled desolation, this young girl of seventy-seven, and she would cry angrily, "You don't understand! You have never understood!"

So much is packed into this short passage. The daughter takes her mother's anxiety personally and feels annihilated by her mother's depression because their connection is so deep that she grounds her mother's emotions as if through a lightning rod. Gornick loses her exuberant mood because her mother didn't see it, didn't acknowledge it, and therefore didn't acknowledge her. Yet all the concerns her mother focused on were ways to protect her child: Is she economically safe? Is she sure no one is exploiting her? Is she dressed warmly against the elements? Ironically, Gornick had felt "safe" in her exuberance, and her mother's concern with her safety dispelled that feeling. The one threat that Mrs. Gornick forgot to protect her daughter against was the threat to her sense of well-being posed by not being seen by her mother.

This passage ends with Gornick's despairing conviction that, were she to try to explain to her mother how her words deflate her, her mother "would cry angrily, 'You don't understand! You have never understood!'" From a daughter's point of view, this shows how oblivious a mother can be to the effect of her words. But from a mother's perspective, it captures a parallel truth: If mothers don't see their daughters, neither do daughters see their mothers. We really *don't* understand our mothers, any more than they understand us. This too is portrayed in Paule Marshall's *Brown Girl, Brownstones.*

The theme driving the novel is Selina's rejection of everything she associates with her mother: her values, her determination to buy the house they live in and then earn money by renting rooms, and most of all, her mother's anger at Selina's father for thwarting her efforts to buy the house. At one point Selina tells her confidante, an older woman, how she disapproves of her mother's life. The woman responds, "Maybe someday you'll understand your momma and then you'll see why she does all of these things." Selina replies, "I never want to understand her, Miss Thompson." Selina seems to sense that with understanding might come acceptance. Later in the novel we see this equation from the mother's point of view. After overhearing her mother talking to her friends about why it is necessary to overcharge roomers, Selina sees her "mother's eyes fixed on her with their mute plea for understanding and tolerance—not only for what she had just said but for all she had ever said or done." Mothers, like daughters, yearn to be understood and accepted—in a word, seen.

## SHE SEES THE OLD ME

Understanding, accepting, and seeing are more complicated than they might at first appear, because people are not fixed in time. This fact presents a particular challenge to mothers and daughters. We change, and we remain the same. So a person who has known us forever may see the person we used to be, not the person we have become. As we change, so does our relationship; another challenge is to know what to keep and what to shed of the relationship that was. And because of the double meaning of connection and control, comments that previously gave comfort may now cause distress.

Tina cringes when her mother begins a sentence "I know you don't like . . ." Tina knows she is about to hear a reference to something that she didn't like at one time in the past but that in all likelihood she has long since changed her attitude toward. For example, her mother might go on to say, "you don't like sushi," because Tina said as much a decade ago. But now sushi is one of her favorite foods. The irony is that on the surface the phrase "I know you don't like . . ." claims closeness by demonstrating intimate knowledge of her daughter's tastes. Such knowledge can certainly work that way, when a mother, say, welcomes her daughter home by preparing her favorite food or by making sure not to serve a food she abhors. But in this case, the effect is the opposite: It gives Tina the impression that her mother regards her as fixed, immutable—as someone she has long since ceased to be.

A student in one of my classes, Heather, described a similar frustration this way:

> When I was younger we lived in Connecticut, so my mother would always bring me to NYC at the prettiest times of the year, which also happened to coincide with the coldest times of the year. I would have to waddle down 5th Ave. in 3 layers of socks, a puffy jacket and two pairs of gloves. So somewhere between the ages of 5 and 8 I must have said that I don't like going to NYC. Now I am 20. I always try to find ways to get to NYC. I always try to go when I am at school, or even when I am home in Florida. And my mother of course says in all seriousness "But you hate NY."

Her mother's remark implies to Heather that she will not let her daughter change. Even worse, it seems to fix her in a time when she was a small child restrained not only by her age but also by immobilizing winter clothes. In any conversation, context is all. I wonder about the contexts in which Heather's mother says, "But you hate NY." Could it be she is trying to dissuade her daughter from cutting short her time at home by going to New York City, or from going to New York instead of making a trip home? Regardless of the reason, the remark annoys Heather because it makes her feel that her mother doesn't see her as the person she is now.

Both daughters and mothers can get stuck in images of the other formed long ago. Many mothers feel that their grown daughters see them as they used to be, not as they are now. For example, a daughter may continue to expect her mother to sew clothes for her grandchildren after the older woman finds it harder to work with her hands and would rather spend her time developing new interests. Indeed, the very way that many of us keep a tally of how our mothers failed us when we were children in itself fixes them in a time long past: a time, moreover, when they may have been young themselves and struggling with the challenges of raising children.

A daughter or a mother can help the other see her in new ways by talking in new ways. For example, many mothers and daughters find themselves replaying a dynamic by which the daughter brings her mother problems to solve, like offerings at the sacred altar of their closeness. There was a time when this was satisfying to both: the mother felt useful and wise, the daughter felt cared for and listened to. But when the daughter is an adult, the familiar conversations may be less satisfying. Her mother's advice may become an irritant: She seems to see her daughter as more problem-ridden than she is. For her part, the mother feels lured into a trap: Her daughter seeks her sympathy and advice, then becomes angry when she gets it. To change the tape—replace the old conversations with new ones more reflective of their new relationship—either could try something different. The daughter could remind herself to tell more stories of her triumphs and fewer of her problems, and the mother might remind herself that she no longer has to solve her daughter's problems. She could respond instead by showing understanding and expressing confidence that her daughter will find a solution.

## WATCH YOUR STEP

Mothers' desire to protect their daughters accounts for many of the patterns that are established when the daughters are young but continue—discomfitingly—when they are grown. The frustration can be even greater for daughters who have brothers, because the difference in how sons are treated sets the daughters' experience in relief. Again the paradox traces to the double meaning of connection and control. When they are teens, a sister may have to be home by 11:00 P.M. while her brother is allowed to stay out into the wee hours of the morning. She may be required to call if she is out after 10:00, while he doesn't have to. This is only realistic; girls are at greater risk of attack than boys are. But regardless of whether the daughter acknowledges these dangers, she is likely to be angered that her freedom is limited in ways her brother's is not. And this contrast can persist into her adult life.

Frances has four grown children, two sons and two daughters. She was not aware while raising her children that she treated her daughters and sons differently, but her daughters certainly were— keenly aware. They frequently point this out to her now that they are grown. "You cut Danny and Kevin more slack," they accuse, and their mother realizes they are right. This applies not only to how strict she was when they lived at home; it applies even now, when her youngest child is thirty. One example is the mother's expectations about staying in touch. As a single mother who worked full-time, Frances always needed to know where her children were, to know they were safe. Now that they're adults, she continues to expect—you might even say demand—to know where her daughters are. But she gradually dropped this requirement for her sons, without giving it conscious thought. She doesn't complain when her sons let weeks pass without calling, whereas she expects her daughters to call every few days. Frances's desire to know where her daughters are reflects her continuing concern for their safety, and she has become accustomed to more connection. Her daughters, however, at times resent the difference, because it implies unfair or even insulting expectations.

Ellen, in her thirties, often works late; she feels slightly nervous as she leaves the deserted office and heads for her car, but this is no more than a fleeting distraction, much as you might feel nervous riding in the car of a friend whose driving you don't completely trust. You put the discomfort aside and get on with your life. So Ellen becomes angry when her mother suggests— which she often does—that Ellen call the security guards to walk her to her car. Ellen's anger focuses on the irrationality of her mother's suggestion: Ellen obviously can't bother the guards night after night. How foolish this would make her feel, since her office is not in a particularly bad neighborhood, and the parking lot is well lit. Furthermore, her mother's repeated suggestions make her more nervous, so instead of being a source of comfort, her mother is a source of anxiety. Worse yet, her mother's ceaseless concern makes her feel like an incompetent, a child in her mother's eyes. And this reinforces the little voice inside that isn't quite sure of her competence either.

Ellen is not alone in hearing her mother's worry as indication that she thinks her daughter can't take care of herself, can't make good decisions, can't do her job. And nothing hurts more—or makes you more angry, since anger is the flip side of hurt—than feeling that the person whose opinion counts most doesn't trust your judgment. How different this is from the quality many women told me they treasure in their mothers: "She is the one who tells me, 'I know you can do it.'" Hearing that kind of encouragement gives you strength. But if your mother does not believe in you, it's harder to believe in yourself. These implications may be far from the mind of a mother who is simply watching out for her daughter's safety and well-being, but intentions do not ensure effects: The message of protection may carry a metamessage of lack of confidence. In situations like these, a mother may do her daughter more good by saying less, not more.

## LIGHTEN UP: HUMOR HELPS

Many of the frustrations that arise between daughters and mothers result from this mismatch between message and metamessage: Something intended in the positive spirit of protection can carry an unintended but hurtful metamessage that you are not measuring up. Even the frequent complaint that mothers are critical of their daughters' appearance is the flip side of a concern that shows connection. And the same topics that are favorites for criticism (or helpful suggestions, depending on your point of view)—the

Big Three: hair, clothes, and weight—can also be material for delightful conversation.

Valerie was one of many women I spoke to who commented that they have much better relationships with their daughters than they had with their mothers. In explaining why this was so, Valerie mentioned that her mother had been overly concerned with her daughter's appearance. "She wanted me to look good to the world," Valerie said. "When I was about forty, I developed some small discolorations on my face. She wanted me to *do* something about those spots." Later in our conversation, Valerie was describing the good relationship she has with her grown daughter. (I later spoke to her daughter, who agreed.) In this regard, Valerie mentioned that her daughter always urges her to spend more money on herself. For example, Valerie said of her daughter, "She's always telling me about these face creams that I ought to buy, to get rid of my wrinkles."

I wondered why Valerie regarded her daughter's suggesting she get rid of her wrinkles as evidence of a good relationship, whereas she saw her mother's suggesting she get rid of her spots as evidence of the opposite. Perhaps she did not feel that her daughter's motivation was to make her "look good to the world," as her mother's had been. Regardless of the motivation, a difference lies in the larger context of their relationships. Here is the context in which Valerie told me about the face creams:

> We love to talk about things like earrings and lipstick and clothes, infinitely, playfully. Last year when I gave the plenary lecture at a conference, my daughter insisted I spend money on my dress. She wanted us to find it together because she thinks I won't spend the money unless she's there. . . . We would go into the store and she'd say to the salesperson, "My mother is a hard sell. She's a tough nut to crack." It's a playful thing. She's always telling me about these face creams that I ought to buy, to get rid of my wrinkles. There's that whole realm that we have a lot of fun with. It's just play.

So one difference between her daughter's and her mother's suggestions is the context—and the spirit—in which they were made. Valerie's interactions with her daughter are playful. With her mother, in contrast, "Nothing was play. Everything was deadly serious." Humor and play are a major reason that Valerie and her daughter can enjoy their connection without tripping the wires of control.

### DON'T MENTION IT

Although play can provide great joy, it must, like all ways of talking, be handled with care. Play can be risky when a daughter (or mother) feels uncertain about her mother's (or daughter's) acceptance of her life choices. Almost any comment by a mother to a daughter (and in some cases, the other way around as well) can be heard as criticism if the subject broached is something of which the mother disapproves. And disapproval often leaks out when mother and daughter have chosen different paths in life.

Jane is a fervent supporter of abortion rights, while her daughter is an equally fervent opponent. When a pro-choice march was to be held in Washington, D.C., the city where Jane's daughter lives, Jane planned to attend the march together with two friends. She called her daughter to say that she'd be coming to town, and to invite her to join her mother and friends at a restaurant one evening. "You're invited to dinner," Jane told her daughter. "You're not invited to the march, ha ha." Jane intended this last quip as a playful, ironic acknowledgment of a difference they both knew existed; the good-natured laugh was meant to imply acceptance of it. But the effect was the opposite; the remark angered her daughter, who perceived it as a dig.

What could Jane have said about the march that would not have irritated her daughter? Nothing. Sometimes when a spot is sore, the best thing to do is leave it alone. Completely alone. No jokes, no references, no nothing. (Saying "I'm not going to say anything about . . ." is not saying nothing.) This is a lesson Jane herself learned. She told me that when her daughter announced she was expecting her fourth child, "This time I didn't ask, 'Are you sure you want another baby?'" Jane had learned a lesson from the reaction she had gotten when she asked that question about her daughter's pregnancy with baby number three. Even the most seemingly harmless reference can be unwise if a topic itself is a source of conflict.

Sometimes it's the daughter who raises a fraught topic, triggering a frustratingly looplike conversation. It's as if we repeatedly return to the points of contention, like running your tongue over a sore spot in your mouth. Margaret, for example, is irritated by her mother's constant criticism of her hair. Her mother tells her it's too long, too unkempt, too wild-looking. So Margaret hears with horror the words that come out of her own mouth when she arrives at her parents' home for a visit. The first thing she says after greeting her mother is "My hair is really wild today; I couldn't get it to stay down." No doubt her motivation, not clearly thought out, was to head off criticism at the pass: If she complained about her hair being wild, her mother couldn't. But the effect was the opposite; Margaret's comment opened the door, and her mother leapt in. She responded with an offer to take her daughter to her own hairdresser, an offer to which Margaret reacted with predictable annoyance—at her mother for her obsession with improving her hair, but also at herself for having triggered this exchange by raising the topic of her hair.

Liz couldn't believe that her daughter Jodie had snapped once again. She had asked an innocent question: "Do you like vegetables?" and Jodie boiled over, accusing her mother of criticizing. Here's how it came about. Jodie and her children were having Thanksgiving dinner at her parents' home, along with her sister and her sister's new boyfriend. The children were intrigued to learn that the boyfriend was vegetarian, and this led to a congenial conversation which Liz described to me this way: "So we were talking about which vegetables everyone liked, which they eat, stuff like that. And I asked Jodie, 'Which vegetables do you like?' Or maybe I said, 'Do you like vegetables?' And she got angry and accused me of being critical of the way she feeds her kids. She said

I always tell her she doesn't give them enough vegetables. It's true I *think* that, but I don't think I ever *said* it. And anyway, all I did was ask a question. I felt like I can't open my mouth without Jodie accusing me of criticizing her."

I had the chance to talk to Jodie as well, so I asked for her take on the conversation. It was almost the same, except for one little word—and a big backstory. When she got to the part where her mother asked the offending question, Jodie said, "So my mother asked me, 'Jodie, do you even like vegetables?'" That little word "even" made the metamessage sound different; it *presupposed* that Jodie did not like vegetables, and this reminded her of a history of conversations: "Whenever my mother visits," she said, "she tells me like ten times that I don't feed the kids enough vegetables." So the biggest difference between Jodie's and Liz's perspectives was their recollections about how often—even whether or not—Liz had mentioned her concern before.

It's not surprising that Jodie would recall, maybe even exaggerate, how often her mother said that she should give her kids more vegetables. After all, this is a way her mother thinks Jodie is failing at her most important job, being a mother. And it's not surprising that Liz would minimize how often she commented on this conviction—or whether she commented at all. It seems likely that what Jodie considers "comments" might have been indirect, as this question was, so Liz might have believed she had not "said" anything, whereas Jodie heard what she was thinking loud and clear. (I was amused by how often, when I spoke to mothers and daughters separately, the mother told me that she disapproved of something about her daughter but never said anything—and the daughter told me that her mother often criticized her on that point.)

Maybe Jodie's children really would be better off if they ate more vegetables. Or maybe they wouldn't. The conviction that vegetables are key to health may turn out to be a fad eventually replaced by another; expert opinion changes quickly, as witness how, in the space of a few years, the role of principal nutritional villain passed from fat to carbohydrates. In any case, it doesn't matter: The children are healthy, they're happy, they're loved. Perhaps the answer is to try to develop some distance and figure, so long as the kids aren't being beaten or starved, they're probably going to turn out all right. (As a woman I talked to quipped, quoting her own reassurance to a new mother, "You just have to not kill the baby.")

When a daughter does not do things the way her mother would wish, or a mother cannot approve her daughter's choices (including her choice of a mate), there is no way out except to leave the issue alone. Otherwise, the distance gets greater. If the mother keeps referring to it, her daughter will want to minimize the time they spend together. This not only gives the mother less time to enjoy her daughter's company but also means she will have less opportunity to influence her, if that is the mother's wish.

### AND NOW FOR SOMETHING DIFFERENT

When a conversation takes a turn we don't like, we usually think of ourselves as reacting to an offense that the other person initiated. We rarely stop and think about whether the other person was reacting to us, or what further response our reaction will provoke. Regardless of who first diverted a conversation from a pleasant to a tense one, either can head off a familiar argument by changing the way she responds. Here again Vivian Gornick's memoir provides an example.

Gornick and her mother are walking together when her mother says, "So I'm reading the biography you gave me." The book was about Josephine Herbst, "a thirties writer, a stubborn willful raging woman grabbing at politics and love and writing, in there punching until the last minute." Gornick is delighted to hear her mother has been reading the book. But when her mother begins to speak, Gornick realizes that they are headed toward an argument:

"Oh!" I smile in wide delight. "Are you enjoying it?"
"Listen," she begins. The smile drops off my face and

my stomach contracts. That "listen" means she is about to trash the book I gave her to read. She is going to say, "What. What's here? What's here that I don't already know? I *lived* through it. I know it all. What can this writer tell me that I don't already know? Nothing. To *you* it's interesting, but to me? How can this be interesting to me?"

Gornick and her mother have had so many conversations over their years together that her prediction of how her mother will speak is exactly right. And she can also predict how she herself will react:

"Listen," my mother says now in the patronizing tone she thinks is conciliatory. "Maybe this is interesting to you, but not to me. I lived through all this. I know it all. What can I learn from this? Nothing. To you it's interesting. Not to me."

Invariably, when she speaks so, my head fills with blood and before the sentences have stopped pouring from her mouth I am lashing out at her. "You're an ignoramus, you know nothing, only a know-nothing talks the way you do. The point of having lived through it, as you say, is only that the background is familiar, so the book is made richer, not that you could have written the book. People a thousand times more educated than you have read and learned from this book, but *you* can't learn from it?"

It's easy to understand why Gornick would be inclined to react this way: She'd be reflecting back the same dismissive, scornful tone in which her mother spoke to her. And the angry reaction would be only natural, since her mother's scorn for the book rejects her daughter's gesture of connection in recommending a book she liked—as well as casting aspersions on her daughter's judgment.

This time, however, the argument does not ensue, because Gornick reacts differently, both verbally and physically. Instead of leaping into the fray with her mother, she steps back and changes the tone of their exchange. She also makes a physical connection by touching her reassuringly:

> I turn to my mother, throw my left arm around her still solid back, place my right hand on her upper arm, and say, "Ma, if this book is not interesting to you, that's fine. You can say that." She looks coyly at me, eyes large, head half-turned; *now* she's interested. "But don't say it has nothing to teach you. That there's nothing here. That's unworthy of you, and of the book, and of me. You demean us all when you say that."

By reacting differently than she usually did, Gornick gets her mother's attention and changes the course of the conversation. After a long silence, her mother makes a very different sort of remark: "That Josephine Herbst," Mrs. Gornick says. "She certainly carried on, didn't she?" At that, her daughter is "relieved and happy." She hugs her mother, who goes on, "I'm jealous. I'm jealous she lived her life, I didn't live mine."

Vivian Gornick changed the way her mother spoke to her by changing the way she spoke to her mother. A key difference in her new response was that it focused attention on the hurtful implications of her mother's remarks rather than simply reacting to them—and reacting in kind. In this, she did what the anthropologist Gregory Bateson called "metacommunication," that is, talking about talk. Metacommunication can be an especially powerful way to reframe a conversation, because it requires you to step out of the interaction and look at it from the outside. This in itself provides a measure of calm, and a new perspective.

Much of the power of Vivian Gornick's metacommunication resided in calling attention to the effect her mother's words had on her. It is common—indeed automatic—to assume that the effects of others' words always reflect their intentions. But that assumption is not always accurate. Checking it out is another useful form of metacommunicating—and of stepping out of the frame.

In telling me how she improved her relationship with her mother, one woman mentioned a simple step, but one that simply doesn't occur to many of us: When something her mother says hurts her feelings, she asks her mother what she means:

> She makes a statement and I don't know whether she's signifying, you know, what her come-from is, and rather than just speculate and just let it hang there, it's like, "What do you mean by that?" or "Do you intend that to be hurtful, do you intend for that to be—What's your come-from on that?"

In other words, the daughter went on, "I took it in a certain way, and she may or may not have meant it that way." By asking her mother to clarify her intentions rather than silently absorbing what to her was a hurtful metamessage, this woman opened a dialogue that improved their relationship. It also let her mother know the effect of her words—whether or not she intended to have that effect.

When we find ourselves having one of our least favorite conversations and feel trapped in it, seeing no way out, it is helpful to remember that if we speak differently than we usually do, the other person will have to react differently too. I can't guarantee that the outcome will always be as satisfying as it was in these examples, but at the very least it will remind us that we have it in our power to change the paths that conversations take.

### *DO* SOMETHING

A linguist, Eleni Petraki, began an interview with two women by saying, "You're mother and daughter." The daughter replied, "Yeah, and we can just sit there and talk for hours and hours and hours." A precious aspect of many women's relationships with their mothers or grown daughters is also the bedrock of women's friendships: shared conversation. Exchanging talk is one of the great joys of closeness for many women. But it's hard to have all that talk without ever touching on topics that one or the other might want to avoid. If that's the case, then something mothers and daughters can do is—something. In other words, rather than just sitting and talking, do something together. In this, women can learn from men, for whom friendship is more often built on doing things together than on talking to each other, just as men can benefit from adopting some of women's ways of creating close relationships by talking more.

Ruth and her daughter were walking through Costco, shopping. As they walked down the aisle, arm in arm, companionably laughing, stopping to examine items, then falling back into their synchronized steps, Ruth noticed her husband regarding them with a smile. "I love to watch the two of you together," he commented later. Ruth and her daughter love to sit and talk, but there is also a special joy in shopping together, where their rhythm is matched, and their focus is on something outside themselves.

When I asked women what they enjoyed about their relationships with their daughters or their mothers, I was amazed at how often they mentioned shopping. Here's how one woman put it, while telling me how she and her mother enjoyed each other:

> We love to shop together. . . . And we do this like guerrilla shopping around Christmas and after Christmas when they have sales. We don't need to save every penny anymore, but it's like a total rush when I get the wrapping paper at half price. . . . And she just gets a total charge off it. . . . Thirty people wanted it, you would crawl between their knees.

I have wondered what it is about shopping that is so appealing to so many daughters and mothers. My conclusion is that what's special is having something that they do together, in addition to—or instead of—the time they spend talking.

Almost any shared activity can be a source of pleasure. For more than one mother-daughter pair, it was attending Weight Watchers. For others it was getting their nails done. Many of these activities are backstage—like an expanded ladies' room where women gather behind the scenes. Perhaps this backstage quality, along with the knowledge that the activity is associated with an in-group—women—adds an extra layer of pleasure. Whatever activity appeals, doing something provides a chance to spend time together, and the doing itself sends a metamessage of rapport.

If you can't get out to do things, or if you'd just as soon not, you can craft new conversations by talking about subjects other than those you usually do. Ask your mother about the past, about family history—a subject on which she is expert. Ask your daughter about her work, if she works outside the home. Talk about movies, TV shows, books you've read. You might even suggest a mother-daughter reading group if you live in the same town. If you usually discuss personal topics, try talking about current events. If you usually avoid personal topics, try telling about what you did the day before or what you plan to do. Sing together. Tell jokes. You can still enjoy that pleasure of shared references, shared rhythms—and avoid the topics that lead to old frustrations.

## CHANGE THE SCRIPT

All these are ways to improve conversations between daughters and mothers. But just being aware of the dynamics that drive conversations is often all that is needed for individuals to find more enjoyment and less irritation in talking to their mothers or daughters. A woman who wrote to me after reading my analysis of the double meaning of caring and criticizing explained how this worked for her. In the past, she said, she had dreaded holidays because she knew that her mother would be critical, and that she would explode in response. Her mother seemed to treat her like a thirteen-year-old rather than a middle-aged woman with a master's degree and a successful career. After she read the chapter, nothing changed—except the way she interpreted her mother's remarks. And that changed everything. Just reframing her mother's comments as expressions of caring rather than criticizing was all that was needed to change the way she experienced her visits home.

For example, the woman showed her mother a new purchase that she was pleased with: two pairs of socks, one black and one dark navy, made of supersoft fabric that was warm to boot. The next day she wore one of the pairs of socks, and she pointed out to her mother how well they matched her outfit. Her mother responded, "Are you sure you're not wearing one of each color?" The woman explained to me how her reaction had changed:

> My immediate thought was "What do you think? That I can't make sure I'm wearing socks of the same color? What kind of incompetent do you think I am?" It's just the sort of thing that would have set me off in the past. But I stopped to think for a moment and realized that she loves me and wants to make sure I look good, or didn't embarrass myself with mismatched socks. I became almost tender toward her for caring in such a small but touching way.

Questioning whether you made sure that you didn't mistake navy blue for black (something, incidentally, we have all done at one time or another) is just the sort of thing that only a mother could do: Who else would worry about the color of your socks? Who else could you show your new socks to in the first place? I'm willing to bet that if you asked this mother whether she seriously doubted that her daughter had put on matching socks, she'd assure you she didn't. Her remark was probably just a way of showing she had paid attention to the purchase, perhaps recalled a time when she mistook navy for black, and was reacting in the way she had learned over a lifetime was her obligation: watching out for her daughter. But it was a perfect setup for her daughter to take offense—until she reframed her understanding of her mother's intentions.

One of my students, Jessie, also found that reframing how she thought about her mother led her to talk to her in new ways, with happy results for them both. Here's how she described in a class assignment the dynamics in her family and the way she began to reframe them:

> This past summer I stayed home with my parents. . . . I found myself having dinner with my parents every night. My father has always dominated every relationship in the family, and it became especially clear to me in the past few months just how often my mother is excluded and cast aside in family debates as we all tend to side with my father. One night we spent nearly an hour arguing against my mother on some topic, barely letting her say a word and condemning anything she said. I really did agree with my father, but I noticed that my brother and sister also side with him and my mother has always been the odd man out.

Jessie reevaluated how she reacted to her mother after class material inspired her to view the dynamics from her mother's perspective. We had discussed in class how mothers are often left out when daughters align with their fathers. As a result of this discussion, Jessie made a change:

> After this summer I realized how out of the loop my mother feels; my father has always been the "favorite" parent to talk to and spend time with, while my mother is constantly trying to be involved in our lives, and my siblings and I see her as intrusive and nagging. I made a conscious effort to spend more time with my mother and to align myself with her whenever possible. She really appreciated my interest in her life and we are closer now as a result. Simply being conscious of certain actions can completely change the emotions and dynamics within a family unit.

Jessie's experience shows how looking at a relationship in a new way can lead to new ways of talking and acting—and improving the relationship.

I am always impressed by individuals' abilities to devise ways to improve communication with those they love once they understand the processes that are causing distress. Though all relationships between mothers and daughters share many characteristics, as I discovered in my research and have shown in this book, each relationship is unique, so no easy solutions will work for all, as daughters and mothers try to find the amount of connection that feels right, without invoking the specters of criticism and intrusion. It might at first seem maddening that there is no correct answer to the question "How much connection is right?" But really, it's good that there isn't, so each family can find the amount that is right for them.

The challenge is greatest when the amount that is comfortable for one is uncomfortable for the other. Yet again, understanding the dynamics can help. I'll explain with an analogy to a nonverbal process described by Edward Hall, an anthropologist who analyzed cross-cultural differences in the use of space. When two people have different senses of how close to stand while having a conversation, the one who expects to stand closer will move in to adjust the space between them, but the one who expects to stand farther away will back off to create the distance that seems appropriate to her. As one inches forward in order to get comfortable, the other inches back for the same reason. Together they move across the room until one is pinned against a wall—or nearly pushed down a flight of stairs. The same can happen in relationships between mothers and daughters. If one—let's say the mother, because it is usually, but not always, the mother—seeks a bit more closeness than the daughter is comfortable with, the daughter will perceive her mother as encroaching and will back off, thereby prodding her mother to intensify her efforts to get closer, and so on, until they end up at the edge of a cliff, if not tumbling over it.

Like moving closer or farther away to adjust the physical

space between us as we talk, we tend to try harder and do more of the same when we are uncomfortable with a conversation—or a relationship. But consider the results of doing that: Each step you take to get comfortable drives the other to take a step in the direction you don't want her to go. And consider the very different results that would ensue if you did something that seems at first counterintuitive: If you stop moving closer, the other person will stop moving farther away. Conversely, if you stop backing up, the other person will stop moving toward you. There may be a moment of discomfort as you stand firm or even take a step in the other direction, but it's surely better than moving inexorably and pointlessly across a room—or into an abyss. That is how doing something different can break a hurtful cycle, or unwind spiraling conversations. And that is how the insights offered in this book provide ways that mothers and daughters can move back from the edge of the cliff and onto the safe ground of more satisfying and comforting mother-daughter conversations.

# AFTERWORD

I was one of those daughters who saw my mother as my enemy when I was a teen. Indeed, I was precocious: I had bitter complaints about and judgments of her from my elementary school days. When I was in my twenties, one of the things that put me off was that my mother seemed to long for my company so much. And I was taken by surprise when, the first time I began a letter to her "Dearest Mom," she replied that she had waited her whole life to hear me say that. I thought this peculiar to her—and peculiar— until, while I was doing research for this book, Rachael Allbritten sent me copies of e-mails she had received from her mother, Wanda Carswell. In one of these e-mails Wanda responded to a Mother's Day card Rachael had sent her (electronically) which expressed her appreciation of the sacrifices her mother had made for her, how much she had learned from her, and how lucky she was to have her for a mother. Her mother's e-mailed response was strikingly similar to my mother's reply to my letter addressing her as "Dearest":

> Oh, Rachael!!!!! That was so WONDERFUL!!! It almost made me cry. I've waited 25 years, 3 months and 7 days to hear something like that. . . .

When I read this, I realized that my mother's reaction had not been anomalous. It made me stop and think about how deep and how passionate the connection between a mother and daughter can be.

As a girl growing up in New York City, I thought I knew all about Freud. I often said of myself that I had an Electra complex, the female version of an Oedipus complex. I said this to acknowledge, sardonically, that I idealized my father and demonized my mother. So I thought of my younger self when I read how Phyllis Chesler reinterpreted the Electra myth to comment on the mother-daughter relationship:

> Electra is not, as Freud's followers would have it, merely competing with her mother for the same man: her father; she is also competing with her father/brother/sisters/ mother's male lover, for the same woman, her mother.

Chesler is right. The relationship between a mother and daughter is like a love affair in the way each can long for, and glory in, the other.

The longer my mother lived—and I am extremely lucky that she lived long—the more I realized that I cherished and sought her love. I didn't think about this earlier because I took it for granted: I counted the ways she had failed me, the ways she had angered and hurt me, because her love and the many ways she showed it were part of the landscape, the background against which her offenses stood in relief. I never questioned that if I came home for a visit, she would be happy to see me, to have me stay as long as I wished, to be available whenever my schedule left me a free day or evening to see her.

As my mother aged and her health gave way, our roles began to blur. I called her daily, mailed her loving notes and small gifts, and visited often, all the while dimly aware that I was treating her like a lover. I held her hand as we walked, slowing my pace to match hers. I helped her get ready for bed, fetching her nightgown and letting her rest her hand on my shoulder for balance as I held out her protective nighttime panties: left foot, right foot, into the leg holes. The older and weaker my mother got, the more caretaking I did—and the more I heard myself talking to her in just the ways she used to talk to me. I asked her if she'd eaten enough for lunch and if she was getting enough sleep. As her lung disease worsened, I learned to operate the nebulizer through which she inhaled medication and pestered her to use it on schedule. Whenever she was hospitalized, I flew to her side and stayed, feeding her, pushing her in a wheelchair. Back in her home, when she proclaimed herself too tired to get off the bed and go to the bathroom to wash up, I suggested we dance to the bathroom and hummed a song, knowing she would never pass up a chance to dance.

By taking care of my mother, I came to understand how much I loved her, and how much she had loved me. And this made it all the more moving when she was able to take her old role back. When I told her during a telephone conversation that I had a sore throat and she said, "I wish I was there to make you some tea," it was almost as if she did make me tea.

One day while writing this book I witnessed a drama. A pair of cardinals had built a nest in a tree right outside the window I face when I write. As I sat at my desk day after day, I watched the parent birds feed their newly hatched chicks, and I watched the chicks grow. At first I could barely spy them over the nest's edge, but soon their heads stretched way out of the nest. I say "heads," but it seemed as if they were barely heads at all, just huge gaping beaks. The parent birds took turns flying in to fill these enormous begging mouths that got bigger and bigger. Each day I could see more of the baby birds as they strained for their food. Then one day the parent birds flew close to the nest—but didn't fly in to feed the chicks. Instead, each time they neared the nest, and the baby birds opened wide to receive their meal, the parent birds changed course and flew away. That was the day the little ones left the nest: One by one, they climbed up onto the nest's edge and eventually hopped clear of it and onto a branch, all the while coaxed by the mother or father, who kept flying by, then flying away.

What surprised and delighted me was that the parent birds did not push the little ones out of the nest. Nor did they simply stop coming by, so the chicks would have to come out to find food. By flying close and then flying away, the parent birds lured their offspring out. It seemed clear to me that the little birds finally left the nest in order to find their parents, who they could see were out there flying around.

If you'd asked me even a few years ago, I'd have said I'd spent my life trying to escape my mother. If you asked me now, I'd say I have spent it trying to find her. Although I lost her while I was writing this book, the writing of it has helped me find her. I hope it helps readers find their mothers and their daughters—in memory or in conversation.

# NOTES

## *1* CAN WE TALK?

p. 17   The quotation comes from Stephanie Staal, *The Love They Lost: Living with the Legacy of Divorce* (New York: Delta, 2001), p. 124. I found it in a paper written by Laura Wright for a seminar I taught in fall 2004.

p. 27   Liv Ullmann made these comments on *The Diane Rehm Show* in 1985. I heard it when a segment of the interview was replayed on *The Diane Rehm Show,* September 21, 2004.

## *2* MY MOTHER, MY HAIR

p. 41   Eder, "Serious and Playful Disputes," pp. 70–71.

p. 43   The article about Andrea Jung is "Calling Avon's Lady," by Ramin Setoodeh, *Newsweek,* December 27, 2004/January 3, 2005, pp. 98–101. The quotation is on p. 101.

p. 43   *the anthropologist Mary Catherine Bateson remarked* I recalled hearing this comment at the time, then checked its accuracy with Bateson herself.

p. 43   *the "refrigerator mother" theory of autism* According to the website Autism Watch (www.autism-watch.org), the term "refrigerator mother" was originated by Leo Kanner in the 1940s but was given widespread popularity by Bruno Bettelheim in the 1950s and 1960s. This shameful and tragic chapter in the history of psychology and medicine is described in a documentary film, *Refrigerator Mothers,* made by David E. Simpson, J. J. Hanley, and Gordon Quinn. The film aired on PBS in July 2002.

p. 46   The article about Ry Russo-Young is "Growing Up with Mom and Mom," by Susan Dominus, *New York Times Magazine,* October 24, 2004, pp. 69–75, 84, 143, 144. The quotation is on p. 71.

p. 55 Matisoff, *Blessings, Curses, Hopes, and Fears,* pp. 58–59. The most frequent way I heard this phrase (which I took to be a single word) used would be a comment like "Look at him eat, kunnahurra," said with a sense of satisfaction that a child is eating well. I always assumed it was an expression of pride or satisfaction.

p. 56 Esmeralda Santiago, *The Turkish Lover* (New York: Da Capo Press, 2004), p. 337.

p. 61 It was Micah Perks, a writer and professor at the University of California, Santa Cruz, who reminded me of the Hawthorne story and suggested that mothers' tendency to scrutinize their daughters and granddaughters might reflect a similar urge to achieve perfection.

### *3* DON'T SHUT ME OUT

p. 63 The e-mail from Joyce Poole was sent June 24, 2003.

p. 64 *Girls' social lives are typically centered on a best friend* Research on gender differences in children's play is summarized by Daniel Maltz and Ruth Borker, "A Cultural Approach to Male-Female Miscommunication," and by Campbell Leaper and Tara Smith, "A Meta-Analytic Review of Gender Variations in Children's Language Use." Many books and articles examining aspects of gender and language begin with or include summaries of research on children's language use, including Penelope Eckert and Sally McConnell-Ginet, *Language and Gender,* Eleanor Maccoby, *The Two Sexes: Growing Up Apart, Coming Together,* and Amy Sheldon, "Pickle Fights: Gendered Talk in Preschool Disputes."

p. 64 Gurian, whose many books include *The Wonder of Boys* (New York: Putnam, 1996), explained to me in an e-mail dated March 28, 2005, that he drew this conclusion based on audience responses to his lectures, which he often begins by asking, "When you give a girl a doll, what does she generally do with it?" and "When you give a boy a doll, what does he generally do with it?"

p. 65 *boys often combine talk with physical action* Among those who have made similar observations are Amy Sheldon (for example, "Preschool Girls' Discourse Competence" and "Pickle Fights"), and Marjorie Harness Goodwin (for example, *He-Said-She-Said*).

p. 65 The cartoon, by Bruce Eric Kaplan, appeared in *The New Yorker,* October 18, 2004, p. 151.

p. 66 *mothers tend to talk to their children more . . . and they talk more to their daughters* Campbell Leaper, Kristin J. Anderson, and Paul Sanders ("Moderators of Gender Effects on Parents' Talk to Their Children") report these findings based on their survey of eighteen published studies that tested mother-father differences in talkativeness (a total of 501 families) and twenty-five studies that tested for differences in mothers' talkativeness with daughters compared to sons (a total of 793 families). Erika Hoff-Ginsberg ("Influences of Mother and Child on Maternal Talkativeness") found that mothers' talkativeness was influenced by their own use of language and by their children's responses to their talk. Thus, one reason mothers talk more to daughters might be that their daughters respond to their talk with more talk. The resultant greater experience talking to each other might also explain why Eleanor Maccoby found, in a study she did with Carol Jacklin, that when they gave mothers, fathers, and male and female children the task of describing one of four ambiguous pictures to another family member, who then had to pick that picture out of a matching set, mothers tended to do better than fathers, daughters tended to do better than sons, and the most successful pairs of all were mothers and daughters (Maccoby, *The Two Sexes,* p. 272).

p. 72   *much of the time most fathers spend with their children* Phyllis Bronstein and Carolyn Pape Cowan survey studies that draw the conclusion that fathers tend to spend their time with children playing. Lauren Weidman called my attention to their paper.

p. 72   Bob Shacochis, "Keeping It All in the Family." In *A Love Like No Other: Stories from Adoptive Parents,* ed. Pamela Kruger and Jill Smolowe (New York: Riverhead, 2005), pp. 176–192; the quotation appears on p. 182.

p. 80   Haru Yamada, *Different Games, Different Rules* (New York: Oxford University Press, 1997), p. 17 (for *haragei*) and p. 37 (for *sasshi*). That the Japanese value indirectness and silence over talk, which they regard with suspicion, is a central point in Yamada's comparison of Japanese and American communication. My understanding of these terms comes not only from her book but also from an e-mail exchange I conducted with Yamada in June 2005.

p. 83   Blum-Kulka's book is *Dinner Talk.*

p. 83   Ochs and Taylor, "Family Narrative as Political Activity" and "The Father Knows Best Dynamic in Family Dinner Narratives."

p. 83   Jefferson, "On the Sequential Organisation of Troubles Talk in Ordinary Conversation."

## 4  SHE'S JUST LIKE ME, SHE'S NOTHING LIKE ME

p. 87   *mothers tend to have more direct physical contact* Studies finding that mothers of newborns engage in more "tactile behaviors" (that is, interactions with their infants that involve skin-to-skin contact such as patting, rubbing, kissing, and touching) with girl babies than with boys include Carl-Philip Hwang, "Mother-Infant Interaction," Monique Robin, "Neonate-Mother Interaction," and Millot, Filiatre, and Montagner, "Maternal Tactile Behavior Correlated with Mother and New-born Infant Characteristics."

p. 89 *Gornick recounts an occasion* This appears in *Fierce Attachments,* pp. 80–81.

p. 90 *"My father smiled at her"* Gornick, *Fierce Attachments,* p. 12.

p. 92 *a video that I made for workplace training* The video, *Talking 9 to 5,* is available through ChartHouse International Learning Corporation (www.charthouse.com).

p. 96 The Erica Jong quotation appears in *Mother's Nature: Timeless Wisdom for the Journey into Motherhood,* created by Andrea Alban Gosline and Lisa Burnett Bossi with Ame Mahler Beanland (Berkeley: Conari Press, 1999), p. 46. I am grateful to Beth Jannery for calling this quotation to my attention.

p. 100 Tesser, "Toward a Self-Evaluation Maintenance Model of Social Behavior."

p. 102 *"I am properly expectant"* Gornick, *Fierce Attachments,* pp. 146–147.

p. 103 the "deprivation litany" quotation: *Fierce Attachments,* p. 17.

p. 104 Ryff, Schmutte, and Lee, "How Children Turn Out," p. 407.

p. 105 *"My sentences got longer"* Gornick, *Fierce Attachments,* p. 108.

p. 106 Paul Preston, *Mother Father Deaf* (Cambridge, Mass.: Harvard University Press, 1994), p. 17.

p. 107 Sue Monk Kidd, *The Secret Life of Bees* (New York: Penguin, 2002), pp. 98–99.

## 5 STOP THIS CONVERSATION, I WANT TO GET OFF

p. 117 Bateson, "Culture Contact and Schismogenesis." The quotation that begins "It is likely that submissiveness" is on p. 68.

p. 123 The concept of alignment comes from Erving Goffman, *Forms of Talk.*

## 6 WANTED: MOTHER, A JOB DESCRIPTION

p. 139 John Richardson was interviewed by Jennifer Ludden on the National Public Radio show *Weekend All Things Considered,* August 13, 2005, about his book *My Father the Spy: An Investigative Memoir* (New York: HarperCollins, 2005).

p. 139 In Kathryn Chetkovich, *Friendly Fire* (Iowa City: University of Iowa Press, 1998), pp. 89–103. The quotations are on pp. 89 and 90.

p. 141 Hall and Langellier, "Storytelling Strategies in Mother-Daughter Communication," p. 113.

p. 143 Santiago, *The Turkish Lover* (New York: Da Capo Press, 2004), pp. 8 and 16, respectively. According to Marlene Gottlieb, Professor of Spanish at Herbert H. Lehman College, *nena* is a term of endearment for "girl" that is used all over the Spanish-speaking world but especially in Puerto Rico.

p. 144 *"Safeguarding my virginity"* Gornick, *Fierce Attachments,* p. 110. The next quotation is from p. 111.

p. 145 Hulbert, *Raising America,* p. 7.

p. 146 Tovares, "Power and Solidarity in Mother–Adolescent Daughter Dating Negotiation."

p. 146 *as the poet Anne Sexton did with her daughter Linda* Linda Sexton, *Searching for Mercy Street* (Boston: Little, Brown, 1994).

p. 151 Polly York was interviewed on a radio magazine show, *This American Life.* The segment, entitled "My Pen Pal," aired on National Public Radio on September 12, 2003.

p. 156 Marie Lee, "Reaching the 'Point of No Return' in Public," *Newsweek,* November 3, 2003, p. 14.

p. 158 *the "ultimate female Olympics."* The caller took part in NPR's *The Diane Rehm Show,* February 12, 2004. The book under discussion was Susan Douglas and Meredith Michaels, *The Mommy Myth* (New York: Free Press, 2004).

p. 158 Smith, *A Potent Spell,* p. 222.

p. 158 Rich, *Of Woman Born,* p. 223.

p. 159 Mary Gordon, *Pearl* (New York: Pantheon, 2005), pp. 38–39.

p. 160 Anna Quindlen, "Flown Away, Left Behind," *Newsweek,* January 12, 2004, p. 64.

## *7* BEST FRIENDS, WORST ENEMIES

p. 163 Laura Dern was interviewed on the National Public Radio show *Fresh Air,* September 9, 2004.

p. 163 Diane Rehm, *Finding My Voice* (New York: Knopf, 1999), p. 4.

p. 163 Tatar, *The Annotated Brothers Grimm,* p. 242.

p. 164 Keller, *Reflections on Gender and Science,* p. 60. Keller cites these lines in connection with her point that scientists in seventeenth-century England believed science proved the existence of witches—a stance that reflected their desire to preserve science as a masculine domain.

p. 168 Chesler, *Woman's Inhumanity to Woman,* p. 284.

p. 169 Rich describes these impulses and fears in *Of Woman Born,* p. 36. The extended quotation is from p. 21.

p. 170 The second quotation is from Rich, *Of Woman Born,* p. 22.

p. 170 Diane Wood Middlebrook, *Anne Sexton* (New York: Vintage, 1992), p. 33.

p. 170 Maushart (*The Mask of Motherhood,* pp. 113–116) quotes Dix (*The New Mother Syndrome,* Sydney: Allen and Unwin, 1986).

p. 171 You can find the lyrics to "Different Tunes" in *The Peggy Seeger Song-*

*book* (New York: Oak Publications, 1998) and listen to it on several of the CDs listed on Seeger's website (www.pegseeger.com).

p. 174 Kahlil Gibran, "On Love," *The Prophet* (New York: Knopf, 1923), p. 11.

p. 174 Smith, *A Potent Spell,* p. 30.

p. 175 This excerpt comes from a novel that Lilika Nakou first wrote in French in 1928 under the title *Le Livre de Mon Pierrot* and later translated into her native Greek. It was published in Athens in 1932 under the title (not of her choosing nor to her liking) *I Xepartheni* (The Deflowered One). The excerpt appears on p. 29 of an edition reprinted by an Athens publisher, Dorikos, in 1980. I discuss the passage in a book I wrote about Nakou's work (*Lilika Nakos* [Boston: G. K. Hall, 1983]). For that book I used the anglicized version of the author's name, Nakos, because it was used when her work was published in English. (In French it appeared as Nacos.) In Greek, women and men have different forms of the same surname. The author's father's surname was Nakos, but hers was Nakou, the feminine (from a cultural perspective) or possessive (from a grammatical one) form of her father's name: literally, the Lilika who belongs to Nakos.

p. 178 Chesler, *Woman's Inhumanity to Woman,* p. 283.

p. 179 Diane Wood Middlebrook, *Anne Sexton* (New York: Vintage, 1992), pp. 20 and 21.

p. 182 Chesler, *Woman's Inhumanity to Woman,* p. 172.

p. 183 Marilynne Robinson's remark appears in "A Moralist of the Midwest," by Meghan O'Rourke, *New York Times Magazine,* October 24, 2004, pp. 63–67. The quotation is on p. 66.

p. 183 Jill Ker Conway, *The Road from Coorain* (New York: Knopf, 1989), pp. 145–146.

p. 184 I found information about foot binding on the BBC website: www .bbc.co.uk/dna/h2g2/brunel/A1155872.

p. 184 The information about Dr. Nour comes from a news item that appeared in *The New York Times,* June 6, 2004, p. 6.

p. 185 Diane Rehm, *Finding My Voice* (New York: Knopf, 1999), p. 152.

p. 189 Donna Brazile made these remarks as a guest on *The Kojo Nnamdi Show,* WAMU (a Washington, D.C., NPR station), August 19, 2004.

p. 190 The quotations from Kathryn Harrison, *The Mother Knot* (New York: Random House, 2004), appear on pp. 28, 41, 42, and 66.

*8* "OH MOM . . . BRB"

p. 211 Bausch made this remark on NPR's *The Diane Rehm Show,* December 12, 2002.

## 9 BLENDING INTIMACY AND INDEPENDENCE

p. 220 Paule Marshall, *Brown Girl, Brownstones* (1959; reprint, New York: Feminist Press, 1981), p. 306.

p. 222 Bea Lewis, "This Day and Age," *Palm Beach Post* July 2, 2005, p. 2D. Lewis asked for my comment on this reader's letter, and she incorporated my analysis into this column.

p. 223 Anndee Hochman, "Growing Pains: Beyond 'One Big Happy Family,'" in *Reading Life: A Writer's Reader,* ed. Inge Fink and Gabrielle Gautreaux (Boston: Thomson, 2005), pp. 131–137. The quotation appears on p. 135. The essay is excerpted from Hochman, *Everyday Acts and Small Subversions* (Portland: The Eighth Mountain Press, 1994).

p. 224 Gornick, *Fierce Attachments,* pp. 103–104.

p. 225 The quotations from Marshall, *Brown Girl, Brownstones,* are on pp. 215 and 226.

p. 235 Gornick, *Fierce Attachments,* pp. 73–74.

p. 238 Petraki, *Relationships and Identities as "Storied Orders,"* p. 359.

## AFTERWORD

p. 246 Chesler, *Woman's Inhumanity to Woman,* p. 198.

# REFERENCES

Bateson, Gregory. 1972 [1935]. "Culture Contact and Schismogenesis." *Steps to an Ecology of Mind*, 61–87. New York: Ballantine.

Blum-Kulka, Shoshana. 1997. *Dinner Talk: Cultural Patterns of Sociability and Socialization in Family Discourse*. Mahwah, N.J.: Erlbaum.

Bronstein, Phyllis, and Carolyn Pape Cowan. 1988. *Fatherhood Today: Men's Changing Role in the Family*. New York: John Wiley & Sons.

Chesler, Phyllis. 2001. *Woman's Inhumanity to Woman*. New York: Thunder's Mouth Press.

Eckert, Penelope, and Sally McConnell-Ginet. 2003. *Language and Gender*. Cambridge, Mass.: Cambridge University Press.

Eder, Donna. 1990. "Serious and Playful Disputes: Variation in Conflict Talk Among Female Adolescents." In Allen Grimshaw, ed., *Conflict Talk*, 67–84. Cambridge: Cambridge University Press.

Furedi, Frank. 2002. *Paranoid Parenting: Why Ignoring the Experts May Be Best for Your Child*. Chicago: Chicago Review Press.

Goffman, Erving. 1981. *Forms of Talk*. Philadelphia: University of Pennsylvania Press.

Goodwin, Marjorie Harness. 1990. *He-Said-She-Said: Talk as Social Organization Among Black Children*. Bloomington: Indiana University Press.

Gornick, Vivian. 1987. *Fierce Attachments: A Memoir*. Boston: Beacon Press.

Hall, Deanna L., and Kristin M. Langellier. 1988. "Storytelling Strategies in Mother-Daughter Communication." In Anita Taylor and Barbara Bate, eds., *Women Communicating: Studies of Women's Talk*, 107–126. Norwood, N.J.: Ablex.

Hall, Edward T. 1959. *The Silent Language*. Garden City: Doubleday.

Hoff-Ginsberg, Erika. 1994. "Influences of Mother and Child on Maternal Talkativeness." *Discourse Processes* 18:105–117.

Hulbert, Ann. 2003. *Raising America: Experts, Parents, and a Century of Advice About Children*. New York: Knopf.

Hwang, Carl-Philip. 1978. "Mother-Infant Interaction: Effects of Sex of Infant on Feeding Behaviour." *Early Human Development* 2 (4):341–349.

Jefferson, Gail. 1988. "On the Sequential Organisation of Troubles Talk in Ordinary Conversation." *Social Problems* 35 (4):418–441.

Keller, Evelyn Fox. 1985. *Reflections on Gender and Science.* New Haven: Yale University Press.

Leaper, Campbell, Kristin J. Anderson, and Paul Sanders. 1998. "Moderators of Gender Effects on Parents' Talk to Their Children: A Meta-Analysis." *Developmental Psychology* 34 (1):3–27.

Leaper, Campbell, and Tara E. Smith. 2004. "A Meta-Analytic Review of Gender Variations in Children's Language Use: Talkativeness, Affiliative Speech, and Assertive Speech." *Developmental Psychology* 40(6): 993-1027.

Maccoby, Eleanor E. 1998. *The Two Sexes: Growing Up Apart, Coming Together.* Cambridge, Mass.: Harvard University Press.

Maltz, Daniel N., and Ruth A. Borker. 1982. "A Cultural Approach to Male-Female Miscommunication." In John J. Gumperz, ed., *Language and Social Identity,* 196–216. Cambridge: Cambridge University Press.

Matisoff, James A. 2000 [1979]. *Blessings, Curses, Hopes, and Fears: Psycho-Ostensive Expressions in Yiddish.* Stanford: Stanford University Press.

Maushart, Susan. 1999. *The Mask of Motherhood.* New York: Penguin.

McFadden, Jennifer. 2005. "Rituals of Family Identity: Prior Text and Prosodic Play in Mother-Daughter Conversation." Paper presented at the Georgetown Linguistics Society conference "The Language and Identity Tapestry," Washington, D.C., February 20.

Millot, J. L., J. C. Filiatre, and H. Montagner. 1988. "Maternal Tactile Behaviour Correlated with Mother and Newborn Infant Characteristics." *Early Human Development* 16:119–129.

Ochs, Elinor, and Carolyn Taylor. 1992. "Family Narrative as Political Activity." *Discourse & Society* 3 (3):301–40.

———. 1996. "The Father Knows Best Dynamic in Family Dinner Narratives." In Kira Hall and Mary Bucholtz, eds., *Gender Articulated,* 97–121. New York and London: Routledge.

Ogilvie, Beverly, and Judith Daniluk. 1995. "Common Themes in the Experiences of Mother-Daughter Incest Survivors: Implications for Counseling." *Journal of Counseling and Development* 73:598–602.

Petraki, Eleni. 2002. *Relationships and Identities as "Storied Orders": A Study in Three Generations of Greek-Australian Women.* Ph.D. dissertation, University of Queensland, St. Lucia, Brisbane, Australia.

Rich, Adrienne. 1986. *Of Woman Born: Motherhood as Experience and Institution.* New York: Norton.

Robin, Monique. 1982. "Neonate-Mother Interaction: Tactile Contacts in the Days Following Birth." *Early Child Development and Care* 9:221–236.

Ryff, Carol D., Pamela S. Schmutte, and Young Hyun Lee. 1996. "How Children Turn Out: Implications for Parental Self-Evaluation." In Carol D. Ryff and Marsha Mailick Seltzer, eds., *The Parental Experience in Midlife,* 383–422. Chicago: University of Chicago Press.

Sheldon, Amy. 1990. "Pickle Fights: Gendered Talk in Preschool Disputes." *Discourse Processes* 13 (1):5–31. Reprinted in Deborah Tannen, ed., *Gender and Conversational Interaction,* 83–109. New York and Oxford: Oxford University Press.

———. 1992. "Preschool Girls' Discourse Competence: Managing Conflict." In Kira Hall, Mary Bucholtz, and Birch Moonwomon, eds., *Locating Power: Proceedings of the Second Berkeley Women and Language Conference,* vol. 2, 528–539. Berkeley: Berkeley Women and Language Group, University of California, Berkeley.

Smith, Janna Malamud. 2003. *A Potent Spell: Mother Love and the Power of Fear.* Boston: Houghton Mifflin.

Tatar, Maria. 2004. *The Annotated Brothers Grimm.* New York: Norton.

Tesser, Abraham. 1988. "Toward a Self-Evaluation Maintenance Model of Social Behavior." *Advances in Experimental Psychology* 21:181–227.

Tovares, Alla Yeliseyeva. 2001. "Power and Solidarity in Mother–Adolescent Daughter Dating Negotiation." Paper presented at the Georgetown University Round Table on Languages and Linguistics, Washington, D.C., March 9.

Vuchinich, Samuel. 1987. "Starting and Stopping Spontaneous Family Conflicts." *Journal of Marriage and the Family* 49(3):591–601.

# ACKNOWLEDGMENTS

This book would not exist if many many women had not opened their lives to me, sharing memories and thoughts about their mothers and their daughters. Whether or not I used specific examples from our conversations or interviews, everyone I talked to helped deepen my understanding of this topic. I am especially grateful to Addie Macovski and Caleen Sinnette Jennings for hosting meals at their homes to which they invited a half dozen friends for group discussions. I have honored individuals' preferences with regard to being identified by name with the examples based on their experiences or remaining anonymous. Those not identified in the book whose examples, insights, or experiences appear in it, or who took the time to be interviewed, are Camille Ashley, Marti Baerg, A. L. Becker, Judith Becker, Margaret Becker, Jane Biba, Anne Marie Blum, Barbara Newman Bonini, Katherine Bradley, Ronde Bradley, Faedra Carpenter, Elizabeth Cohen, Larry Cole, Elizabeth Collins, Claire Convey, Elton Couch, Darryle Craig, Sarah Crump, Gay Daly, Bronwyn Davies, Angela J. Davis, Janice Delaney, Becky Dye, Michael Eckenrode, Patricia Elam, Adrienne Erickson, Maura Flaherty, Ila Griffith Forster, Erica Frank, Thaisa Frank, Anne Glusker, Jennifer Goldstein, Cynthia Gordon, Sarah Hafer, Kristina Hamilton, Cindy Handler, Sara M. Holmes, Jane Houston, Dennie Hughes, Spencer Humphrey, Debra Iverson, Marielena Ivory, Beth Jannery, Barbara Kirsch, Linda B. (Sprechman) Jacobson, Barbara Johnstone, Susan Joseph,

Donna Leinwand, Molly Myerowitz Levine, Bea Lewis, Molly Loughney, Jodi Lyons, Alison Mackey, Dorothy Ester Madden, Devra Marcus, Robin Alva Marcus, Julia Marter, Jean Martin, Kay Martin, Gabe Marx, Josh Marx, Susan Mather, Larry McGrael, Dory McKenzie, Nell Minow, Janine Murphy-Neilson, Rachel Myerowitz, Azar Nafisi, Patricia O'Brien, Lisa Page, Meghan Pelley, Micah Perks, Rebekah Perks, Angela Perrone, Terri Pilkerton, Cynthia Read, Diane Rehm, Louis Reith, Amy Repp, Olivia Richardson, Jill Holmes Robinson, Suzanne Romaine, Regina Romero, Cynthia Roy, Kathleen Santora, Milena Santoro, Deborah Schiffrin, Denise Sheehan, Monica Sheehan, Susan Richards Shreve, Elinor DesVerney Sinnette, Esther Willa Stillwell, Kate Stoddard, Elizabeth Stone, Carole Suarez, Amy Tan, Miriam Tannen, Jane Turner, Marianne Walters, Suzanna Walters, Molly Wille, and Haru Yamada.

I count myself inordinately lucky to teach in a program at Georgetown University in which colleagues and students share my research interests. During the spring term 2004 I taught a graduate seminar on mother-daughter conversations. The talented students who participated in that seminar helped enormously by locating relevant articles and by taking part in discussions that enriched my understanding of the topic. They are: Shanna Gonzalez, Jennifer McFadden, Barbara Soukup, Ingrid Stockburger, Anna Marie Trester, and Laura Wright. I am also grateful to the undergraduate students who have taken my Cross-Cultural Communication course. Many of their observations on their own interactions, described in written assignments, provided examples and insights into them.

I am overwhelmed by the generosity of those who read early drafts and offered incisive comments as well as, in many cases, their own experiences which became examples in later drafts. For their gifts of time and wisdom I thank Sally Arteseros, Pete Becker, Harriet Grant, Addie and Al Macovski, Michael Macovski, Susan Philips, Phyllis Richman, Naomi Tannen, and David Wise.

My agent, Suzanne Gluck, has been my trusted and treasured

guide for nearly two decades. No more passionate and inspired an advocate could an author wish for. David Robinson, whose able assistance I have been fortunate to have for a decade, helped by tracking down a dizzying variety of information on breathtakingly short notice. The book was greatly improved by the incisive comments of my editor, Caroline Sutton.

Words are paltry indeed to express my gratitude to Michael Macovski, my husband, my heart. In this as in all things, he has been a life companion in every sense of the word. For the many ways he has helped and for being who he is, I daily give thanks.

# INDEX

# YOU'RE WEARING *That?*

## DEBORAH TANNEN

*A Reader's Guide*

READING GROUP QUESTIONS AND
TOPICS FOR DISCUSSION

1. According to Tannen, talk between mothers and daughters can be the best and worst of all possible conversations; we talk to our daughters and mothers in better and worse ways than we talk to anyone else. What are some of the best aspects of mother-daughter conversations? What are some of the worst?

2. In a chapter entitled "My Mother, My Hair," Tannen calls hair, clothes, and weight the Big Three that mothers and daughters critique in each other. Why, according to Tannen, do girls and women tend to criticize their mothers and daughters on these aspects of appearance? Can you think of other reasons? What other characteristics are also frequent topics of comments that come across as criticism?

3. How could a comment like "Do you like your hair that long?" be interpreted as criticism? How could it not? What other comments that are not critical on the surface have you heard and interpreted as criticism? What do these comments have in common?

4. Look around the room and consider the range of hairstyles you observe among the women and, in contrast, the men. Ask yourself how many of these hairstyles you think are the most flattering possible—but keep your observations to yourself! Then

ask (again, privately) what impression you get of the character or lifestyle of each individual, based on hairstyle, or choice of clothes. Do you draw as many conclusions about men as about women based on these style choices? Does this play a role in women's tendency to critique their daughters' or mothers' appearance?

5. Tannen claims that the mother-daughter relationship is especially intense and complex because both are women. How does the role of talk in relationships tend to differ for women and men? How does this affect mothers and daughters? (You may want to refer to Tannen's earlier book *You Just Don't Understand* for a discussion of how women and men use language.)

6. An aspect of girls' and women's friendships is "troubles talk." Why does troubles talk present a special challenge for mothers and daughters? How would a friend be likely to respond when you tell about a problem? How would a mother be likely to respond? How would you be likely to react to those responses?

7. Another aspect of girls' and women's friendships is the focus on sameness. If you have daughters, have you observed this in their friendships or experienced this with regard to yourself or other family members? Do you sometimes think about ways you and your mother or daughter are the same or different? Does this bring you closer or create distance? Does it affect how you, or your mother or daughter, think about your own life? How do you think your mother or daughter feels, or felt, about similarities or differences between you?

8. Girls at play often punish a girl they don't like by locking her out ("You can't come to my birthday"), and women are often sensitive to being excluded as well. How does feeling left out often cause pain for mothers of adult daughters? How can either the mother or the daughter address this discomfort?

9. How often do you think it is appropriate for a mother and daughter to talk on the phone, visit, or exchange e-mails? What happens when a mother and daughter—or sisters and brothers— have different ideas about what amount of contact is desirable, appropriate, or healthy?

10. Tannen points out that women often expect more of daughters than sons, and of mothers than fathers. Can you think of examples when you observed or experienced this? Why would this be so? What are some of the advantages and disadvantages of these greater expectations? Can anything be done to change this—and should it be changed? Do you think this pattern is avoidable, inescapable, or even preferable?

11. Tannen points out many ways that a woman's relationship with her mother changes when she has children of her own. For example, sharing interest in the (grand)children can bring them closer, but if the (grand)mother criticizes the (grand)children, their mother may hold back on talking about them, and the criticism may remind her of how she herself was criticized or not accepted by her mother. All mothers worry that they are not good enough mothers, so criticism of how a woman is raising her children proves especially troubling to the woman criticized. Have you noticed other ways that having children affects a woman's relationship with her mother? Are there positive or negative effects that Tannen did not note?

12. Many women told Tannen that they sense their daughters' or their mothers' moods instantly and often absorb that mood. How strong is the experience of such a transfer of emotions? Are there other ways that a mother can be a lightning rod in the storm of family emotions? Why do daughters sometimes express anger more freely at mothers than fathers?

13. In a chapter entitled "Oh Mom . . . brb," Tannen discusses how e-mail and Instant Messaging can change mother/daughter

relationships. Did you recognize the meaning of "brb"? Do you routinely use e-mail, IM, or text messaging? How do these means of communication differ from telephones, letters, and face-to-face conversation? Have you used these new media with your mother or daughter? How has this affected your relationship?

14. In a chapter entitled "Wanted: Mother, A Job Description," Tannen lists many requirements of the job of mother, and notes that it's impossible for any one person to fulfill them all. What are the job requirements she lists? Can you think of others? Are some of them contradictory?

15. One woman said, "My relationship with my mother keeps changing; she's been dead twenty years." The mother-daughter relationship lasts a lifetime, including after the mother's death. Tannen gives examples of women who felt their mothers' influence was positive, and some who felt it was negative, after they were gone. If your mother has passed on, what are some ways that you still have a relationship with her? If she is still alive, how do you think your relationship may evolve after she's gone?

16. What is "complementary schismogenesis"? Have you ever experienced such a mutually aggravating spiral? You might note, when an argument breaks out, what each person said, and how each offending comment might have been triggered by the one that came before it. You might even tape-record conversations in order to catch the one that ends in an argument, so you can go back and see where things went awry. Then ask, what could you have said differently to change the response and therefore the outcome?

17. A lot of what we hear focuses on the positive side of mothering, especially around Mother's Day. Tannen discusses these aspects, but she also discusses the dark side: ways that mothers can cause their daughters pain, undercut their confidence, clip their

wings, even physically beat them. Abuse can also flow from daughter to mother, especially if the mother is old or dependent. How prevalent, in your experience, is this dark side? How often is it talked about? Can the positive and negative co-exist in the same mother-daughter pair?

18. Tannen makes many suggestions for improving mother-daughter conversations, and hence relationships. Among them are: Adopt the mantra "Don't advise, don't criticize"; offer praise; reframe criticism as caring; if talk leads to arguments, talk differently (tell jokes; change topics); spend less time talking and more time doing things together; use humor. Are these suggestions realistic? Can you think of others that you have used or would like to try?

19. Tannen points out that much of what she says about mothers and daughters may also be true of mothers and sons, fathers and daughters, or fathers and sons. Describe some ways that you have observed or experienced similar phenomena in these other relationships. Are they as widespread, frequent, and intense in these other relationships? If so, how? If not, why not?

20. Many women told Tannen that they have better communication, and better relationships, with their daughters than they had with their mothers. Why do you think this is? Is this cause for hope? What other causes for hope can you think of?

DEBORAH TANNEN is on the Linguistics Department faculty at Georgetown University, where she is one of only two in the College of Arts and Sciences who hold the distinguished rank of university professor. Her book *You Just Don't Understand: Women and Men in Conversation,* which has sold more than two million copies and has been translated into twenty-nine languages, was on the *New York Times* bestseller list for more than three years, including eight months as number one. It was also on bestseller lists in Brazil, Canada, England, Germany, Holland, and Hong Kong. This is the book that brought gender differences in communication style to the forefront of public awareness. Among her other books, *Talking from 9 to 5: Women and Men at Work* was a *New York Times* business bestseller; *The Argument Culture: Stopping America's War of Words* won the Common Ground book award; and *I Only Say This Because I Love You: Talking to Your Parents, Partner, Sibs, and Kids When You're All Adults* won a Books for a Better Life award. *You're Wearing THAT?* is her twentieth book.

Deborah Tannen is a frequent guest on television and radio. *Nightline, The NewsHour with Jim Lehrer, 20/20, The Oprah Winfrey Show,* the *Today* show, *Good Morning America,* ABC's *World News Tonight, The Diane Rehm Show, Fresh Air with Terry Gross,* and *All Things Considered* are among the programs on which she has appeared. She has written for most major magazines and newspapers including *The New York Times, The Washington Post, USA Today, Time, Newsweek,* and *The Harvard Business Review.*

Tannen is an internationally recognized scholar who has received fellowships and grants from the Rockefeller Foundation, the National Endowment for the Humanities, the National Science Foundation, the American Council of Learned Societies, and the Alfred P. Sloan Foundation. She holds a Ph.D. from the University of California, Berkeley, as well as five honorary doctorates. She has been McGraw Distinguished Lecturer at Princeton University and was a fellow at the Center for Advanced Study in the Behavioral Sciences in Stanford, California, following a term in residence at the Institute for Advanced Study in Princeton, N.J.

In addition to her linguistic research and writing, Deborah Tannen has published poetry, short stories, and personal essays. Her first play, "An Act of Devotion," is included in *The Best American Short Plays: 1993–1994*. It was produced, together with her play "Sisters," by Horizons Theater in Arlington, Virginia.

Her website is www.deborahtannen.com.